Surprise, Strategy and *'Vijay'*

20 Years of Kargil and Beyond

Surprise, Strategy and *'Vijay'*

20 Years of Kargil and Beyond

Editors

Lt Gen (Dr) VK Ahluwalia

and

Col Narjit Singh

Centre for Land Warfare Studies

PENTAGON PRESS LLP

The Centre for Land Warfare Studies (CLAWS), New Delhi, is an autonomous think tank dealing with contemporary issues of national security and conceptual aspects of land warfare, including conventional and sub-conventional conflicts and terrorism. CLAWS conducts research that is futuristic in outlook and policy-oriented in approach.

Centre for Land Warfare Studies
RPSO Complex, Parade Road, Delhi Cantt, New Delhi-110010
Phone: 011-25691308 • Fax: 011-25692347
email: landwarfare@gmail.com • website: www.claws.in

First Published in 2019

ISBN 978-93-86618-94-8

Published by
PENTAGON PRESS LLP
206, Peacock Lane, Shahpur Jat,
New Delhi-110049
Phones: 011-64706243, 26491568
Telefax: 011-26490600
email: rajan@pentagonpress.in
website: www.pentagon-press.com

Printed at Aegean Offset Printers, Greater Noida, U.P.

Poor is the nation that has no heroes, but poorer still is the nation that having heroes, fails to remember and honor them
— **Marcus Tullius Cicero**

DEDICATED TO

THE BRAVEHEARTS OF THE KARGIL CONFLICT (1999)

Contents

General NC Vij
PVSM, UYSM, AVSM (Retd)
Hony Col of the DOGRA Regt & DOGRA Scouts

Former -
*Chief of the Army Staff
*Founder Vice Chairman
 National Disaster Management Authority
*Director
 Vivekanand International Foundation

House No - 4500A, Sector-23A
Gurgaon (Haryana)
PIN - 122017
Ph : 0124-4364500
E-mail : gncvij@gmail.com

FOREWORD

2019 marks 20 years of the Kargil Conflict. Yet, the saga of great battles of the capture of Tololing, Point 4875 (Batra Top) and Tiger Hill etc are as vivid in our memory, as if they were only yesterday. The victories won in the various battles of Kargil, in its two months duration, will always remain a symbol of pride for the Nation and serve as an inspiration for every soldier of the Indian Armed Forces.

The enemy had surprised us and occupied tactical heights in the previous winter months along Srinagar-Leh Road from where they could effectively dominate our movements by observation and fire. The time for recapture of the occupied positions was of utmost priority, and these definitely had to be cleared in the earliest time frame. Any delay in accomplishing the set objectives would have had a disastrous effect on our logistics and future sustenance. Had we failed, the enemy would have had a full season to consolidate their presence, cut off the Valley from the Ladakh Sector and consequentially lay claim on the area of ingress, and redraw the Line of Control (LoC).

Yet, the Indian Army remained undaunted. They were determined to recapture these impregnable heights irrespective of what was the cost in terms of lives. The fact that these attacks were to be up hill along treacherous heights against very well coordinated Pakistani ground and artillery fire, did not deter them. Exemplary leadership at all levels, wherein platoon and company commanders physically led from the front without a second thought to the risk to their lives, left the Pakistani soldiers gasping with surprise. In such rarefied high-altitude terrain, our troops derived their oxygen from just one single thought- 'Victory'. Resourcefulness and ingenuity of the highest order was displayed wherein, Bofors guns were used in direct firing role for bunker bursting like tank guns. This left the Pakistani soldiers completely bewildered and all advantage of occupying hill features greatly negated.

The then Pakistani Army Chief, General Parvez Musharraf believed to have given his broad plan of capture of these heights on the Indian side of the LoC within hours of taking over his appointment on 7 October, 1998. The political leadership of Pakistan has claimed that they were kept in the dark even though it is difficult to believe that. The operational and the execution plans were shared by the Pakistani top brass with a chosen few only. Against this backdrop, the violent and speedy response by the Indian Army took the enemy by complete surprise. The recapture of these heights helped resume the strategic vehicular movement, which the ingresses had made nearly impossible.

It is true that due to the lack of intelligence at the national level and poor surveillance at the local level because of our predominant occupation with counter insurgency operations, it took time to clear the initial fog of war. However, when Pakistani dispositions were identified, they were subjected to unprecedented volume of artillery fire and air attacks. The earlier bravado of the Pakistani army started to buckle as a chain of military reversals commenced. The tide had started turning since mid-June 1999 until their final capitulation in the end July, 1999.

Credit must also go to our brothers-in-arms, the Air Force, who carried out 'Op Safed Sagar to great effect. The biggest gain from the air attacks was that it exhibited the national will. It literally broke the enemy's back when the Air Force subjected them to relentless attacks by their fighters and bombers. This coupled with the fearsome ground attacks hastened the Pakistani collapse.

Reflections on the Kargil conflict can never be complete without recounting the heroic accounts of the brilliant junior leadership. Some of the junior commanders who had led these suicidal ground attacks became household names. Their legendary tales of courage and sacrifice deserve mention in the school textbooks to serve as a reminder and inspiration for our youth. To all those who fought, and many of whom sacrificed their lives for the nation, the country will ever remain grateful.

Internationally too, these illegal intrusions by Pakistan, in the face of failure, left them hugely embarrassed. The world was also worried on account of the danger of further escalation into a full-fledged war between two nuclear powers.

In the end, Pakistan Prime Minister Nawaj Sharif went rushing to Washington to beg the US President to save their face. Pakistan Army was once again reduced to making lame excuses for their failures like they did in 1965 and 1971 wars.

Whereas the Armed Forces will always try and live upto their reputation, I do hope that we have learnt our lessons seriously at the strategic level to ever remain prepared to fight future wars, should they ever be once against forced upon us!

New Delhi
24 June 2019

(NC Vij)
General

List of Abbreviations

AAD	Army Air Defence
AGL	Automatic Grenade Launcher
AGPL	Actual Ground Position Line
AI	Artificial Intelligence
AMS	Acute Mountain Sickness
AMSL	Above Mean Sea Level
AOC	Army Ordinance Corps
AOP	Air Observation Pilot
Approx.	Approximately
AP	Ammunition Point
AREN	Army Radio Engineering Network
Arty	Artillery
ASC	Army Service Corps
ASCON	Army Static Switched Communication Network
AT	Animal Transport
AWACS	Airborne Warning and Control System
1 BIHAR	1st Battalion of The Bihar Regiment
BRI	Belt and Road Initiative
BSF	Border Security Force
CCS	Cabinet Committee on Security
CEMA	Cyber Electromagnetic Activities
CDS	Chief of Defence Staff
CI	Counter Insurgency
CNP	Comprehensive National Power
C4I2SR	Command, Control, Communications, Computers, Intelligence, Information, Surveillance and Reconnaissance

CMD	Credible Minimum Deterrence
COAS	Chief of the Army Staff
COSC	Chiefs of Staff Committee
CPEC	China-Pakistan Economic Corridor
DCN	Defence Communication Network
DF (SOS)	Defensive Fire (Save Our Souls)
DGMI	Director General of Military Intelligence
DGMO	Director General of Military Operations
DIA	Defence Intelligence Agency
DRDO	Defence Research and Development Organisation
EME	Electrical and Mechanical Engineers
ELINT	Electronic intelligence
EW	Electronic Warfare
FCNA	Force Commander Northern Area
FDL	Forward Defended Locality
FOO	Forward Observation Officer
18 GARHWAL	18th Battalion of The Garhwal Rifles
GDP	Gross Domestic Product
GOC	General Officer Commanding (of a division or corps)
GOC-in-C	General Officer Commanding-in-Chief (of the Army)
GoM	Group of Ministers
GPI	Global Peace Index
GPS	Global Positioning System
18 GRENADIERS	18th Battalion of The Grenadiers Regiment
1/11 GR	1st Battalion of The 11th Gorkha Rifles
HAA	High Altitude Area
HQ	Headquarters
IA	Indian Army
IAF	Indian Air Force
IB	International Boundary
IDS	Integrated Defence Staff
IFF	Identification of Friend or Foe
IOR	Indian Ocean Region

IoT	Internet of Things
IPB	Intelligence Preparation of the Battlefield
IRNSS	Indian Regional Navigation Satellite System
ISI	Inter-Services Intelligence
ISIS	Islamic State of Iraq and Syria
ISPR	Inter Services Public Relations
ISR	Intelligence, Surveillance and Reconnaissance
ISRO	Indian Space Research Organisation
ITBP	Indo Tibetan Border Police
JeM	Jaish-e-Mohammad
12 JAK LI	12th Battalion of The Jammu and Kashmir Light Infantry
13 JAK RIF	13th Battalion of The Jammu and Kashmir Rifles
17 JAT	17th Battalion of The Jat Regiment
JCO	Junior Commissioned Officer
JIC	Joint Intelligence Committee
KRC	Kargil Review Committee
13 KUMAON	13th Battalion of The Kumaon Regiment
LAC	Line of Actual Control
LeT	Lashkar-e-Tayibba
LIC	Low Intensity Conflict
LoC	Line of Control (in J&K) after 1971 War
LRP	Long Range Patrol
LGB	Laser Guided Bombs
LTIPP	Long-term Integrated Perspective Plans
12 MAHAR	12th Battalion of The Mahar Regiment
MCCS	Mobile Cellular Communication System
MHA	Ministry of Home Affairs
MMG	Medium Machine Gun
MoD	Ministry of Defence
MSL	Mean Sea Level
Mtrs	Metres
2 NAGA	2nd Battalion of The Naga Regiment
NCO	Non-Commissioned Officer

NLI	Northern Light Infantry (Pakistan)
NSG	Nuclear Suppliers Group
NTRO	National Technical Research Organisation
NVDs	Night Vision Devices
OODA	Observe, Orient, Decide and Act
OMP	Ordnance Maintenance Park/Platoon
OP	Observation Post
Op KP	Operation Koh Paima
PAF	Pakistan Air Force
5 PARA	5th Battalion of the Parachute Regiment
10 PARA(SF)	10th Battalion (Special Forces) of the Parachute Regiment
PGMs	Precision Guided Munitions
PoK	Pakistan Occupied Kashmir
3 PUNJAB	3rd Battalion of The Punjab Regiment
2 RAJ RIF	2nd Rajputana Rifles
RAW	Research and Analysis Wing
RPA	Remotely Piloted Aircrafts
RPG	Rocket Propelled Grenade
RVC	Remount and Veterinary Corps
SAM	Surface to Air Missiles
SF	Special Forces
8 SIKH	8th Battalion of The Sikh Battalion
SLOC	Sea Lanes of Communication
SSG	Special Service Group
Tac HQ	Tactical Headquarters
UAV	Unmanned Aerial Vehicle
UNSC	United Nations Security Council
5 VIKAS	Specialist high altitude/mountain warfare troops
WMD	Weapons of Mass Destruction

Preface

I feel privileged and honoured to be able to re-ignite the embers of "Operation Vijay" or the Kargil Conflict of 1999. Twenty years have passed since our great nation woke up to a disbelief, announcing intrusions by Pakistanis along the Line of Control (LoC) in the Kargil region. The resultant war that ensured the rout of the treacherous Pakistan Army has been one of the most remarkable episodes in the history of independent India.

I have also had the honour of commanding the 8 Mountain Division (8 Mtn Div), which was the formation in 1999, that, along with other formations, gave the first flicker of victory to the unified citizens of the country, who supported the Indian Armed Forces to the hilt. The Indian Armed Forces were overwhelmed by the spontaneous positive response from the instruments of national power and the people. 8 Mtn Div with its war cry motto "Forever in Operations" generated the push and momentum to take mountain warfare to new heights, and to display immense courage. Now, 20 years down the line, the Centre for Land Warfare Studies (CLAWS) felt that it will only be befitting to re-enforce citizens' gratitude to those who made the supreme sacrifice in upholding the Nation's pride and dignity. I continue to remain emotionally connected with "Forever in Operations" Division more, as later in 2008-09, I was also the Corps Commander of the Leh-based Corps and was able to get a much bigger overview of the war fought in such chilling conditions and circumstances.

Therefore, the faculty at CLAWS has endeavoured to recapitulate many battles while also introspecting upon the measures institutionalised to safeguard safeguard the frontiers of our hinterland. To do so, the importance of upgrading our war machine remains an ongoing process. In effect, the man behind the machine must always have at his command, a superior and effective weaponry and skill to annihilate his enemy. During the initial days of Op Vijay, it was important to overcome the nightmare of every soldier, which was of going into battle in a dark, undefined terrain. Yet, we gave a bloody nose to the intruders through a humiliating defeat. Getting the wounded out was a daunting task and entailed at least 8 to 12 troops depending upon the altitude and the distances involved, to carry a wounded soldier on a stretcher. The Air Force launched Operation Safed Sagar on 26 May 1999, which brought cheers to the troops, as also raised their motivation and morale. Similarly, as the Indian Naval fleets carried out aggresive surveillance and patroling in the Arabian Sea, it sent a strong message of its capabilities to Pakistan's Navy. The entire nation was witness to the Kargil conflict unfolding before their eyes through household TV sets. Mass hysteria was generated to inflict severe defeat on the Pakistani forces who had, with their warlord ethos, dared to test and provoke the Indians. CLAWS faculty was enthusiastic to study the Kargil Conflict and review the thought process originating now after two decades of its conclusion. Therefore, in accordance with the methodology for seeking new answers, we wrote to a host of contemporary and retired officers to send us their side of the facts, impressions and interpretation for compiling this book. The response was indeed positive, just like going back 20 years when so many of our veterans had approached the army and volunteered to render their services during the war.

It would be relevant to briefly look at the changes in the security matrix over the past two decades. With the introduction of a plethora of disruptive technologies, communications, asymmetric threats and revolution in autonomous weapon systems, the geo-political and regional security environment has been in a state of flux. Resultantly, the envisaged threats and challenges to national security have also undergone a change, especially so on the Indian sub-continent. Keeping in mind the unsettled boundary disputes and the Sino-Pakistan nexus, it is even more important to analyse our operational preparedness. While looking at the battles fought during the Kargil Conflict, the role of diplomacy, media and perception management, and the lessons learnt, this book also addresses the high points, the threats and some of our weaknesses which merit immediate attention.

A basic point to ponder upon is, "Was the Kargil imbroglio a war or a conflict?" It is felt that the connotation of war implies an open declaration of war by the government, general mobilisation of the Armed Forces, employability of unrestricted force levels, unrestricted space to conduct manoeuvre and attrition operations, and a political-cum-military aim to wage war in enemy territory. In this case, the aims, the force levels, geographical space and the mobilisation were restrictive. Also, the government did not declare a total war or mobilisation. Therefore, there is an element of interchangeability in the word "war" versus "conflict" as reflected in the chapters in this book. This is based on the perception of the individual authors. In fact, a few historians and authors have also termed the Kargil Conflict a border skirmish.

The Book has been divided into five parts. The first part, titled "Blood, Guts and Glory," briefly discusses the actual battles fought in Dras, Mushkoh, Batalik, Kaksar and Turtuk sub-sectors , to evict the Pakistani intruders from the dominating heights in the Kargil region. The aim was to restore the LoC to its originally held positions. The second part analyses the supporting forces that synergised the effort to victory, in the true spirit of Op Vijay. In the third part, individual officers, associated with Kargil, have shared their perceptions and opinions about the Kargil conflict and the scenario after 20 years. The fourth part focuses on "Motivation"; it has been our endeavour to pay tribute to our bravehearts who made us proud. Some of these articles have been published in CLAWS' publications recently and are being reproduced in the book. The next part (Part 5), "Emerging Challenges and the Way Ahead" looks at the emerging global-cum-regional scenario, the envisaged threats, and our preparedness, and makes substantial recommendations to face the conflicts in the future.

I am grateful to the units, formations and training centres who have made available their war accounts. I would also like to acknowledge and convey our sincere thanks to Gen VP Malik, the COAS during Kargil conflict, Lt Gen Mohinder Puri, the then GOC, 8 Mountain Division, Air Marshal Anil Chopra, Lt Gen Rajeev Sabherwal, Maj Gen Alok Deb, Maj Gen PK Chakravorty, Brig Akhelesh Bhargava Col Sushil Chander, Col Madhusudan M Dave, Col BM Cariappa, Col Rajeev Kapoor, Col Vivek Murthy, and Maj Saurav Pandey, who agreed to share their valuable impressions and have contributed thought-provoking chapters to enrich the Book. Our thanks are due to Gen NC Vij (Former COAS) for the foreword ; Lt Gen KM Seth, Lt Gen AK Singh, and Prof Gautam Sen, for writing a blurb; and to Brig Ganapathy V and Lt Col Jignesh Prakash for all the support provided for the book. I would also like to place on record my appreciation for the entire CLAWS faculty, particularly the positive contribution of Col HS Burn, Col Amit Hajela, Col Sunil Gupta, Dr Manjari Singh, Ms Shreya D Barman, Mr Raghunandan and Ms Tejusvi Shukla. They had voluntarily undertaken additional work to edit and check the correctness of the facts.

A special word of thanks to Col Narjit Singh, who had spontaneously accepted the proposal to co-edit the book. A soldier to the core, he brings good experience of mountain warfare, as he had served in 8 Mountain Division in 2005-06, with distinction.

Surprise, Strategy and '*Vijay*': 20 Years of Kargil and Beyond would be of a great interest to policy makers, and to military and civilian personnel alike. Besides the Kargil Conflict, it has examined a host of issues relating to global security, threats and challenges to India's security, and the way forward. In addition, the personal accounts of officers given in this book would interest the youth of the country as it reflects the saga of the courage and valour of the Indian Armed Forces, and the junior leadership, which remains unmatched the world over.

VK Ahluwalia and Narjit Singh

Introduction

Lieutenant General (Dr) VK Ahluwalia

On 2 July 1999, Mian Nawaz Sharif chaired Pakistan Defense Committee of the Cabinet (DCC). It was nearing midnight, and the Prime Minister had already decided in his mind to withdraw from Kargil. According to Nasim Zehra, a Lahore-based journalist and writer, the Prime Minister sought this urgent meeting, which was attended by the three Chiefs of the Pakistan Armed Forces, Director Inter-Services Intelligence (ISI), Defense Secretary and other cabinet ministers. The air was tense and in the light of reports stating that the Indian Army had reclaimed the Tololing Hill Complex, a Pakistani cabinet minister even remarked, "*Pakistani Army had climbed up a pole without considering how it would get down*".[1]

The Pakistan's Kargil misadventure, code-named "Koh-Paima" (*Operation KP*), raised endless questions as to who gave the go ahead? Who participated? Why and what should have been public known facts that had transformed into deep mysteries? Was Operation KP approved by the government? Was this covert military injunction proving to be economically unsustainable? Had it hurt India in any way? Obviously, there was a clear and visible rift between the civilian and military leaderships. As the military side of the briefing continued, the main thrust of the Pakistani PM's question was, *What you are now telling me, you should have told me earlier*.[2] At this, an agitated Musharraf pulled out his pocket diary and gave out seven dates on which he had personally briefed the PM on the military situation. So, the inevitable blame game was also in parallel progress of the same meeting.

Mian Nawaz Sharif was rather quiet as the scales in the Pakistani power power equation was tilted in favour of the army. At this stage, Chaudhry Shujaat Hussain (then Minister of the Interior, Pakistan) recommended that a message of unity and a spirit of collective responsibility must be aired to the media and the people of Pakistan through this meeting. He suggested that a joint effort should be made to manage the situation. Chaudhry Shujaat's interaction eased the tension and everyone's body language also relaxed. This meeting lasted five hours and ended inconclusively. Two incontestable facts about the 2 July 1999 DCC meeting emerged. Firstly, there was no decision taken on any future move on the Kargil ingress. Secondly, at no point did Musharraf recommend a military withdrawal. However, the civilians in the meeting did feel palpable signs that the army actually wanted to get "out" of Kargil.[3] Their discomfort was quite discernible from the recurrent military setbacks and the building diplomatic backlash. Indeed, the high casualties plus losses of Tololing and Tiger Hill had put the military under pressure. Interestingly, the day the DCC met, the US Congress passed a resolution by a 20 to 5 vote asking Pakistan to vacate Kargil.

In the light of such prevailing circumstances, Mian Nawaz Sharif, without any further consultations, decided on taking Pakistan on a path to bring Op KP to a close. Sharif, as his usual routine, flew to Lahore, his hometown and the next day spoke from the Governor's House with the US President. The clock was ticking towards the closure of Pakistan's fourth military encounter with India. The indication from Washington was as clear as "get out", thus leaving no more space for deliberations and negotiations.

US President Bill Clinton agreed to meet Sharif on a national holiday, i.e., 4 July (the American Independence Day). Musharraf was in Murree for the weekend. In the dead of the night, post 1 am, the Pakistani Army Chief along with others, held a 90-minute meeting at Islamabad, Chakala airport. Thus, at 2.30 am on the same day, the Pakistani PM took off by a commercial, New York bound, PIA flight. Pakistan also woke up stunned to hear to their PM's hasty departure for talks with Clinton. There was little fight left in Sharif, and he appeared drained during his discussions with Clinton. The Americans found him nervous and finally after a 2-hour-long meeting, at about 3 pm, the meeting concluded with the Washington statement, the text of which reads,

President Clinton and Prime Minister Sharif share the view that the current fighting in the Kargil region of Kashmir is dangerous and contains the seeds of a wider conflict.

They also agreed that it was vital for the peace of South Asia that the Line of Control in Kashmir be respected by both parties, in accordance with their 1972 Simla Accord.

It was agreed between the President and the Prime Minister that concrete steps will be taken for the restoration of the Line of Control, in accordance with the Simla Agreement. The President urged an immediate cessation of the hostilities once these steps are taken. The Prime Minister and the President agreed that the bilateral dialogue begin in Lahore in February provides the best forum for resolving all issues dividing India and Pakistan, including Kashmir. The President said he would take a personal interest in encouraging an expeditious resumption and intensification of those bilateral efforts, once the sanctity of the Line of Control has been fully restored. The President reaffirmed his intent to pay an early visit to South Asia.[4]

The Washington Statement had no legal binding, but it reflected the personal commitment made by the Prime Minister of Pakistan to the global community. It was not a bilateral statement between two interlocutors directly engaged in conflict that would have made the undertaking in the agreement binding. As the statement called for the "restoration of LoC" in accordance with the Simla Agreement, Pakistan committed itself to unconditional withdrawal from Kargil.

Concurrently, the Indian Army had mobilised with great speed to launch Op VIJAY to evict the Pakistani intruders to restore the sanctity of the LoC. Despite the politically dictated operational restrictions of not crossing the LoC, both the Army and the Air Force modified their strategy and tactics to deliver a dreadful blow to the intruders at the dominating heights. As the Navy also mobilised themselves and carried out aggresive patroling and manoeuvres, it sent a strong signal to Pakistan, and acted as a viable deterrent.

Surprise, Strategy and '*Vijay*': 20 Years of Kargil and Beyond is a tribute to the valour and fighting spirit of the Indian Soldiers, the bravehearts, who made the nation proud by showcasing unflinching courage throughout the Operation and for assaulting the impregnable heights of Kargil to restore the sanctity of the LoC. The book brings out that due to the synergy between the three services, and support of other elements of the national power, we were able to achieve our aim of Operation Vijay. The book also delves into the changing and emerging global security environment, threats and challenges of the future conflicts in the Indian sub-continent, and our preparedness to face them.

NOTES

1. Owen Bennet Jones, *Pakistan: Eye of the Storm* (Yale university Press, New Haven and London, 2002), p. 94.
2. Nasim Zehra, *From Kargil to the Coup: Events that Shook Pakistan* (Sang-e-Meel Publications, Lahore, 2018), p. 282.
3. Ibid., p. 285.
4. *"Clinton, Sharif Statement on Kashmir"*, Reuters, 4 July 1999. Accessed at http://www.jammu-kashmir.com/archives/archives1999/99july4b.html.

•

PART I
BLOOD, GUTS AND GLORY

Blood, Guts and Glory

Colonel Narjit Singh
Assisted by Raghunandan MC and Tejusvi Shukla

हतो वा प्राप्स्यसि स्वर्गं जित्वा वा भोक्ष्यसे महीम्।
तस्मादुत्तिष्ठ कौन्तेय युद्धाय कृतनिश्चयः॥

"Either you will be killed on the battlefield and attain the heavenly planets, or you will conquer and enjoy the earthly kingdom. Therefore get up and fight with determination."

— *The Bhagwat Gita,* Chapter 2, Verse 37

My posting to 8 Mountain Division coincided with the same time in June when five years earlier, every man in the formation was waging a relentless war to eliminate the deceitful Pakistani Army from the Kargil peaks.

My posting to Ladakh (on my vehement request) opened my vision to the bigger and brighter world of soldiering. Almost immediately on arrival, I was self-initiated to scale the heights of the Tololing Complex, which symbolised the rawest form of courageous assaults undertaken in the midst of intense enemy fire. In the extreme high-altitude areas of Kargil, I was gasping for air, with every moving step going up towards the Tololing. I really wondered how our soldiers really cantered up to their objectives under bullets and splinter bursts in 1999. My mind, which had felt invincible only a while back, started to feel terrified.

Having spent over two memorable years in the midst of the Kargil heights in 2005-07, I have had the privilege of gathering a sound knowledge of its vast terrain and formidable features. Besides that, I have also had the advantage of reading a number of books on this subject, written by eminent authors like Captain Amarinder Singh,

Lt Gen YM Bammi, Maj Gen Ashok Kalyan Varma, Harinder Baweja, General VP Malik, and Nasim Zehra (a Pakistani journalist and the author of *'From Kargil to Coup'*), which I have consulted to compile this Part of the Book. These books give detailed accounts of the operations undertaken during Operation VIJAY. Therefore, this part is not an official account of the Battles, or of the Conflict. Every victory along the 170-km long rarefied mountainous terrain was accomplished by surpassing new challenges, thus, leading to a new brand of personal leadership. The foregoing part of the actual war front is a concise recollection of many such battles, along with the remembrance of the valiant troops whose sacrifices ushered a new dawn in the Indian minds.

To facilitate easier understanding of the battles and the Conflict, I have divided this part into five sub parts, each describing the battles (which were taking place almost simultaneously) in the five sub-sectors of Kargil: Mushkoh, Dras, Kaksar, Batalik and Turtuk.

> "There's not to reason why, enemy guns to the right, guns to the left, and guns in front of them, yet the Indian rank and file wrote new lessons of bravery and fight, as all the world wondered how and why"
>
> **(Modified from Tennyson's 'The Charge of the Light Brigade')**

Summer of 1999

Kargil was a limited war that was fought with the collective backing of the whole nation, between May 1999 and July 1999 – a "bloody" two months. The officers, the junior commissioned officers and the fearless soldiers valiantly took on the back-stabbing Pakistanis head on. Not only did the Indian troops relentlessly attack uphill over the rugged terrain against a well dug-in enemy, but also managed to overcome the highly rarefied air while regaining every inch of occupied territory. The war in Kargil will always be remembered as a saga of unmatched bravery, and an unprecedented triumphant show of sheer dedication, determination and raw courage exhibited by our soldiers against all odds.

The Line of Control (LoC), delineated in 1972 by senior commanders from India and Pakistan, runs for approximately 220 km eastwards, beginning from the Kaobol Gali. This unseen line had remained quite intact and quiet for over 27 years (till 1999), except for some artillery firing by the Pakistanis, mainly to interdict the arterial road of National Highway 1A (NH-1A, now NH-1D), and also terrorise the local inhabitants of Kargil. The LoC in the Kargil region runs along the rugged mountainous Himalayan terrain varying in altitudes between 14000 and 19000 feet. This region was guarded by 121 (Independent) Infantry Brigade comprising a few Infantry units strung along the entire length of the LoC. Quite naturally, there were a few large unguarded gaps which were covered by foot patrols. A similar arrangement existed on the Pakistani side of the LoC.

However, all this changed in one stroke in early 1999, when Pakistani troops in civilian attire, intruded through the unguarded gaps and occupied the vacant mountain tops and ridgelines. These chosen routes of intrusions varied from 4 to 12 km inside the Indian territory. Consolidation followed, wherein locally improvised bunkers or *sangars* (*defensive walls with loopholes to fire weapons, made of stones and boulders, with or without the use of mud plaster, or cement-like material*) were built. This was followed by induction of heavy weaponry, ammunition, rations and other military hardware.[1] The Pakistanis established forward administrative bases inside Indian territory to sustain their troops (later, as the Conflict progressed, our valiant men of the Indian Air Force also made merry in reducing some such targets to ashes.) Simultaneously, the artillery guns and heavy mortars were moved up close to the LoC so as to provide fire support. Therefore, like the ghost in the darkness, the Pakistanis had in fact succeeded in giving India an absolutely unexpected tactical surprise. They appeared well-entrenched, as well as adequately armed and fed, to draw and proclaim a new LoC. It is ironic to recall that the Lahore Declaration was signed on 21 February 1999, only three months before the Kargil Conflict began.

The Lahore Declaration

Some pertinent recollections of the declaration were as follows:
- *Sharing a vision of peace and stability between the Republic of India and the Islamic Republic of Pakistan.*
- *Reiterating the determination to implement Simla Agreement of 1972.*
- *Convinced of the importance of mutually agreed confidence building measures.*
- *Shall refrain from intervention and interference.*

Lahore Declaration 1999: Exchange of pleasantries between the then Prime Minister of India Atal Bihari Vajpayee and Prime Minister of Pakistan Nawaz Sharif in February 1999

Sinister Design

Despite the signing of the Lahore Declaration between the political leaderships of the two countries, a sinister plan was being hatched by the Pakistani military leadership to change the geographical alignment of a 200-km long sanctified line (LoC) in the Kargil region. In the backdrop of such contemporary developments at the political level, some of the primary reasons that motivated the Pakistan military to embark upon such a sensational venture, appeared to be as follows: -

- To internationalise Kashmir as a nuclear flashpoint requiring urgent third-party intervention.
- Inject a fresh serum to revive the flagging *Jehad (a struggle or holy war against the infidels, on behalf of Islam).*
- To alter the LoC and disrupt its sanctity by capturing unguarded areas in Kargil.
- To achieve a better bargaining position for a possible trade-off against positions held by India in Siachen.[2]

There were several military designs incorporated in the need to carry out such an audacious military operation. Having intruded into advantageous areas, their army aimed to achieve their aforementioned motives by severing the Srinagar-Leh Highway (NH-1A). This highway, connecting Srinagar and Leh, passed through Kargil and was considered to be the lifeline of this region. By cutting this artery to Leh, Kargil district would have been left completely isolated. This would have enabled them in choking road-bound supplies, movement of troops, and other military hardware to the battle heights in the Siachen Glacier. In effect, this region was to be controlled by new masters who would establish a firm base in the Indian side of the LoC and bring life to a standstill at their will. Such ingress inside Indian Territory would have also opened new routes for armed militants to enter Doda-Kishtwar-Bhaderwah region located south of the Pir Panjal Range. Furthermore, by establishing a firm base in the Batalik Sector, they could move along the Shyok River and cut the only road link from Leh to the Siachen Brigade.

Hints of a long drawn-out plan: Later realisations

Interestingly, in the spring of 1999, the up-gradation of road communication opposite Dras by the Pakistanis was also reported. It was done by the Pakistanis with a supposed aim of moving its artillery to the forward post to dominate the Dras region and change the status quo. This movement proved to be an inherent part of this sinister plan, which was realised by the Indian troops only later, as the events unfolded in the forthcoming days.

('Kargil: Turning The Tide' by Lt Gen Mohinder Puri)

Additionally, the capture of 12 trained Pakistani mercenaries by Indian troops in the Turtuk region brought out their need to spread Islamic fundamentalism in Ladakh, as a long-term measure.

It may be interesting to note Nasim Zehra, a Pakistani Journalist, gives an account of intrusions by the NLI troops, duly supported by a map on the next page (Not to scale).

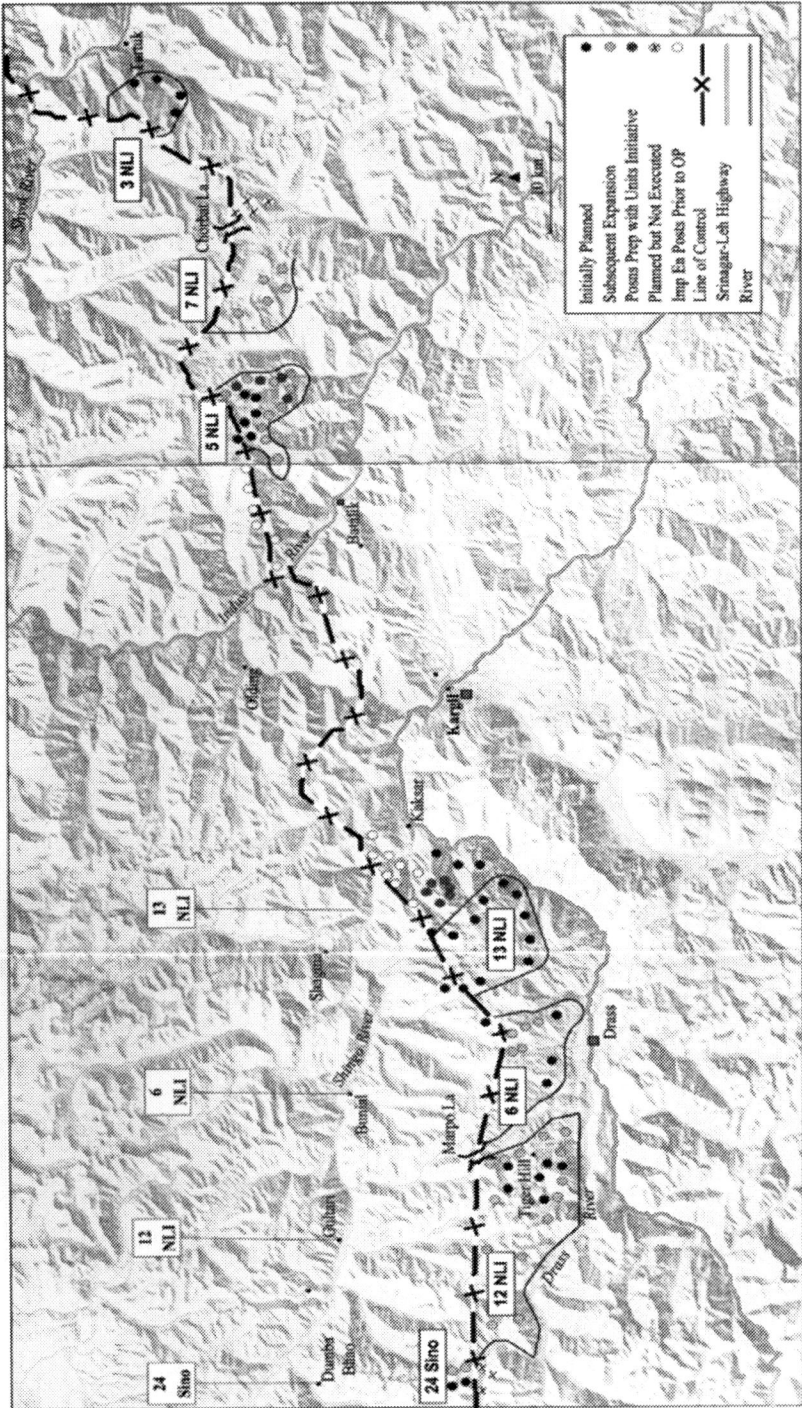

Operation Koh Paima

Source: Nasim Zehra, From Kargil to The Coup: Events That Shook Pakistan

The Ides of May '99

A considerable political euphoria and goodwill in Indo-Pak relations was generated on the Indian side in the backdrop of the Lahore Declaration of February 1999. Despite the Lahore visit and signing of the declaration, the Indian Prime Minister conveyed to his counterpart Mian Nawaz Sharif, on a number of occasions, that there was no reduction in Pakistani militant infiltration into India. Sharif replied that he 'would use his influence to correct the situation'[3]. Thereafter, in frequent inquiries, both the Indian Defence Minister and the Prime Minister sought answers of any drop in militancy numbers from the then Army Chief, Gen VP Malik. Unfortunately, the situations on the ground continued to remain unchanged. All formations in Northern Command were committed to counter infiltrations and counter-terrorist activities at this point, and there was no hint or intelligence of any Pakistani intrusions taking place into the Indian side of the LoC. The LoC was after all a *Laxman Rekha*[4] which was expected to be mutually accepted as status quo. It was anyway unthinkable that intrusions could be undertaken in such a rugged terrain, and that too when it was in the grip of the Himalayan winters.

The situational reports since 3 May and the visit by the Director General Military Operations (DGMO) to Leh and Kargil on 4-5 May had indicated presence of a few Mujahids on the dominating heights and ridgelines. Interestingly, reports of sightings of some unknown armed elements stationed at heights given to the nearest unit (3 PUNJAB) and the Headquarters 121 (I) Infantry Brigade by some locals, had not filtered down to the Army Headquarters. More so, even when the Pakistani shelling in Kargil scored a direct hit on the Brigade Ammunition Point, that too was brushed away as another routine event.[5] At the same time, an officer-led patrol had also gone missing in the Kaksar sector. Perhaps, a close reading of the situational reports, linking incidents of some Indian units already having skirmishes with the intruders, to the patrol that went missing, may have given an answer to the magnitude of the problem.

As the reports of increased sighting of the intruders kept emanating, Pakistani media also reported that Pakistani Mujahideen had captured some Indian areas near the LoC in J&K. Gen VP Malik, as mentioned in his book (*Kargil: From Surprise To Victory*), perhaps sensed a different situation and remarked, "Jehadi Militants do not usually capture territories". But, the Corps Commander, 15 Corps, stated that these intrusions were a 'local situation to be dealt with locally'[6].

The Army Chief, who was on an official visit abroad, reached New Delhi on 20 May 1999 and carried out an assessment with senior officers. The assessment was as follows:

- The exact numbers of intruders could not be ascertained.
- Identity of the intruders was still unknown.
- Extent of the Infiltrators was unknown/unidentified, but they appeared strung out all along the LoC in the Kargil region.

The extent of the deployment, their positions, the quantum as well as the type of machine gun firing, mortar fire and use of artillery, indicated that a major role had been played by the Pakistani Army. Based on an analysis, the latest assessment of the Headquarters Northern Command reflected that at least 250 to 300 intruders had occupied positions in the Kargil region.

Enemy preparations for an extended fight

An interesting insight based on the recovery of material after routing the enemy from their well-fortified posts revealed that they had catered to the finest details. Sophisticated plastic mines, barely decipherable in the snow had been laid to cover the assaulting lanes. Corrugated sheets had been brought up to cover sangars, and so had fibre huts been constructed for their officers. Their clothing kit also seemed very well calculated. Snow jackets and other winter clothing had been purchased and worn by the troops to endure the freezing temperatures. Shelters were pinned with family photographs, and there were envelopes to dispatch private mail to their kith and kin. Other paraphernalia included medicines, Urdu books and notebooks, in which their soldiers wrote accounts of their daily existence. In fact, they even had time to pen little poems. Leave applications, pay books, and other military documentation were also present in their locations, much on the lines of our own army. The sangars were well-stocked with rations and a reasonably efficient communication system was laid out in various locations.

(*'A Soldier's Diary: Kargil The Inside Story*' by Harinder Baweja)

Various government agencies such as the R&AW, the Intelligence Bureau, and even the Secretary of the National Security Council Secretariat (NSCS) opined that the intruders comprised 70% Jehadis and 30% Pakistani regulars. But, on further review by the NSCS, and in the light of intercepting telephonic conversations between the Pakistani Army Chief and the Pakistan Chief of General Staff, the same assessment got reversed stating the presence of 70 percent Pakistani army regulars and 30% Jehadi Militants. However, as events unfolded in the coming days, a general belief prevailed indicating 100% involvement of the Pakistani Army. It is interesting, in this context to have the then Indian Army Chief, Gen VP Malik, bring out in his book *Kargil: From Surprise To Victory*, as to how the Secretary NSCS whispered in his ear, "*Inki bhi to laaj rakhni hai*" (We have to save their honour too).

The War Begins

The Cabinet Committee on Security (CCS), along with the three service chiefs and others all came together after 24 May 1999. The message was clear: although the Indian territory was a victim of Pakistani intrusions, it was fully determined to evict every single enemy footprint at the earliest. However, as the Army, the Air Force or the Navy was not to cross the International Boundaries (IBs) or the LoC, no formal mobilisation or declaration of war was ordered. Considering the magnitude of the intrusions and the likely impact on other areas, the immediate tasks cut out for the Army were as follows: -

1. Forces to be in a state of readiness for orders to mobilise. In fact, forces to be ready to launch an offensive anywhere along the IB at a short notice.
2. Induct additional troops into J&K, particularly the Kargil region and create a force superiority.[7]
3. Maintain vigil on the border with China.
4. Monitor the military situation in J&K.

Since the Srinagar-Kargil-Leh road was under constant enemy threat, therefore induction of additional troops was to optimally utilise the alternate route of Pathankot-Manali-Upshi-Leh road. Such a measure would require enhancing the logistic infrastructure and facilities along this road.

The depth of Pakistani intrusions and the extent of their preparations had started to become evident by this time. It was also realised that the capture of each of the ridge lines from well-entrenched Pakistani regular forces, would entail extremely difficult military operations. Eviction meant that infantry assaults would be undertaken along narrow high-altitude approaches, all done under a relentless volume of enemy fire. This fire would be directed from different directions and features. Further detailed appreciation brought out the need for maximum artillery fire power which could support the assaulting troops almost right up to the objectives.

Surprise Catch: Telephonic Conversations

It becomes relevant to replay the texts of the telephonic conversations, held between Gen Pervez Musharraf (who was visiting China then) and Lieutenant General Mohammad Aziz Khan (Pakistan Chief of General Staff).

Conversation dated 26 May, 1999:

Musharraf (M): What else is the news on that side?

Aziz Khan (AK): No change in ground situation but they (Indians) have started rocketing and strafing. Today high altitude bombings have been done.

M: On their side, in those positions?

AK: Yes, in those positions, but three bombs landed in our side of the LoC.

M: So what was he (Indian Army DGMO) saying?

AK: Very interesting. I'll play the audio to you when you come back. It says that these infiltrators who are sitting here have your (Pak) help and support. He (DGMO) would stress on 3 points again and again. These militants should not be supported, without your support they could not be there, we will not let them stay there.

M: Anything else? Is Mian Sahib ok. (Nawaz Sharif)

AK: OK. He was confident. Today for the last two hours BBC has been reporting on the airstrikes by India. You may have seen in Press about UN Secretary General Kofi Annan's appeal that both countries should sit and talk.

Conversation dated 29 May, 1999:

AK: the situation on ground is OK. One of their (Indian) MI-17 armed helicopters was brought down. Have you listened to yesterday's news of Mian Sahib speaking to his Indian counterpart. He (Sharif) told him (Vajpayee) that escalation has been done by your people (Indians). He told Vajpayee that they should have waited before upping the ante by using Air Force and other means.

AK: Today we have a meeting with him (Nawaz Sharif) in the foreign office. GOC II Corps and the acting chief is supposed to attend.

M: OK. You may have to go as others don't know about the ground situation.

('Kargil: From Surprise to Victory' by Gen VP Malik)

Based on politico-military deliberations, the might of the Indian Air Force was requisitioned and made readily available for carrying out strikes on enemy positions, particularly those which were not discernible to the ground troops. The first air-to-ground strike by fighter ground-attack aircrafts was launched on 26 May.

The Battlefield

Ladakh, the northernmost region in the state of Jammu and Kashmir, formed the centre of the area of operations during Operation VIJAY. It is divided into two sectors: Leh and Kargil. Dominated by high-altitude mountain ranges, the Great Himalayan Mountain Range separates the Ladakh region from the Kashmir Valley. Three other major ranges, the Zanskar, Ladakh and the Karakoram ranges, also pass through the region, with peaks in Kargil district ranging from altitudes between 16,000 feet (4,880 m) and 18,000 feet (5,485 m).

> The cold arid high-altitude desert and its atmosphere makes this region an inhospitable and sparsely populated land. A local Ladakhi saying in this regard states,
>
> *"The passes are so high, and the land so barren, that only the best of friends or the fiercest of enemies would want to visit us."*

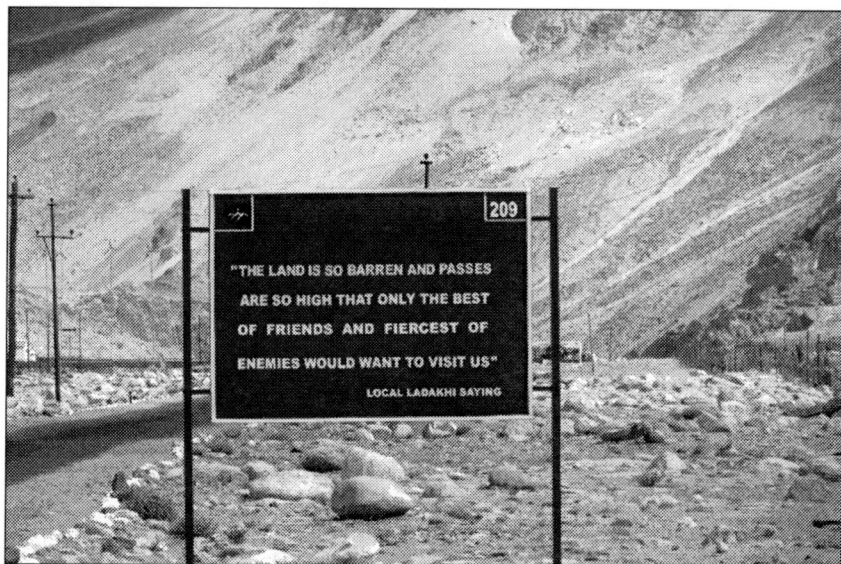

The main approach is the 434-km long Srinagar-Leh highway, called NH 1A (now NH-1D), which is most vulnerable near Dras and Kargil. The road winds through the critical Zoji La (Pass), which is the gateway to Ladakh, a chokepoint at an altitude of 11,575 feet (3,535 m) between Baltal and Dras. The highway further passes close to the LoC in the Kargil district. The Kargil and Turtuk sectors put together comprise five sub-sectors, namely, Mushkoh, Dras, Kaksar, Batalik and Turtuk.

The extremely high altitude, sub-arctic temperatures, rarefied thin air, rugged mountains, very high solar radiation exaggerated by very high velocity winds coupled with reduced oxygen levels compound the range of physiological and psychological ailments which had adverse effects on the troops and their equipment. High altitudes limit the functioning of the machines, as well as the pay load carrying capacity of aircrafts. Moreover, the mountainous terrain with steep slopes makes the movement of troops incredibly slow and vulnerable to enemy fire, thus making it an unforgiving battlefield. Thus, the natural landscape in this region posed as much deadly a challenge for the troops, as the enemy, on the mountain tops and the ridge lines.

DRAS SUB-SECTOR

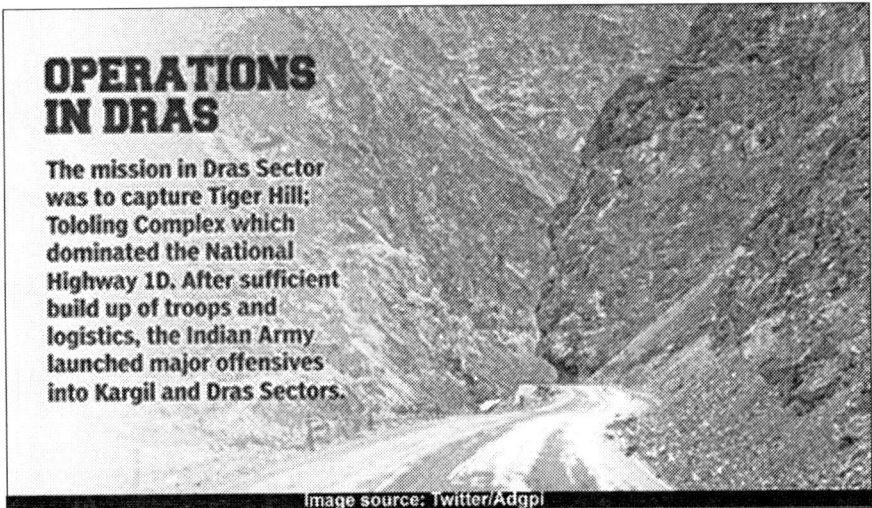

OPERATIONS IN DRAS

The mission in Dras Sector was to capture Tiger Hill; Tololing Complex which dominated the National Highway 1D. After sufficient build up of troops and logistics, the Indian Army launched major offensives into Kargil and Dras Sectors.

Image source: Twitter/Adgpi

The scene at the Traffic Check Post (TCP) at Sonamarg, was chaotic and choked with hastily inducting units coming to Dras from counter-insurgency locations near Srinagar. Endless convoys choked both sides of the road. Some units were awaiting transfer orders after a gruelling stint in Siachen, and most of their troops were on leave. 16 GRENADIERS, which was the holding unit for the Dras-Kargil sector, still had their families staying with them. The three-tonner vehicles of an inducting unit groaned while negotiating the turns and sharp bends on the road to Kargil. One such convoy, on 13 May, was hastily waved down by a Colonel, camped on the side of the road, who thrust his head into the Commanding Officers vehicle and told him to stop or else get killed. 'They (Pakistanis) are dominating the road, you'll all be killed.' The Colonel, an artillery officer, had already had a taste of the enemy firepower and had been under incessant rain of shells fired from across the LoC and from nearby heights of Dras sub-sector. Soon, the shells rained down on this vehicle column too, and there was dust everywhere. Through the haze, the CO asked as to where they could find the Brigade Commander, Brigadier Surinder Singh. They located him sitting in a bunker and reported their arrival. The Brigade Commander opened the conversation with,

> *"Don't worry, some atankwadis (militants) have come in. We will catch them by the scruff of their necks and throw them out."*[8]

All night, the newly inducted unit personnel remained huddled in their vehicles. The unit in question was 1 NAGA, and the thoughts of the CO amidst the thunder of artillery fire, were that his brave unit was now headed into a deadly war zone. The enemy they had to face was not just gunfire alone, but also the formidable weather and the rugged terrain. In fact, so vague was the nomenclature of the people who had intruded inside Indian Territory that the reference to the intruders was with the word *"they"*, and *"they"* had to be thrown out[9]. Despite these, the Nagas were determined to face these challenges head-on.

Initial Retaliation

By mid-May, the appreciation of the situations as per the 121 (I) Infantry Brigade was *(Refer to Image 1)*:

1. Approximately 15 or 16 "they" (militants) were present.
2. Distribution of these 15 or 16 militants was shown against Tololing, Point 5140, Point 4700 and Point 5100.

The plight of 1 NAGA, which was the first battalion to be inducted into the Kargil region within 48 hours (of earlier fighting counter-insurgency in Srinagar), was quite different. Major Sharma, who was the officiating Commanding Officer, even highlighted the absence of any recce by his troops or acclimatisation or orientation for the attacks. The unit had not even carried out any recce of the objectives before they were asked to move from Kashmir Valley to Dras[10]. The problems for the Nagas were further compounded with the absence of any adequate guides or terrain maps, and the actual strength of each company was just 50 to 55 men. Despite all of this, as Baweja mentions, the Brigade Commander brushed these necessities aside by telling the CO that speed was of paramount importance in launching an offensive, as the militants would barely be able to stand the might of the Infantry battalion.

The officiating Commanding Officer of 1 NAGA was given his operational orders on 15 May, which were *(Refer to Image 2)*:

- One Company was to move through Bimbat Nullah to attack Pt 5140 (Tololing Top) and capture it by morning of 17 May.
- Three Companies were to move along axis Dras-Sando-Point 5100[11] via Gorkha Nullah, and capture Pt 5100, hold feature with one platoon and secure area Pt 4700.
- Thereafter, these companies were to link up with the company at Pt 5140 and capture area Hump and Pt 4590 with one company.

Identifying the Enemy?

At the outset, the numerical assumptions that guided the unit's immediate response stated the presence of mere 10-15 militants with their small arms against our otherwise fully equipped infantry battalion. But, the general perception that prevailed and that remained unanswered was, that if only militants were occupying these heights, why was the Pakistani army raining down artillery shells at such a large scale?

Marching towards the enemy: 1 NAGA launch operations

Having marched 10 km through slush and snow, the unit reached Sando as dawn set off on 16 May. Thus, the Indian side of the war had finally commenced by the last light of 15 May, 1999, when the brave and resolute 1 NAGA moved to accomplish their given objectives. Patrols from Sando tried to reach the ridgeline but could not succeed due to the lack of snow equipment for negotiating the hard and slippery snow. After establishing harbour, the assaulting company commanders moved forward for recce of Pt 5100 when their movement got stalled due to accurate and intense artillery fire hitting them, probably directed from an observation post from Tiger Hill. 1 NAGA reached the base of Pt 5100-Pt 5353 ridgeline on 17 May. Without waiting, this unit launched an attack, but the leading elements encountered sheer cliffs with thick and hard standing snow. Despite all odds, the Nagas continued, and reached the ridgeline before sunrise. Unfortunately, this is when the assessed militants opened fire from the machine guns deployed on the ridge line, thus preventing any further move.

The sound and quantum of fire was easily heard in Dras and the Brigade Headquarters. Against disbelief, it ultimately dawned on the Commander that a lot was amiss. The attack plan of Pt 5140 also met a similar fate where the troop's encountered snow-covered steep cliffs and intense machine gun fire. The entrenched Pakistanis covered every move of 1 NAGA, by firing parachute illuminating flares at night. The enemy was firing at them from three sides and the company patrols suffered a few fatal and other non-fatal casualties. But, despite the hardships, the Nagas, with undeterred determination, continued their operations to achieve their objectives.

An account by an officer on 1 NAGA states,

"We returned fire but firing uphill was useless. The enemy was dominating the ridgeline and contradictory to our plight, they also had complete cover. The morning of 17 May 99 had come and gone and we were still shivering in the snow, chilled to our bones, while the militants continued to remain in their positions."

('A Soldier's Diary: Kargil The Inside Story' by Harinder Baweja)

First Attack on Tiger Hill: *"The Sartaj"*

On 16 May, after having some idea of the fate which had befallen 1 NAGA, the atmosphere and mood in the Brigade Headquarters had completely changed. The Adjutant's office in 8 SIKH received an urgent call from the Brigade to launch a company for emergency operations. "Send the company commander for a briefing", was the terse message. Major Arun Suri, Second-in-Command (2IC) of the battalion, took his vehicle, and driving through the night without any headlights, he reached the headquarters in Pandras. The mood of the Commander had become very sombre. His instructions to the young Major were to divide his company into section groups and place them around the Tiger Hill. The points which the men were to occupy were marked on a map laid out on a rickety table. While Arun was being briefed by the staff, Brig Surinder Singh rang up the CO, and complaining about his 2IC, remarked that he was being quite argumentative. In a raised voice, he ordered that the task be done. On returning from the Brigade Headquarters (as Harinder Baweja mentions in her book *'A Soldier's Diary Kargil: An Inside Story'*), an agitated Major Suri stated that,

> *"They (Brigade staff) have no information, they can't give any guides, they can't even tell me where the feature is and how we should get to the objective."*

8 SIKH was actually on the move to the Valley, when, following this episode, it was ordered to proceed to Dras for operations in the Kargil Sector. This unit reached Pandras on 12 May. Unfortunately, like 1 NAGA, this unit too, neither possessed any adequate snow-clothing, nor got any time to acclimatise to the formidable situations. Overall, there were deficiency of most of the required support weapons and radio sets, but the determination of the resolute troops continued to remain incredibly high. The story was the same.

Climbing up the Tiger Hill

Meanwhile, some infiltrators had been seen on Pts 4195, 4460 and Tiger Hill, which were at altitudes ranging from 4500 to 5600 m. Initially assumed no challenge against the trained Indian troops, the Sikhs were ordered to launch companies immediately, encircle the Mujahideen, and liquidate them. Since 16 GRENADIERS, which was in Dras and the holding battalion, did not have prior knowledge or idea of the enemy or features, they were of little help to 8 SIKH. On 16 May, the unit was tasked to send one company on a special mission by forming nine smaller parties and encircle Tiger Hill from all sides. But, just next morning, as some enemy presence had also been spotted on Pt 4875 and Pt 4540 in Mushkoh Valley, the orders changed, and this battalion (less one company) was tasked to attack Tiger Hill from the northeast and northwest. The objective was to be captured by 18 May. *(Refer to Image 3).*

Struggling against odds

At a later stage, one section of the jawans (soldiers) led by a JCO, could walk no more and even took off their shoes to stretch their legs and feet. Some even managed to fall asleep in the bitter cold. Such were the effects of non-acclimatisation and hasty response to launch operations.

('A Soldier's Diary: Kargil The Inside Story' by Harinder Baweja)

The company commander reached Pt 4460 without any mishap and radioed that he had seen tent marks. As there was no firing, the southern spur of Tiger Hill appeared unguarded. With this, a fresh set of orders came in, ordering an entire battalion (less one company) to move up towards the Tiger Hill. En route to Sando Top, another new order came through the operator which was to divert and move to "Pariyon Ka Talab" *(Refer to Image 3)*. The men were taking steps in robot-like motions, with officers in the lead.

By dawn of 18 May, the leading elements started climbing along a nullah to Tiger Hill. A patrol led by Subedar Joginder Singh was sent to open up a route, but came under intense fire from Tiger Hill. Subedar Joginder was killed and some jawans were wounded. Another platoon came under intense fire and was forced to fall back to Tingal Nullah. It was thus clear to the CO that Tiger Hill was held by at least one company and adequately supported by artillery fire. It was realised that the capture of Tiger Hill would entail at least three infantry battalions attacking in a coordinated manner.

By now, 8 SIKH was left with just one company to capture "Pariyon Ka Talab". This company reached the area only by 28 May, and after having established a firm base, sent a patrol under Lieutenant Kant to secure the features Rock Fall and Pariyon ka Talab. This patrol too came under intense firing from Tiger Hill, wherein an officer and a few jawans suffered casualties, which thereby forced the patrol to fall back. Thus, the enemy's route of maintenance continued to remain open, and though 8 SIKH made a few futile attempts to regain lost ground, as well as to close in with the Pakistanis, their attempts repeatedly met stiff resistance.

Worsening situations

By 21 May, there was blood everywhere in the Kargil sector. The enemy was effectively dominating the road in Mushkoh and Dras. In Kaksar, it was equally serious. The demeanour and optimism in the Brigade Headquarters had transformed. Their assessment had fallen apart, and all heads were shaking in disbelief. The patrols led by 1 NAGA and 8 SIKH had established contact with Pakistanis. This had brought out some clarity in the situation. Tololing, Pt 5140 and Pt 4875 (which overlooked the highway and Mushkoh Valley), had to revert into Indian hands in order to ensure regular movement of troops and supplies into Kargil. The battle of Dras sector was to commence after inducting 56 Mountain Brigade from Counter Insurgency Operations in the Valley.

Fighting the Unknown

Some texts of the conversation between a wounded soldier of 8 SIKH and the stretcher bearers substantiate the complete ignorance about the enemy:

"I'll die, I'll die, saale, they almost roasted us alive"

"Don't worry, we are almost there," replied one of the stretcher bearers. *They had been carrying the multiple gunshot injured jawan for an hour, and would continue to do so for another hour.*

"Hoya ki?" (What happened?)

"They were all well-equipped and sitting high. How will we ever reach them?"

"Did you see them?"

"Nahi yaar," he groaned. *("Not really")*

"Pata nahi, (do not know) how are they managing to stay in so much snow and carry those machine guns."

"They must have orders too from some Karnail, or some Jarnail"

"Theek hai, (Good enough) we are faujis, we have to fight or why are we wearing this uniform"

"I am willing to die but what kind of a war is this? We don't even know who we are fighting and how many!"

(*'A Soldier's Diary: Kargil The Inside Story'* by Harinder Baweja)

This Brigade had already shed 1 NAGA earlier, hence, the Brigade Headquarters moved 1 BIHAR to Dras on 16 May, followed by their third battalion, 18 GRENADIERS. The formation was placed under the command of 3 Infantry Division. 1 BIHAR was moved further up to Batalik and placed under the 70 Infantry Brigade. 18 GRENADIERS carried out acclimatisation and orientation for the impending operations. In another shift, on 1 June, 8 Mountain Division was inducted from the Valley into Dras, and subsequently, 56 Mountain Brigade was reverted to its parent formation of 8 Mountain Division. The Division also took over the Operational Control of Dras and Mushkoh sectors.[12]

The First Attack on Tololing

Tololing was perhaps the most important feature to be captured during the Conflict, as it bestowed the Pakistanis a clear dominance over the only lifeline to Kargil, that is, the NH-1A. The Tololing-Pt 4590 complex overlooked the Dras village and directly the Dras-Kargil highway from a distance of just about 5 km. The firmly entrenched enemy could at will interfere with the movement of vehicular traffic moving on this highway, especially, with the observed artillery fire. Such a precarious situation meant that all vehicular movement was possible only during bad and foggy weather, or at night.

On 20 May, another meeting took place between Brig Surinder Singh and Commanding Officers of 18 GRENADIERS, 8 SIKH and 1 NAGA. Major General Budhwar, the GOC of 3 Infantry Division, had also come from Kargil to the Brigade Headquarters. Herein lay the irony of the macabre situation. 1 NAGA and 8 SIKH had just paid a heavy price when launched into operations, and had to come under such accurate, intense and voluminous fire, that their movement got almost instantly seized. Yet again, according to Harinder Baweja, the GOC (who was briefing in a volatile theatre) commented, "There are only a handful of mercenaries there. There is no need to worry."[13]

The task to evict the handful of intruders fell on 18 GRENADIERS/ 56 Mountain Brigade. Interestingly, since induction into Dras, the battalion had been given only four days to carry out reconnaissance, conduct acclimatisation training for high-altitude conditions, and prepare for the attack.

On being given the task to capture Tololing and Pt 4590, Col Kushal Thakur (CO 18 GRENADIERS) and his 2IC Lt Col R Vishwanathan, went up to the fire base of 16 GRENADIERS, whose troops were in contact with the enemy at distances ranging between 900 and 1200 m.

The Commanding Officer ordered dumping of ammunition along the Bimbat Nullah, followed by establishment of a fire base on the South-Eastern approach, where a platoon of 16 GRENADIERS was already positioned. Apparently, the enemy was observing the movements of Thakur's party. Heavy machine gun and mortar fire was brought down on them. Undeterred, the motivated and dedicated soldiers of 18 GRENADIERS continued to give their attack plans a definite shape. While A Company was commanded by Major Randhir Singh Rathore, B Company was under Maj Adhikari, Captain J Das Gupta was with the C Company, and Major Vishal, was commanding the D Company. Two spirited young officers, Lieutenant Balwan and Captain Nimbalkar, were with the Ghatak Platoon. Finally, the attack plan of the unit was as follows *(Refer Image 4)*:

- Ghataks to move along the South-Eastern approach through 16 GRENADIERS and secure Pt 4590 from North, followed by A Company.
- B Company to follow the Southern approach to Pt 4590 via fire base of the 16 GRENADIERS.
- C and D Companies to move along Tololing Nullah and attack the feature from the west.
- Simultaneously, 1 NAGA were to attack Pt 5140.
- D-Day: night 22/23 May 1999.

The Nation Watches: Recapturing Tololing

The attack on the Tololing complex commenced as planned. It was an uphill task with icy winds and frequent rains, compounding the degree of difficulty. Many were stumbling and falling due to the slippery slopes. Therefore, the attack did not go as planned and by first light on 23 May, the leading elements were still 1 km short of the objective. Adding to the hurdles, the unit came under intense enemy machine gun fire. Captain SA Nimbalkar moved up the south-eastern spur on all fours under heavy enemy fire. They were pinned down, but the unit did not really suffer any serious casualties. At this time, the CO and 2IC, had also moved up from the fire base and Col Thakur decided to launch A Company along the eastern spur. This was all happening under bad weather conditions coupled with poor visibility, which acted as a cover for the progressing Indian troops. Consequentially,

A Company managed to close in up to 300 to 400 metres of the enemy by the same evening. Unfortunately, at this juncture, the weather cleared up. On sighting the Indian forces, the entrenched Pakistanis unleashed their fire power at their disposal. This included Heavy Machine Guns (HMGs), Medium Machine Guns (MMGs) and even Air Defence (AD) guns being used in the ground role. Falling darkness saved the defending troops further attrition as the firing became inaccurate.

Throughout the next day, Maj Adhikari and his men remained pinned down in the open, with only boulders to protect them. Meanwhile, along the southern approach, one company of 18 GRENADIERS came 300 yards (approximately 274 m) short of Pt 4590 when all his troops came under intense firing. The CO launched A company under Maj RS Rathore along the eastern spur who again came as close as 300 yards but attracted a very heavy volume of assorted weapons fire. (An added disadvantage for the troops was them carrying at least 20 kg of weight in their rucksacks comprising emergency rations, clothing, ammunition, and so on.) Additionally, foothold on the slippery snow was near impossible, and in the assault stage, many troops just slid down the slippery mountain side, almost back to their starting points.

Reality dawns: First encounter with the Enemy

The eye opener was when for the first time they saw their enemy – men in black outfits with red headgears. About 15 of them were on the western side of Pt 4590 and another 15-20 were sitting on top. The number was almost three times than what the Division had stated. The dilemma for the CO was acute: if they withdrew, they would have lost precious ground. Subedar Randhir Singh of the unit had also remarked that if they fell back, then a second attempt would not bring them so close to the enemy unless the weather turns foggy again. The enemy was shouting, *"Allah ho Akbar"* and raising their weapons in victory. They were in great numbers and fully trained in employing all Battalion support weapons, plus adequately trained to rain down artillery fire, as well as execute all aspects of fighting in a coordinated manner. When many lives were already lost due to the sheer blindness of the situation, it finally dawned in the Divisional and Brigade Headquarters that these infiltrators were not militants or Mujahideens.

Detailed operational discussions followed. The leaders at all levels rose to the occasion to infuse that 'kill spirit' among the rank and file. It proved fatal to the intruders.

The stalemate continued with heavy exchanges of firing from both sides. On 26-27 May, the first air strikes by the Indian Air Force took place, which resulted in the downing of our two MiG aircrafts. Although the effect of the Air Force strikes did not lead to any tangible results, it raised the motivation and morale of the Indian troops and led to the Pakistanis becoming downcast. Armed MI-17 helicopters were also pressed into service but had little results. In fact, one MI-17 machine was shot down by a Stinger missile fired from Pt 4590. Thereafter, the use of helicopters was withdrawn. During this period, there were only five fire units employed, which were grossly insufficient, and there were no additional officers in the Observation Posts to give target coordinates and corrections.

From the battleground: Verbal Duels

"If you have the guts, come and collect the officers' body" to which an enraged Nimbalkar replied, *"You bastard, I've come to take your body."*

(*'A Soldier's Diary Kargil: The Inside Story'* by Harinder Baweja)

The Second Attack on Tololing

A detailed fire plan incorporating Bofors, Light and Heavy Mortars was drawn up. D-Day for the second attack was postponed from 28 May to 29 May. Finally, after heavy preparatory bombardment lasting for two hours, the second attack got under way on the night of 29/30 May. *(Refer to Image 4)* As per the plan, Maj Adhikari led an assault on Tololing's Southern ridge, and two elements led by Captain Nimbalkar and Lieutenant Balwan progressed towards the Tololing Top. Maj Adhikari and about 40 men were able to reach up to 30 m of a bunker but could not secure it. He then personally crawled another 10 m forward to silence a machinegun, but was hit fatally in the head. Words of his operator, Lance Naik Rajinder Singh, echoed in the CO's ears, "We can't move left or right...do something to save us". The CO and 2IC, Lt Col Vishwanathan, rushed towards Maj Adhikari, but had to take cover. Sitting behind a boulder they were told by a Lance Naik that the Major and his operator had been killed. Daylight came and they could see the bodies of Maj Adhikari and others from behind the boulder. This was also the first time that verbal duels were exchanged between the Pakistanis and Capt Nimbalkar. The bodies of Major Adhikari and others lay there, while the enemy reinforced Pt 4590, and Tololing, from Pt 5140, which was just behind.

After observing the enemy's strength, dispositions and automatic weapons, Col Thakur concluded that at least one enemy rifle company was positioned on the Tololing Complex. He also noticed that during engagements by own artillery, the enemy took cover in caves and no sooner had the fire lifted, they again occupied pre-planned positions, fully armed with machine guns and stocked with adequate ammunition. Their movement between Pt 5140 and Tololing meant that reinforcement plans had been well-rehearsed.

On 1 June, Headquarters 8 Mountain Division, had assumed the operational responsibility of Dras and Mushkoh Sectors. By early next day, the *sangars* on Tololing and Pt 4590 were well identified and subjected to intense artillery bombardment. Col Thakur, along with his 2IC, Vishu, and his gallant troops, continued to hold their last positions, fortifying themselves behind boulders and other types of cover. On the same night, in another assault personally led by the 2IC, an intense fire-fight took place at ranges between 30 and 50 metres, where he sustained a machine gun burst and breathed his last in the CO's arms. The attack was replete with the acts of the Grenadier's heroism over and over again.

Vishu: Lt Col R Vishwanathan

An interesting episode occurred just before this attack was launched, wherein a discussion regarding the change of this Commanding Officer occurred between the Corps Commander and the Brigade Commander. As mentioned in Lt Gen Bammi's book (Kargil 1999: The Impregnable Conquered), they ordered the 2IC to take over command, or rather Col Thakur to be relieved of command. On the other hand, Vishu, a true soldier, refused and implored to the senior leadership "not to destabilise the battalion at this juncture", which led the order to be shortly reversed.

(*'Kargil 1999: The Impregnable Conquered'* by Lt Gen YM Bammi)

Although some ground had been gained through the attack in the battle for Tololing on 2 June, the battle was not over yet. The valiant

Grenadiers continued to hang onto their perilous perch. Tasked to capture Pt 5140 in conjunction with 18 GRENADIERS, 1 NAGA at that stage could just muster adequate strength for the attack. On 27 May, the unit reached 150 m below the ridgeline when they encountered a sheer vertical cliff. The enemy also had readjusted their weapons on the likely approach route of 1 NAGA and brought down intense fire on them. Attempts to move up were futile and casualties were mounting. At this juncture, the company commander decided to fall back and was ordered by GOC 8 Mountain Division to return to base and re-organise for future impending operations.

First Decisive Victory: Tololing Recaptured

Tololing was the operational juggernaut of the Kargil War. 8 SIKH, 1 NAGA and 18 GRENADIERS had done more than their bit to wrest the Tololing and Tiger Hill complexes from Pakistani intrusions. For the final capture, it required detailed planning, fresh troops, adequate artillery, and logistical support. Thus, in order to fully regain the Indian Pride, the GOC allotted two additional units, 2 RAJPUTANA RIFLES and 18 GARHWAL RIFLES to 56 Mountain Brigade. A marvel of improvisation was carried out by using the Bofors gun in the direct firing role, duly incorporated by the Artillery Commander, Brig Lakhvinder Singh.

The attack plan was as follows:

- 2 RAJ RIF to attack Tololing from South
- 18 GARH RIF to attack Pt 5140 from North East
- 18 GRENADIERS to provide firm base in Phase 1
- In Phase 2, after capture of Tololing, 18 GRENADIERS were tasked to secure Hump
- D-Day: Night 12/13 June

Prior to the commencement of battle, an amazing build-up had been carried out by 2 RAJ RIF. Two fire bases each with four MMGs, two grenade launchers, four rocket launchers and two 51 mm mortars were established under Subedar Man Singh and Subedar RKS Lamba. Approximately 400 porters worked over four nights to dump nearly two second lines of ammunition for all weapons of the fire base. Local population remained fully supportive to provide all possible assistance to the army, at all stages of the Conflict. Even the Regimental Aid Post (RAP) was moved up to 750 m of Tololing and had life-saving medicines and six stretches. Every soldier clerk, and even a partially blind trade man, climbed up and down at least four times to dump these stores. An interesting point was to defer the assault from 11 June (being Friday and auspicious for Pakistanis) to 12 June. Accordingly, as dusk fell on 12 June, the full might of artillery gunfire commenced, and the Tololing feature turned into a ferociously burning red hill. This fire ball was given a small gap to catch the enemy who had been crouching on reverse slopes, who could come back to their defences in the open, and again savour the splintering effects of artillery fire. Consequentially, enemy casualties occurred in large numbers, but they were able to recover.

Bofors guns firing

The Bofors guns were firing in direct firing role, enabling the troops to advance up to 200 m from the ridgeline. Amidst this, the Pakistanis discovered the movement of the Indian troops from Pt 4590, who then brought down intense fire, but fortunately, the resolute troops had already established a foothold by then *(Refer to Image 4)*. At this stage, another company launched its assault on Tololing Top, which ultimately came down to hand-to-hand fighting. Maj Vivek Gupta suffered grievous wounds, and at this critical moment Captain Mridul Kumar, a young Forward Observation Officer (FOO) took over the company to complete the capture of the objective. The Pakistanis made some desperate attempts to recapture Tololing, but their attempts were foiled single-handedly by Company Havaldar Major Yashveer Singh who kept lobbing hand grenades at them from a distance of barely 30 m.

Almost in immediate succession, the CO 2 RAJ RIF Col M B Ravindranath, launched one of the companies to capture the rest of Pt 4590. Despite the proximity to own troops at the Tololing Top, effective Artillery fire was unleashed on Pt 4590 again. Meanwhile, another company was ordered to clear the northern slopes of Tololing. By the following day, 2 RAJ RIF had given India the first decisive victory and success of Operation VIJAY. The Queen of the battle stood solid and victorious on its objective.

> ### "My Son is now the son of the Motherland"
>
> *Said Magodu Basappa, a retired school teacher, proudly. He had a reason to be proud. His son Ravindranath, a Colonel and Commanding Officer In-Charge of the 2 Rajputana Rifles, was tasked to capture the mighty Tololing Peak back from Pakistani intruders. On June 14, the family received the call they had been waiting for; Col Ravindranath telephoned to say,* **"Operation Successful**, *We have captured the Tololing Peak".*
>
> **"It was the happiest moment of my life,"** *said Basappa, with tears in his eyes.*

The reverse slopes of this feature had the Pakistani administrative bunkers in which our victorious troops found good stock of ghee, butter and honey, which was put to good use in the prevailing -5°C temperature. Additionally, the capture of large stocks of ammunition and different calibre weapons broke the myth created by the Pakistanis that the ingress into Indian territory was by mujahideens.

Eliminating the residual enemy footprints

Having punished the enemy with large volume of infantry and artillery fire, the men of 18 GRENADIERS were able to recover the bodies of their fallen comrades. At the same time, this unit prepared to assault another feature of the Tololing complex called Hump *(Refer to Image 4)*. Hump was a whale back feature that was connected to Tololing by another feature called Saddle. Just before the H-hour, this unit came under air burst shelling, and in one swish of the hand lost some of its men, with an additional few injured. Subsequently, the CO, Col Thakur, regrouped and infused their spirit to attack, after a readjustment delay of 30 minutes in their H-hour. The reserves for phase 2, C and D Companies were now tasked to capture the Hump under Major Joy Dasgupta. Like their previous acts of heroism displayed during the attack to capture Tololing, 18 GRENADIERS, who were seething with anger at the loss of their comrades, rushed uphill and in one swoop simply vanquished the intruding Pakistanis, thus inflicting heavy casualties on them.

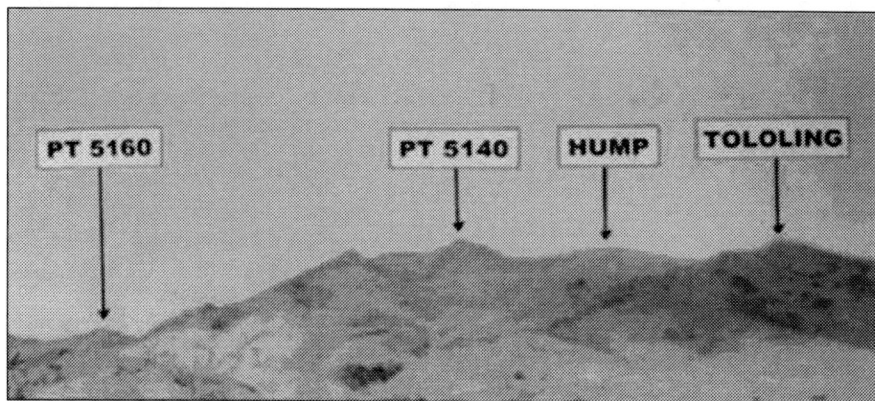

Source: ADGPI (Not to the scale)

Point 5140 Captured

Pt 5140 is a dominating feature adjacent to the Tololing (*Refer to Image 4*), and Pakistani troops had been reinforcing the Tololing feature from this point. The task of capturing this feature was a part of operations of the Mountain Brigade, and to be executed by 13 JAK RIF. As nightfall came on 15 June, the battalion launched their attack towards the objective. This was preceded by intense artillery shelling on the adjacent Rocky Knob, as well as, at Pt 5140. However, the advance of the troops was stalled by midnight due to effective fire from well-sited and impregnable bunkers positioned at the area Hump and Base of Pt 5140. Even direct rocket fire failed to destroy the bunkers or dislodge the enemy.

Amidst this, CO had to be evacuated on medical grounds, leaving the huge responsibility of the command on the young shoulders of Maj YK Joshi, 2IC, who was immediately promoted as a Lieutenant Colonel. As the enemy *sangars* were strongly holding up the forward momentum of attack to secure the objectives, any further daylight

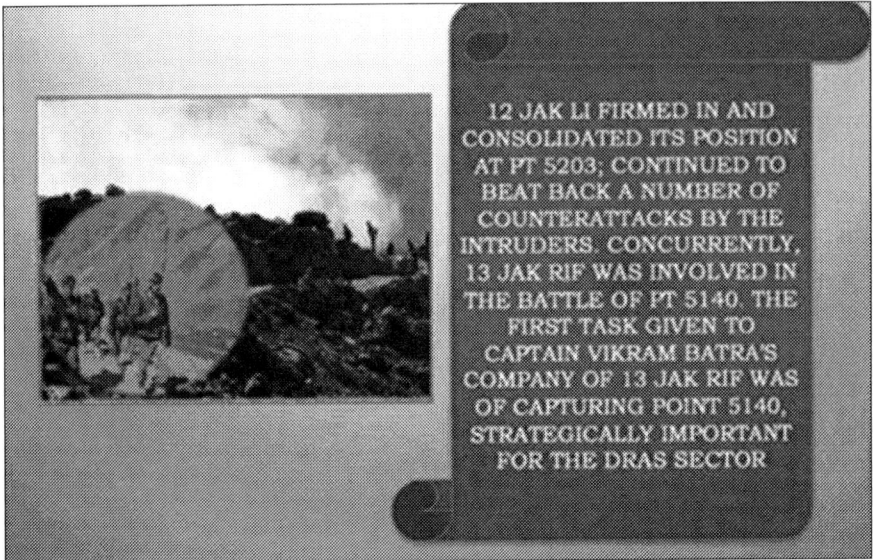

12 JAK LI FIRMED IN AND CONSOLIDATED ITS POSITION AT PT 5203; CONTINUED TO BEAT BACK A NUMBER OF COUNTERATTACKS BY THE INTRUDERS. CONCURRENTLY, 13 JAK RIF WAS INVOLVED IN THE BATTLE OF PT 5140. THE FIRST TASK GIVEN TO CAPTAIN VIKRAM BATRA'S COMPANY OF 13 JAK RIF WAS OF CAPTURING POINT 5140, STRATEGICALLY IMPORTANT FOR THE DRAS SECTOR

Source: ADGPI

attacks would have entailed quite heavy casualties. The Bofors 155 mm medium guns were again pressed into the attack in a direct firing role on the *sangars* that had stalled 13 JAK RIF further movement towards the enemy. The coordinated firing commenced by late noon on 17 June and was complimented by all the available direct firing weapons of 13 JAK RIF. The ferocity of the attack by 13 JAK RIF completely annihilated the enemy, who were either dead or were forced to make a rearward run to Pt 5140. 13 JAK RIF had now reached the base of Pt 5140. This unit was joined by 18 GARH RIF and 1 NAGA, so that a multidirectional attack could be launched to erase any Pakistani footprint there in. Over 100 guns opened up on Pt 5140 two days later, and expectedly, 13 JAK RIF raced up the southern slope. D Company was led by Captain Vikram Batra who personally killed four Pakistanis in a hand-to-hand fight. The swiftness of their climb and ferocious assault, unnerved the enemy, and one by one, each of the seven solid bunkers was taken physically. By next morning, the Pakistanis were either dead or had fled using rappelling ropes down the feature.

Sartaj Captured: Regaining Tiger Hill

After the Tololing, the next most prominent feature still held by the

Pakistanis in Dras sector was Tiger Hill. Tiger Hill was comparatively less important than the Tololing Top as it was located 10 kilometres from the highway. But the wide media coverage had caught the imagination of every Indian home which turned the capture of Tiger Hill into a national objective and made it the ultimate pinnacle of Operation VIJAY. Accordingly, Maj General Puri, decided to infuse a fresh Brigade Headquarters for the capture of Tiger Hill. The gauntlet fell on 192 Mountain Brigade, and its commander Brigadier MPS Bajwa. Assessment of the stretch and panorama indicated that the defence of Tiger Hill spread from the Top to the V-cut, which was approximately more than 300 metres long *(Refer to Image 3)*. The area between Collar and Rhino Horn was very difficult to climb because it was full of loose gravel and additionally covered with slippery ice. Therefore, the key for a successful attack lay in securing Tiger Hilltop, for which, the features Tooth, Tongue and Collar formed the most likely approaches.

By now, it was assessed that the enemy had about two companies deployed in the area of Tiger Hill and Pt 4875. The automatic weapons of the enemy covered all likely approaches effectively as had been experienced at the Tololing. The mission to recapture Tiger Hill was assigned to 18 GRENADIERS and 8 SIKH. 8 SIKH were already deployed at the base of the Tiger Hill. The highly motivated Indian troops were in high spirit, having just had Tololing captured. As the preparations for the battle commenced, the focus of the camera lenses of all TV Channels on the impending battle also turned towards the Tiger Hill Complex.

The brave soldiers of 18 GRENADIERS left the firm base by evening of 03 July. The progress was relatively slow for the company under Capt Nimbalkar, who were accompanied by a column of Ghataks (commando force of each battalion) under Lieutenant Balwan. Defying all odds, by the following morning, Balwan reached 20 m short of Top, so much so that he could even hear the unsuspecting enemy talking amongst themselves. The surprised enemy reacted with ferocity and realising that he could not wait for another company to build up, Balwan assaulted the position with just six men. *Sangar* by *sangar* had to be taken, and these brave Grenadiers fixed ropes to climb further up to the Top. The other company was also just 50 metres short of the objective. At this point, Grenadier Yogendra Singh Yadav, despite being shot by at least seven bullets in his left arm, crawled and single-handedly cut down the Pakistanis manning their defences. His daredevilry infused greater courage in the balance of men of his section, who further killed 12 Pakistanis and took control of the Tiger Hill Top. Subsequently, counter-attacks by the enemy in small groups were also successfully beaten back.

According to the first-hand accounts, the sheer heroism of the Indian troops had demoralised the enemy to an extent that their panic became evident in their responsive actions, particularly in the half-hearted counter-attacks that thence followed. Consequentially, they suffered heavy casualties.

Psychological Victory: Premature Media Declarations

By 6 am, the GOC 15 Corps informed the Army Chief that Tiger Hill had been successfully recaptured. But the fact was that only a part of the mountain had been wrested by the Indian troops by this time. However, Star News prematurely beamed that Tiger Hill had been recaptured, which also hit the Pakistani Prime Minister who was waiting in New York for his talks with US President Bill Clinton. The news was beamed all over the world and acted as a major physical and psychological blow for the Pakistani military and political leadership.

In the meantime, in the raging battle to capture Tiger Hill, 8 SIKH, who had provided the firm base for 18 GRENADIERS, were ordered to attack and capture area Helmet and area India Gate (*Refer to Image 3*). Success of their attrition would ensure that while on one hand the enemy's ability to reinforce the troops was cut short, on the other hand, his supply lines were also severed. The deafening sound of their battle cry **'Jo Bole So Nihal, Sat Sri Akal'** pulverised the Pakistanis, and led to the eviction and death of several enemy troops. In fact, a column led by Subedar Nirmal Singh, fought hand-to-hand, with bayonets thwarting a counter-attack, to secure area Helmet by the morning of 05 July. India Gate too had been captured by the troops of 8 SIKHS, and the Pakistani telephone lines to Tiger Top were consequentially severed. Naib Suberdar Karnail Singh and Sepoy Satpal Singh, who were deployed on the reverse slope of area Helmet, repulsed enemy counter-attacks in a hand-to-hand combat. Both of them sacrificed their lives, but with 8 SIKH having captured Helmet, India Gate, and Rocky Knob, their sacrifice had paved the way for the complete eviction of all Pakistanis from the Tiger Hill.

The following day, Col Thakur moved the fire bases on the eastern and the north-eastern ridges to facilitate effective fire. Thus, while the attacks by 8 SIKH were on, the remaining Ghataks of 18 GRENADIERS and Capt Nimbalkar's men had joined the fight for the complete capture of Tiger Hill Top. Nimbalkar, code named *'Sholapur'*, led the assault, and despite abuses (such as 'bastards come up, we will teach you a lesson') the enemy was totally demolished by the Indian troops. The Tiger Hill Top was well secured by the Indian soldiers. Amidst this, came a wave of counter-attacks led by a Pakistani officer, Capt Karnail Sher, along with another SSG officer, Maj Iqbal. These attacks were aptly repulsed, and both enemy officers were killed. By late evening, the situation somewhat stabilized, and finally on 08 July, the Indian Tricolour was hoisted on the Tiger Hill Top by 18 GRENADIERS. The nation finally rejoiced *'Vijay'* (victory) in its truest sense.

Three Pimples and Point 4700

The Three Pimples or the area of Black Rocks on ridgeline is a massive cluster of imposing peaks emanating from Pt 5100. This feature, along with Pt 4700, was occupied since it effectively dominates the NH-1A. The task for recapturing 'Three Pimples' (along with Pt 5100), was given to 2 RAJ RIF. Pt 4700 was to be captured by 18 GARH RIF who were to further exploit up to Pt 5100, and finally, link up with 2 RAJ RIF. Pt 4700 mutually supported Three Pimples, implying that both the attacks had to be undertaken simultaneously. 16 GRENADIERS were to launch a feint attack from southwest. The attack was finally launched on 28 June, preceded by heavy artillery fire with Bofors firing in the direct role. Intense fighting took place in the area and despite heavy casualties, by evening of 29 June, the unit succeeded in capturing Three Pimples.

18 GARH RIF carried out a simultaneous attack on Pt 4700 with 2 RAJ RIF, and by 4.30 am on the same day, Pt 4700 complex was also cleared by the unit. The enemy engaged with the Indian troops from the nearby 'Saddle', which was also wrested from him in no time. Under panic, the Pakistanis had to withdraw in haste, leaving their dead behind. (What appeared most shameful and unfortunate was that the

enemy refused to acknowledge and accept their own dead later.) The unit continued to exploit further success by capturing Rocky, Sandra and Junction, fully securing the feature by 02 July. Subsequent assessment of the Pt 4700 revealed that one company had been deployed here, and stocking was complete for a long drawn-out fight.

Image 1: The Rugged Terrain of Dras Sub-Sector

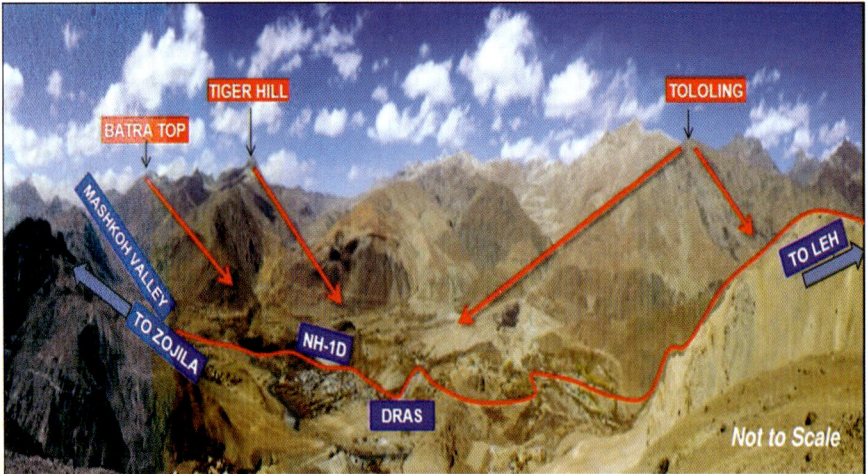

Image 2: Domination of the Dras Bowl

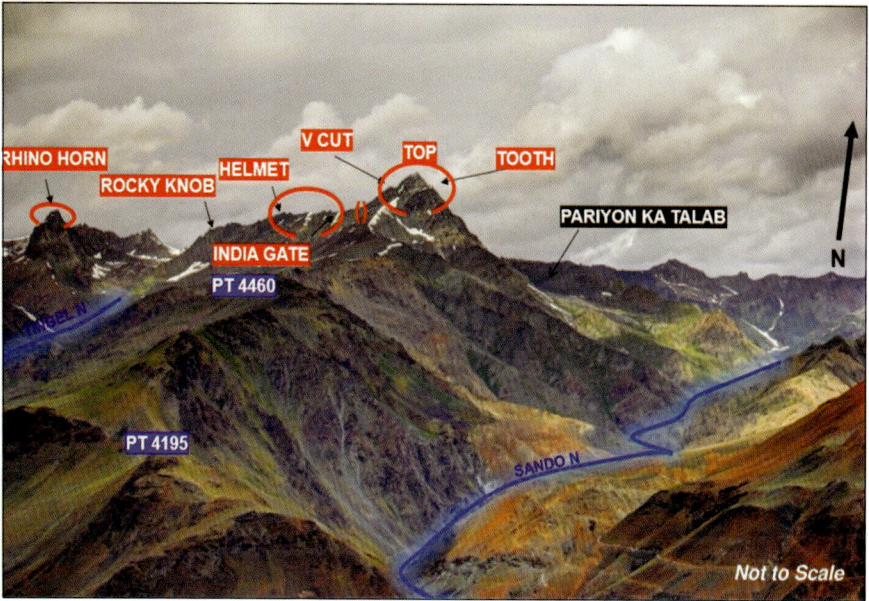

Image 3: Enemy deployment at Tiger Hill

Image 4: Enemy deployment at Tololing Complex

Image 5: Batalik Sub-Sector

Image 6: Chorbat La and River Hanu Lungpa

MUSHKOH VALLEY SUB-SECTOR

The area of Mushkoh valley has heights ranging from 3300 to 5368 m (10000 to 18000 feet). The upper regions are glaciated, and the slopes towards Indian Territory are steep. The Mushkoh valley provided a possible route of infiltration into the valley and also a passage into Doda-Kishtwar-Bhaderwah areas of the Jammu Division. The Kargil Infantry Brigade had carried out counter infiltration operations in 1998 in the Valley, but these positions remained unguarded in 1999.

In early June 1999, a message was received from DDG (Special Operations) ordering the battalion to move to Kashmir to take part in the impending operations. Upon arrival in Kashmir, the battalion was attached to the Parachute Brigade along with two other battalions of the same brigade, which was commanded by a brigadier.

Special Forces were given the task of evicting the Pakistani infiltrators from the western part of the Mushkoh Valley. The main route of the infiltrators into the Mushkoh Valley was through a deep ravine called Kirdi Nala. On either side of Kirdi Nala, were two mountain peaks – namely Point 4745 and Point 4700, which were held in strength by the enemy. Kirdi Nala had to be secured in order to seal-off the main infiltration route of the intruders into the Mushkoh Valley. Troops from the Para brigade also had contributed to the success in the Mushkoh sub-sector.

Roped to Assault Point 4745 and Point 4700

Point 4745 is a massive feature which dominated the region and was also a strategic point. An initial reconnaissance was made, and a foothold was secured at the base of Point 4745. The reconnaissance showed no sign of the enemy. However, on the night of 04 July, an observation post reported the presence of enemy soldiers on a ledge on the northern slope of Point 4745. Therefore, a meticulous plan was drawn up to evict the enemy off Point 4745. The attack was scheduled to begin on 07 July at nightfall by the Para brigade, who were supported by expert mountaineers by fixing ropes along the steep slope of the Mountain.

The attack commenced as per schedule, men of Para swarmed up the steep and treacherous slope of the mountain. Swiftly and stealthily, they crawled close to the enemy positions and then leaping to their feet charged the unsuspecting Pakistanis. The swiftness of the attack unnerved the enemy troops who then took to their heels leaving behind a large quantity of supplies and ammunition. The triumphant Indians found themselves in possession of Point 4745.

Simultaneously, another attack had been launched on the adjoining feature called Point 4700 by the troopers of another battalion of Para brigade. This was in accordance with the master plan, the purpose of which was to ensure that both "shoulders" of the Kirdi Nala were in possession of the Indian troops in order to facilitate movement through the ravine. Unfortunately, this brigade's attack got stalled due to heavy enemy resistance. Thereby, one Team from a Para battalion was ordered to assist the hard-pressed troopers of Para by making a wide flanking movement from the East of Point 4700 in order to hit the enemy from the rear. At about the same time, one Troop from another team was tasked to cut across the Kirdi Nala.

And so, on 10 July, braving exploding artillery shells, mortar bombs and whining machine-gun bullets, the troopers of the Para brigade waded through the icy waters flowing through the Kirdi Nala while another team carried out a wide encircling movement along the eastern side. This turning movement brought them on to the northern slopes of Point 4700. This was observed by the enemy and fearing the prospect of being caught in the jaws of a pincer attack, they hastily vacated their positions and fled from Point 4700 which was soon recaptured by the troops.

The pursuit of the enemy now began in the direction of the Line of Control (LoC). Chased relentlessly by the vengeful Indians, the enemy vacated all the positions they had so treacherously occupied and fled across the Line of Control. By 20 July, the brave para troopers had reached the LoC having completed a difficult assignment in an exemplary manner.

Capturing Pt 4875

There was a total vacuum about enemy information in Mushkoh sector, and only after 18 May, a few air photos showing enemy *sangars* located on the most important feature of Pt 4875, were noticed. This feature dominated the NH 1A by observation for nearly 30 kilometres from Moghalpura to Dras. At this stage, the enemy had at least one company holding this feature securely, which could easily spot convoys moving on the main highway *(Refer to Image 2)*. This had restricted the travel of army convoys to night moves, along with even the flying of helicopters being jeopardized, who had to resort to low flying, hugging the ridgeline. Hence, it became imperative to clear Pt 4875 forthwith, and completely remove all the footprints of the Pakistani intruders.

The capture of this objective was assigned to 13 JAK RIF, the battalion that had earlier distinguished itself at Pt 5140 in Dras sector. Here again, Lt Col YK Joshi who had just earlier been promoted for command of this unit, met the Brigade Commander, responsible for the Mushkoh sector. The artillery fire-plan commenced raining deadly bombs by the evening of 04 July, lighting up the objective.[14] Finally, at the H-Hour at 9 pm, the attack commenced with Maj S Bhaskar's company going for Flat Top which was adjacent to Pt 4875. C company under Maj Gurpreet Singh proceeded to the same objective from the western slope. MMGs from the fire base commanded by Capt Vikram Batra, fired tracer rounds to assist the assaulting companies in maintaining direction. By attacking from two sides they had managed to divert the enemies' attention, but when the troops of 13 JAK RIF came close to the objective of Flat Top, they were pinned down with accurate small arms and MMG fire. Having been bogged down in open during daylight, on 05 July, there was a need for change of tactics, wherein both FOOs with two companies called for intense artillery fire. Faggot missiles were also fired to destroy enemy *sangars,* and the CO of one company personally fired Rocket Propelled Grenades (RPGs) on the enemy entrenchments.

Meanwhile, the CO of 17 JAT, who was on the nearby Whale Back feature in the vicinity, reported to 13 JAK RIF that quite a few enemy intruders were seen extricating from their positions at Pt 4875 and running away. Sensing that the time was ripe to assault, both the companies of 13 JAK RIF rose with their battle-cry **'Durga Mata Ki Jai'** and fell upon the remaining bewildered enemy. Supreme acts of valour were on display, especially by Riflemen Sanjay Kumar who single-handedly charged and destroyed enemy *sangars* and killed numerous Pakistanis in hand-to-hand combat. He was seriously wounded and bleeding, but he refused to give up. He continued to fire by his Universal Machine Gun on the fleeing Pakistani soldiers and shot them dead. Another case of outstanding bravery was that of the valiant and single-handed charge by Rifleman Shyam Singh who bayoneted the enemy at a short distance from Pt 4875. Victory was achieved the same day by noon, with both Flat Top and Pt 4875 back in Indian hands.

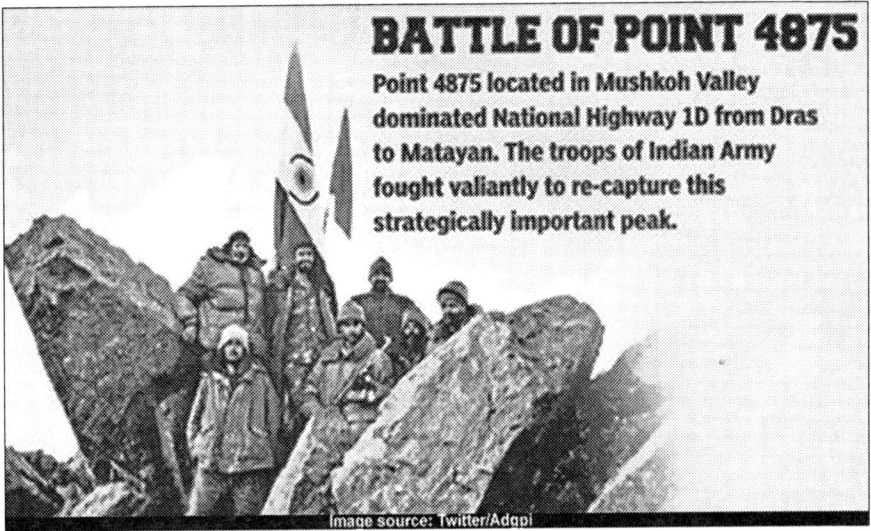

BATTLE OF POINT 4875

Point 4875 located in Mushkoh Valley dominated National Highway 1D from Dras to Matayan. The troops of Indian Army fought valiantly to re-capture this strategically important peak.

Image source: Twitter/Adgpi

Guarding the gains: *'Sher Shah's'* Batra Top

However, holding on to these important pieces of territory was as tumultuous as its capture. The troops were subjected to heavy artillery shelling and MMG fire, and though both positions were reinforced by another company of 13 JAK RIF, the enemy and the Indian troops were in constant combat wherein one side was desperately holding on to their gains and the other side was trying to wrest it back. The additional company commander Capt NA Nagappa observed 8-10 enemy troops still holed up behind boulders on Pt 4875. So close were both sides that a constant exchange of verbal abuses was being hurled between them. Firing from close quarters carried on, but by early morning of the following day, the officer reported a scarcity of ammunition. This carried on till the night, and the enemy even crawled close to the officer's location and lobbed grenades. The young captain was wounded, but held on. At this point of time, another braveheart of 13 JAK RIF, Capt Vikram Batra (codenamed *'Sher Shah'*), volunteered to take ammunition and reinforce Capt Nagappa. He was able to identify a previously unseen enemy *sangar, from* where dangerous machine gun fire was stalling the final capture of Pt 4875. The officer single-handedly pounced upon the enemy and firing from his hip, killed five Pakistanis and destroyed the *sangar.* In having exposed himself, he was felled by a sniper's bullet with a successive direct hit from a rocket launcher. In the process, he had averted the Pakistanis from regaining their hold on Pt 4875 and ensured that 13 JAK RIF was credited with another masterful victory. Most deservedly, Pt 4875 was named as Batra Top, and continues to inspire subsequent generations of officers and troops who come to serve in this area.

Capture of Pimple 1, Pimple 2 and Twin Bumps

Para Brigade was also inducted into Mushkoh Valley in the third week of June. The task to recapture Pimples 1 and 2 was assigned to 17 JAT, and that of the clearance of Twin Bumps was given to 2 NAGA. 17 JAT launched operations on the night of 04-05 July, having to confront heavy artillery fire from a well-entrenched enemy. At the same time, one company of the unit was assigned to capture Whale Back feature, which offered an unhindered observation of the Mushkoh Valley, Dras and Matayin. After some bitter fighting, Pimple 1 was captured, thus leaving the remaining enemy to withdraw to Pimple 2. The same day, Whale Back feature too had been captured, and secured by the Indians despite heavy counter-attacks. The impending attack on Pimple 2 commenced by early morning of the following day. During the attack, one of the company commanders got seriously injured, which led to the leadership being restored the respective 2IC, Captain Anuj Nayyar. This brave officer exhibited extraordinary valour during the attack, until he too was brought down by a hit from an enemy's rocket fire. The leadership crisis was again averted by the FOO, Capt Shashi Ghildyal, who took charge and continued the attack with the same momentum. At this stage, further progress of the company was stalled due to heavy artillery and automatic weapons fire from the enemy, but the troops still continued to move forward and set about to consolidate their gains. On 08 July, after having reinforced, a broad daylight attack was launched, and Pimple 2 was restored in Indian hands.

Since 2 NAGA was to assault in Phase 2 to clear Twin Bumps, they had some time to complete their preparations. Additionally, this feature was given heavy artillery bombardment, by the guns and rockets deployed in Dras and Mushkoh valley sub-sectors, due to which the enemy effectiveness was also substantially reduced.

The Nagas commenced their assault during the night on 05 July, but because of the steep climb, the operations continued till the next morning. The troops perforce conducted operations in broad daylight. They were subjected to a counter-attack by the enemy, which was successfully repulsed. With their war cry of *"Jai Durga Naga"* in the daylight, they fought right through their objective till its capture on 06 July. With the success of 2 NAGA, the presence of the enemy had been effectively eliminated from interfering with NH 1A in the Mushkoh Valley sub-sector.

Zulu Spur

All was still not over in the Mushkoh Valley sub-sector. Despite the ceasefire and withdrawal agreement, the Pakistani intruders refused to vacate Zulu spur[15], which comprised important features including Tri-junction, Zulu Ridge and Sando Top. Commander 192 Infantry Brigade, Brigadier MPS Bajwa, tasked 3/3 GORKHA RIFLES, along with two teams of 9 PARA (SF), for this eviction operation. High on confidence, 3/3 GR commenced the planned operation to capture Tri-junction on 22 July, in broad daylight, as Brigade Phase 1. Their movement to glory was preceded by intense artillery fire on the entrenched enemy *sangars*. By evening, Tri-junction had been captured. Further ingress into the enemy-held positions along the spur continued, resulting in enemy eviction and their subsequent forced withdrawal to Zulu Top. Further, the Gorkhas had another task of supreme importance at their disposal: to remove approximately 550 mines and improvised booby traps for the next five days.

In the meantime, a firm base had been established for 192 Infantry Brigade to launch further clearing operations without losing any momentum. One Team of 9 PARA (SF) began their climb towards Zulu Top the same night (area Ledge had already been secured by 3/3 GR by noon of the day when the climb was to begin).[16] By 25 July, the team commander had succeeded in opening a route and subsequently reaching the crest line. Simultaneously, a series of see-saw battles was in progress between the Pakistanis and the Indian commandoes. Although the Para Commandoes reached Zulu Top with 20 comrades, and managed to clear a few *sangars*, the enemy reactions were equally stiff with counter-attacks, thus limiting their earlier success. The situation was restored after Captain Amit Aul (of 3/3 GR) fetched up to inject the desired fire power, thus finally restoring Indian dominance on Zulu Top, from where the PoK side of the LoC was exposed and interdicted successfully. Catapulting against the Indian tenacity, the Pakistanis asked for a flag meeting on 27 July, and requested the army for the return of their dead. This was when the guns finally fell silent in the Mushkoh valley.

BATALIK SUB-SECTOR

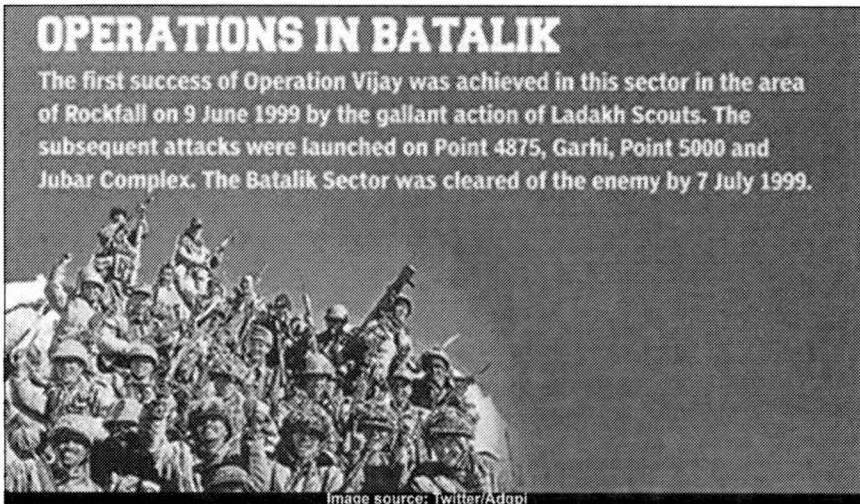

OPERATIONS IN BATALIK

The first success of Operation Vijay was achieved in this sector in the area of Rockfall on 9 June 1999 by the gallant action of Ladakh Scouts. The subsequent attacks were launched on Point 4875, Garhi, Point 5000 and Jubar Complex. The Batalik Sector was cleared of the enemy by 7 July 1999.

Image source: Twitter/Adgpi

By 8 May, there was enough information that the Pakistani troops had carried out large scale intrusions into the Batalik Sector. It had emerged that 5 NLI had come in at least 8-10 km inside the Indian territory, and had occupied four ridgelines (varying from 4572 to 5120 m), which were Jubar, Kukarthang, Khalubar and Pt 5203-Churbar Po *(Refer to Image 5)*. These ridgelines projected into the Indian territory and threatened the Kargil-Batalik-Leh road (another road between Kargil and Leh that runs for a fair portion of its length along River Indus). 70 Infantry Brigade (under Brig Devinder Singh) was guarding the NH 1A from Zoji La to Kargil and was in the process of moving its HQ to

Kargil. Between 3 and 7 May, GOC 3 Infantry Division, on seeing the gravity of the situation, became aware of the large-scale intrusions into the Indian territory in the Batalik Sector. Immediately, the tasking of 70 Mountain Brigade was revised, which was now ordered to move to Batalik. Further assessment revealed that a grazier from this area had trudged up looking for his Yaks. On coming down, he informed a sentry of 3 PUNJAB at Batalik, about the presence of men in black *salwar kameez (a traditional dress worn in some regions by men, in South Asia, as well as Central Asia, which comprises loose trousers that, wide at the waist, narrow towards a cuffed bottom, along with a long shirt)* constructing some shelters with stones. He enquired if any personnel of 3 PUNJAB had been carrying out any such activities or training there. Drawing a blank, 3 PUNJAB, immediately dispatched one patrol without any fire support, medical support, or logistic cover, to find the exact details about the intruders, and destroy the reported constructions, if any. The patrol went out of communication by 5 May, and some vague information of armed clashes and casualties near Jubar and Kukarthang ridges began trickling in. There was no prior information regarding the dispatched patrol of 3 PUNJAB with its Infantry Brigade HQ.

On 7 May, the enemy shelled the Battalion Headquarters of 3 PUNJAB destroying their officers' mess, offices and stores. By then, there was enough proof of heavily armed Pakistani troops, who were supported by artillery, having intruded well inside the Indian territory. Two days later, an Observation Post Assistant, Gunner Sanjeev Pillai of the 4 Field Regiment, effectively engaged with the enemy intruders with effective fire. The Observation Post Assistant and his team came under heavy machine gun fire, and he suffered several gun-shot wounds. None the less, using his rifle to fire back, he kept providing technical data to the FOO, until his evacuation.

Meanwhile, when the reports of the missing patrol of 3 PUNJAB reached the Brigade Commander of 121 Infantry Brigade, additional patrols from 16 GRENADIERS and 10 GARH RIF were immediately pressed forward to locate the missing patrol of 3 PUNJAB. Unfortunately, these patrols met the same fate.

Conundrum Galore: Attempts to a hasty enemy eviction

Sensing serious trouble, the GOC 3 Infantry Division hastily diverted 70 Mountain Brigade to the region to handle the Batalik situation. On being tasked to do so, Commander 70 Infantry Brigade embarked upon an aerial recce and had an MI-17 flown in to extricate the stranded patrols and remove the casualties. He was aware that the two new units being allotted to him, which were 12 JAK LI and 1/11 GR, had no prior knowledge of the area in consideration. Besides, having just been de-inducted from the Siachen glacier, the fighting strength of both the units was also comparatively less. On the other hand, the infiltrators who had been observed constructing bunkers and engaging with the patrols with heavy machine gun and artillery fire, had clearly indicated their intention to hold ground, instead of laying ambushes or conducting raids. Though the unfolding events indicated towards the extreme urgency to drive out these infiltrators, it was also known that launching troops in penny packets without adequate information could lead to a greater number of casualties. Thus, it was made clear that all offensive operations would be undertaken only after proper arming, training and rehearsals of the troops.

The Division Commander assured the Brigade of artillery, air, logistic, communication and engineering support. A composite logistic area at Dah (on the Kargil–Batalik-Leh road) was planned, which would ensure faster administrative turn round of all essential elements. But unfortunately, because of the abject embarrassment that these infiltrations had caused to the nation, a haste to evict every infiltrator at the earliest got majorly emphasised. A preliminary operation was launched by 1 BIHAR on Pt 4268, which was carried out on 28 May. Despite the lack of enemy information and artillery support, a few enemy *sangars* were captured in the attack led by Maj H Sarvanan. This attack also tremendously showcased the bravery of Naik GP Yadav and Naik Shatrughan Singh of the same regiment. However, despite heroic efforts, the unit could not hold on to the feature.

Victory Route to the Khalubar Ridgeline: Point 5203 Captured

The unsuccessful preliminary operations meant going back to the planning boards. It was realised that if the main effort was shifted from the present western side to the east, it would bear fruit. Therefore, the capture of Pt 5203, which would provide the springboard for further operations along the Khalubar Ridgeline and Chorbat La, was made the next immediate objective. On 6 June, HQ 70 Infantry Brigade handed this task to 12 JAK LI, along with a company of 5 PARA. The battalion secured a foothold, but was embroiled in a fierce enemy counter-attack. Both, 12 JAK LI and 5 PARA, remained engaged with enemy from the foothold on Pt 5203 for the next twelve. On 7 June, near midnight, 12 JAK LI reached quite close to their objective of Pt 5203, and established a foothold. The CO ordered them to remain hidden for the subsequent attack on the following day. However, an enemy soldier unexpectedly strayed into the platoon of Captain Amol Kalia the following morning, and was killed. This gave away their position, and 5 PARA, who had encountered steep cliffs, had to conceal their move forwards till nightfall. When the enemy rained down menacing artillery and small arms fire on Indian troops, Lance Naik Ghulam Mohammad Khan emerged with his rocket launcher, killing three Pakistanis of a group of twenty Pakistanis advancing towards his team. Unfortunately, he sustained gun-shot wounds while reloading his own weapon, thus India cried at the loss of yet another brave-heart.

The Brigade Commander moved forwards on 21 June to expedite the capture of Pt 5203. For this, a three-pronged attack by 12 JAK LI, one company of 5 PARA, and two companies of LADAKH Scouts was planned. Probing attacks had already been launched on the preceding days. Finally, on 20 June, a multidirectional attack was launched with LADAKH Scouts and 5 PARA taking circuitous routes to evict the enemy from Pt 5203. The victory route to evict the enemy from Khalubar Ridgeline, thus, got opened. On the same night, after the preceding attack with selective artillery fire, as our troops were already in close contact, the main assault commenced. The startled enemy was literally gutted out of their defences who ran down using slithering ropes leaving their dead and large quantities of stores behind. Pt 5203 was fully in possession of Indian hands by 22 June.

Encircling the Enemy: Capture of Point 4812

12 JAK LI was assigned the task of capturing Pt 4812 with the aim to cut off the enemy's routes of maintenance and withdrawal, and drive

them out of Jubar, Kukarthang and Tharu. *(Refer to Image 5)* The attack was preceded by intense artillery fire on the objective.

On the morning of 30 June, when the assaulting troops commenced their mission, they soon came under heavy machine gun fire. Fighting men know instinctively that during an attack, the safest place is the objective. Undeterred, one of the officers, Captain Nongrum, charged an enemy *sangar*, and despite serious wounds, led his men to overcome this position. Havaldar Satish Chander ran towards another *sangar*, amidst a hail of bullets, and lobbed grenades to silence the enemy. By the first light of the following day, one column of 12 JAK LI succeeded in cutting off the enemy's route of reinforcements and supplies. However, this column remained cut off for two days. Meanwhile, the rest of the strung-out unit after reinforcements, launched fresh assaults, which culminated in hosting the tricolour on Pt 4812 on 03 July. The first Pakistani Prisoner of War (PoW) was also captured by 12 JAK LI, while the coward enemy troops were making their escape.

Khalubar

Khalubar was the hub of the enemy defences in the Batalik Sector. Its capture entailed entirely cutting off the enemy's maintenance and supply routes, thereby rendering the defences of Pakistani 8 NLI, untenable. The Commander 70 Infantry Brigade planned simultaneous attacks, wherein Pt 5000, Stangba and Padma Go were to be captured by LADAKH Scouts. *(Refer to Image 5)* In the centre, 22 GRENADIERS were tasked to establish lodgements astride Pt 5287, which were to be further enlarged by 1/11 GR. Preceding this multipronged attack, 17 GARH RIF was tasked to capture area Bumps.

The initial assault on Khalubar was launched by 22 GRENADIERS on the night of 30 June-01 July. The troops were assisted up the steep slopes by expert mountaineers from the VIKAS battalion. They overcame stiff resistance and ensured their hold on two small lodgements on the Khalubar ridgeline, south of Pt 5287. Maj Ajit Singh, the company commander, tenaciously held on to the lower lodgement with a handful of men, but the Grenadiers were dislodged from the upper lodgement. All through the day, Maj Ajit Singh and his men held on to their precarious territory despite heavy fire by the enemy. No reinforcements could reach these men of 22 GRENADIERS. With no stores, ammunitions, or food coming up, a sepoy named Amrit Lal from another company overtook others and joined the handful of troops under Maj Ajit Singh. Luckily, he was carrying a bagful of *puris (wheat flour bread, fried in oil)* which were distributed and relished by everyone.

An enemy counter-attack was repulsed the same day, but casualties were already mounting. Just the following day, another Pakistani counter-attack was launched, which too was beaten back, but with additional Indian casualties, thereby further reducing their fighting strength. Herein, Grenadier Azim, using his machine gun to great effect ensured that the ledge position remained in Indian hands. He even got a bullet hit in his helmet, but miraculously survived.

Catching the enemy by Precision: Major Dhingra

Recalling being stuck in the middle of raining enemy artillery, Col Rai once remarked, "The situation was desperate. We were just a handful on Khalubar and could not have beaten back a major counter-attack about to be launched by the Pakistanis. Despite their proximity, I had no choice but to call for artillery fire on my own troops."

But, the brilliance of the gun position officer, Maj Deepak Dhingra, ensured that the fire landed on to the exposed Pakistanis who were in the process of counter-attacking. The Pakistanis caught in the open, and amidst the intense artillery shelling, suffered heavy casualties.

(*'Kargil 1999: Conquering The Impregnable'* by Lt Gen YM Bammi)

By early morning on 03 July, Col Lalit Rai, CO, 1/11 GR and eight Gorkhas joined Maj Ajit Singh. Col Rai decided to launch a counter-attack on the enemy *sangar*, but was beaten back. As the sun came down on the same day, the next enemy counter-attack was launched, which came so close that both sides got intermingled amongst the boulders. The stage was such that the Pakistani company commander who was barely 15 metres away, began enticing the Grenadiers to surrender. Despite injuries, Maj Ajit Singh shouted that 'they (Indians) will make you (Pakistanis) surrender'. There was also a lull in the firing and now Maj Ajit Singh and Col Lalit Rai, with the remaining troops, fired onto the Pakistanis. Quite a few Pakistanis were killed which, as it turned out later, also had the company commander Maj Sayeed of NLI in the bag.

The Gorkhas roar: *"Na Chhornu!"* (Khalubar Top Captured)

Lt Col Amul Asthana, the 2IC, company reserves, and Kranti Task Force (KFT) of 1/11 GR joined the battle for Khalubar ridge on 04 July. This battle continued for three days and as operations progressed towards Khalubar Top, many heroes were born from this unit. Lance Naik Gyanendra made daring raids on enemy gun positions and was even captured by the Pakistanis. Despite serious injuries, he escaped from captivity from a *sangar* and re-joined the CO's party. Havaldar Bhim Bahadur Diwan showed utmost courage in reducing two *sangars* before being fatally injured. *"Na chhornu"* (don't leave them), exhorted the Gorkhas for the kill and victory.

However, the epitome of courage was on display by a young officer, Lt Manoj Kumar Pandey, of 1/11 GR, who fearlessly led attacks at Khalubar. When after an arduous climb, his platoon came under intense fire from the surrounding heights, he strode fearlessly to clear four intimidating enemy *sangars* which were not letting the attack progress. Having killed the enemy and destroyed two *sangars,* while clearing the third one, he was grievously injured by the enemy fire. Undaunted, he led another attack on to *sangar* number 4, and succeeded in destroying it. In doing so, he sustained a burst from a machine gun in the head at point blank range and met his heroic end. The capture of this area of bunkers by Lt Manoj Pandey and his troops facilitated the capture of Khalubar. Col Lalit Rai, too, was injured in the knee, but carried on leading his troops, and engaged in a hand-to-hand combat with the Pakistanis. 1/11 GR eventually routed the enemy from Khalubar on 06 July and linked up with 12 JAK LI.

Padma Go Ridge

Features Stangba, Pt 5000 and Dog Hill lie on the Padma Go ridge, which further meet the LoC further south. Eviction of the enemy was necessary so that operations towards the west could commence unhindered. 70 Infantry Brigade planned to capture Pt 5000 first. The task to capture Pt 5000 was given to the Indus and Karakoram Wings of LADAKH Scouts. On the night of 30 June-01 July, one column of LADAKH Scouts launched an attack and despite steep slope and waist level snow, succeeded in capturing the objective. Thereafter, the Padma

Go objective was softened over the next few days with concentrated artillery and infantry mortar fire. *(Refer to Image 5)*

In renewed attacks on 05-06 July, Dog Hill was captured, and a foothold was established. Here again, further operations were deliberated, and troops were prepared for the final roll over. Padma Go was finally captured in a daylight operation by LADAKH Scouts on 09 July. Keeping the momentum going, the LADAKH Scouts captured Pt 5229 close to the LoC. The loss of this ridgeline due to sustained and determined attacks, broke the back of the Pakistani soldiers of 8 NLI, and succeeded in cutting off all the maintenance and withdrawal routes of the enemy. While this success was being lauded, other battalions of 70 Infantry Brigade were simultaneously launching assaults on Pakistani-held positions at Jubar, Tharu and Kukarthang. *(Refer to Image 5)*

Jubar, Three Bumps and Kukarthang

Initial attacks to capture Jubar and Pt 4924 had proved unsuccessful. Consequentially, the Brigade Commander devised a level plan wherein 1 BIHAR was tasked to capture Jubar and Pt 4924, 17 GARH RIF was to go further north and 1/11 GR was to focus on the Kukarthang ridge *(Refer to Image 5)*. As per the plan, coordinated artillery fire commenced on the night of 06/07 July, and in accurate firing, set the ammunition bunker of the enemy on fire. Immediately, the Pakistanis started to withdraw resulting in 1 BIHAR racing upwards to their objective and linking up with 17 GARH RIF. The bodies of Maj Sarvanan of 1 BIHAR, Naik Ganesh Prasad, and two others were recovered in the process. In this attack, the artillery innovated the employability of 122 mm Grad multi-barrel rocket launchers, deployed on the Batalik-Kargil road where these weapons were positioned on the same height as Jubar, in a direct firing role. The following day, the feature Tharu (Pt 5103) was captured, and the unit carried its momentum to link up with 1/11 GR at Kukarthang. Boys were seen in high spirit to take on the withdrawing enemy as the bodies of their dead lay scattered on the erstwhile intruded areas.

Area Bumps, Kala Pathar, and Pt 5285

Preceding the main Brigade attack on Khalubar, 17 GARH RIF launched simultaneous attacks on Area Bumps and Kala Pathar. Having secured the western spur and area Flat, and having established their firm bases, the Garhwalis attacked at dawn on 30 June. All companies were exposed during daylight, except one platoon of Capt Jintu Gogoi, who made steady progress and reached Kala Pathar. The Pakistanis surrounded his platoon, leading to a hand-to-hand combat. With his personal acts of bravery, despite being surrounded, the officer averted the danger that had befallen his platoon, but in doing so, he himself got grievously wounded.

Fresh snowfall occurred in the following days, which stalled any further movement for a short while. The Garhwalis finally captured Area Bumps and opened the route to Pt 5285, which was subsequently wiped out the Pakistani presence.

Freed from Intruders: The Last Battle at Batalik

The long-awaited attack on Kukarthang was launched by 1/11 GR on 08 July, preceded by devastating artillery fire. In the run up to their objective, 1/11 GR captured Pt 4821 and Ring Contour, and by 09 July, the Kukarthang ridge was back in Indian hands. *(Refer to Image 5)*

The Pakistanis were on the run by 11 July, when 1/11 GR launched their attack on Pt 5300. Holding this feature would have given the Indian troops a dominant observation of PoK, as well as the Pakistani positions on their side of the LoC. Just when the Gorkhas were about to initiate the attack, the alarm for ceasefire was sounded, and the Gorkhas halted barely 500 metres from their objective. But, true to their colours, the Pakistanis did not vacate the peak. The Gorkhas, on 22 July, were signalled to proceed with the capture of Pt 5300. Unleashing their *khukhris*, the Gorkhas fell upon the bewildered Pakistanis who just collapsed and made a dash backwards without caring for their wounded or dead comrades. Meanwhile, Special Forces, who had also launched a simultaneous attack, successfully secured another feature, Conical, on 23 July. Quite naturally, our artillery OP officers had a grand day of shelling and interdicting the Pakistani supply lines to their battalions on the enemy side of the LoC. The fight for the eviction of the enemy continued with the capture of Ring Contour and Tekri by 1/11 GR and 5 PARA. In a simultaneous action that night, a team of 10 PARA (SF) and Indus Wing of LADAKH Scouts attacked and succeeded in capturing another adjacent feature, South Saddle. Finally, the guns fell silent in the Batalik sub-sector on 26 July.

KAKSAR SUB-SECTOR

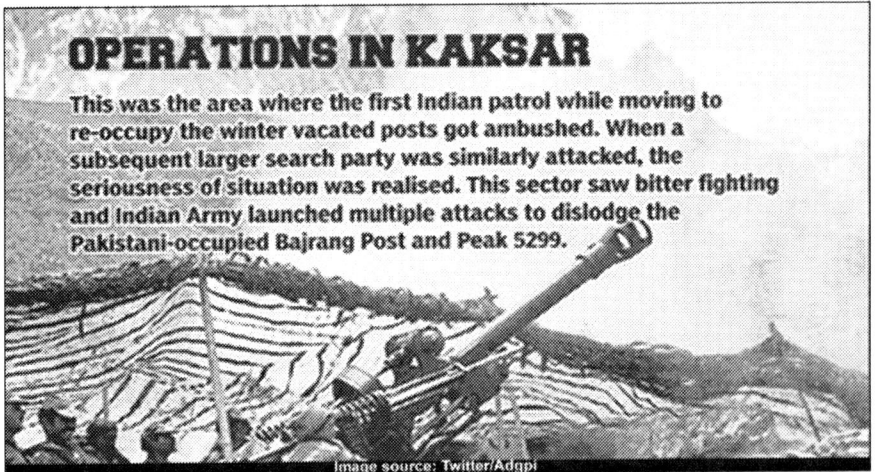

OPERATIONS IN KAKSAR

This was the area where the first Indian patrol while moving to re-occupy the winter vacated posts got ambushed. When a subsequent larger search party was similarly attacked, the seriousness of situation was realised. This sector saw bitter fighting and Indian Army launched multiple attacks to dislodge the Pakistani-occupied Bajrang Post and Peak 5299.

Image source: Twitter/Adgpi

ADGPI Twitter Handle

The terrain of the Kaksar area along the LoC is glaciated with heights as high as 15000 feet (4572 metres). The main ridge comprising Pt 5608, Pt 5065, and Pt 5280 remains snow-bound throughout the year and consists of a number of glaciated valleys. One Indian post of prominence in the Kaksar region is the 'Bajrang' post, which was always occupied even during winters, by approximately 8-10 troops, who kept a watch on the open glaciated flank. However, sometime in March of 1999, the troops manning this post were allowed to fall back due to heavy snowfall. On 14 May, a five-men patrol of 4 JAT, led by Lt Saurabh Kalia, had disappeared in the Kaksar area. Pakistani troops had reportedly taken them as PoWs, and after gruesome torture, had returned their bodies on 10 June. Since there was no contact with Lt Kalia since 14 May, 4 JAT had dispatched another patrol led by Lt Amit Bharadwaj, which had come under intense enemy fire. This officer also went missing and it was only after the ceasefire that the soldiers' bodies, along with that of Lt Amit Bharadwaj, were recovered from the site.

Almost till the third week of June, the intensity of operations in this region remained comparatively low. Meanwhile, there was also a change in the commanders of the Kargil Infantry Brigade, and the new commander, Brig OP Nanderjog, had taken over command. Full-fledged operations resumed only by 05 July but were subsequently called off as the Pakistanis had offered to withdraw. The enemy had suffered heavy casualties, which prompted them to request the Indian troops to stop firing. White flags, being waived by the Pakistani troops from the Bajrang post, were all too visible to suggest their withdrawal. In fact, Kaksar was the first sector to be vacated by the Pakistani forces who completed their retreat by 11 July. 'Bajrang' post was finally reclaimed by 15 July.

TURTUK SUB-SECTOR

The southern glacier and sub-sector west (Sub-sector West-Turtuk-Chalunka) were also brimming with enemy activity. Due to the inhospitable terrain, initially, most features at altitudes up to 21000 feet (6400 m) were unguarded by either side, thus resulting in wide gaps between the actual holdings by troops on both sides. In early May, after a patrol clash in this area, when some intrusions up to 500 m were discovered, the commander ordered the occupation of all defences along important features up to Chorbat La and Turtuk Lungpa. Prevention of any further enemy movement, with a simultaneous establishment of a firm base for launching attacks, was recognized as the immediate motive *(Refer to Image 6)*. Although initially detected by 12 JAT, the main action in this region against enemy intrusion was carried out by 11 RAJ RIF, which was also the first unit to be deployed in this area. It assumed the operational responsibility of Sub-sector Turtuk, close on the heels of their de-induction from Operation MEGHDOOT on 11 May. It was a challenging task and an acid test of the physical and mental robustness of the troops. This challenge called for a very high level of motivation and aggressive spirit, and was readily accepted by all the ranks of the unit with enthusiasm. Smaller successful actions in this area were also fought by 9 MAHAR, 13 KUMAON and 3 RAJPUT.

High Morale of the troops

It was towards April of 1999, that the news of Pakistani Puma helicopter sorties being spotted along Mian Lungpa, along with the sounds of blasting, started pouring in. The Brigade Commander, Brigadier PC Katoch, having evaluated the situation, immediately dispatched a patrol, after due assurance of artillery, medical and communication support, to the area. The task was given to the patrol master of LADAKH Scouts, who was to identify and clear the enemy intrusion across the LoC, and occupy Pt 5283.

While leading a patrol at dawn on 19 May, Subedar Lobzand Chhotok, spotted an enemy*sangar* southeast of Pt 5283. A fire-fight ensued wherein Subedar Chhotak, hit by machine gun fire, breathed his last. Meanwhile, confirmations of similar intrusions akin to Dras and Batalik had been made in the glaciated region. After firming in, the first attempt to capture Pt 5990 (18400 ft) was made by a patrol led by Captain Haneef Uddin and Subedar Mangej Singh of 11 RAJ RIF on 6-7 June. The patrol came close to 200 m of the objective, when the mayhem erupted from the Pakistani intruders. The young captain who was leading with two of his buddies had to bear the brunt of the enemy fire and was injured in the firing. Despite his grave wounds, he took position and fired back till the remainder patrol succeeded in establishing a foothold on the mountain. He continued to lead his troops against the heaviest odds and was successful in eliminating several enemies perched on dominating positions. Inspired by their leader, the troops continued to move forward and succeeded in killing the enemies and silencing the fire. Haneef had to take another gun shot before succumbing to his injuries. Eight enemy bunkers had been identified by this patrol, along with details of automatic weapons sited on Pt 5590 and Pt 6041. The bravery of the patrol led by this officer and his able JCO, Naib Subedar Mangej, took them to such close proximity that even their bodies could not be recovered until later operations.

11 RAJ RIF was now employed to capture Pt 5590 on 14 July, but on the request of the CO, for additional preparation time, the date was moved forward. On 2 August, the unit reached 40 metres short of the top. Almost by daylight, the unit returned to their respective release points, and then again on the night of the following day, re-launched themselves for the desired conclusion. Since the threat of day light eluded any further movement to attack, in order to stay oblivious from the Pakistanis, they hid themselves amongst the rocks. But, they were soon detected and fired upon from the neighbouring features, as also Pt 5590. This time, they were stuck in a 'do or die' situation, and they ferociously retaliated. By 5 August, the feature was captured along with an adjoining feature named Saddle, by 11 RAJ RIF. The capture of Pt 5590 and Saddle gave our troops the direct observation of the sole Pakistani supply route to their troops in Chorbat La. It also provided observation between Pt 6041 and Pt 5590, which could be a gateway for the infiltration of sizeable Pakistani force levels, inside Indian territory. Hence, the capture of this mountain top provided major tactical advantages. This sector has been named as sub-sector Haneef, in recognition of the incredible frontline leadership displayed by this young soldier, Captain Haneef Uddin, at an altitude of 18000 ft, against such daunting conditions and formidable heights.

Victory Moments: Point 5590 captured

'Blood, Guts, and Glory' signifies the legendary bravery of the Indian soldiers, who undeterred, stormed the deceitful Pakistani bastions regardless of their own safety. The scenes were actually 'hell under fire, weather and terrain' to accomplish victory. Therefore, this chapter is a tribute, as well as, a reminder of a collection of victorious battles fought to regain territorial losses and bring status quo to the Line of Control. In doing so, it has been our endeavour to cover the battle roles of the maximum number of units deployed in the operational front and rewrite very briefly their unforgotten contributions on the road to the final victory – 'Vijay'.

AN OVERVIEW

It was evident from the information and documents seized from the PoW, that regular Pakistani troops had moved close to the LoC in late 1998 and January 1999. They had crossed over, primarily in February, and occupied full-fledged defences by the month of April in 1999. Apparently, the early opening of Zoji La had upset their plans for extended occupations. They had prepared their defences with cunningness under rocky patches, and in caves, which were well stocked with ammunitions, rations, clothing and other military hardware. Carrier cables too were laid out between various defensive positions. The defences were well-sited and covered all approaches with observation and fire. They had even constructed fibre-glass huts to help themselves keep warm during the harsh winters. Clearly, the Pakistanis had made detailed plans to hold the Indian territory across the LoC, and had thereby adequately dug themselves to ensure long term territorial gains. On the war front, the Pakistanis displayed an inability, fear and hesitancy to carry out offensive patrolling outside their defences. They also did not launch any raids with their special forces to disrupt and cause attrition to the Indian troops. Their military leadership was quite certainly under the impression that the Indian forces or political leadership were inept and weak to counter their territorial losses.

Delving into the Indian side of the Kargil conflict, it was quite conspicuous that the harsh reality of intrusions (or information of additional activities) involving the Pakistani Army, could not be detected by the military or civil intelligence agencies. Till late May, the ingresses were being referred to as a localized affair made by a handful of jehadis. Lt Gen Kishen Pal, then GOC 15 Corps (who was the security advisor to the Chief Minister), stated that army convoys were moving unhindered to Kargil, and soon civilian traffic will be allowed.[17] In the initial stages, this sense of pseudo-realism had apparently manifested in the military leadership right up to the apex.

The initial counter moves by pushing the Indian troops up the mountain tops, brought home the stark reality of the well-entrenched Pakistani troops, only unluckily at the cost of the lives several Indian brave hearts. What was even more unfortunate was that while the Pakistanis were busy beating their hollow drums proclaiming their superior fighting capabilities, the Indian military leadership was in a quandary, unwilling to accept the realities despite the grave challenges already faced by 1 NAGA, and later by 18 GRENADIERS and 8 SIKH. The commanders at the Brigade, Division and Corps levels refused to see the writing on the wall for quite some time. It was finally 8 Mountain Division that was moved from the Valley, and in keeping with the motto i.e. *'Forever in Operations'*, turned the dynamics of this volatile area into India's favour. Additional formations were simultaneously moved into the Batalik sub-sector.

In the initial operations, there was no semblance of forward logistic bases, or casualty evacuation plans. Due to lack of porters, the fighting troops were committed to organise the move of battalion support weapons and ammunition to vantage points. Such move involved almost 8-12 hours of walking at a time. Casualty evacuation was also being done by the fighting troops, wherein 8-12 personnel were involved in the carriage of casualties. These carriages costed the troops at least 6 hours or more to reach the nearest advanced dressing stations. This meant a depleted fighting strength of the troops who were simultaneously engaged at close quarters against a well-fortified enemy.

It was ultimately the victory of Tololing, Tiger Hill, Batra Top (Pt 4875) in Dras and Mushkoh sub-sectors; and other vantage peaks like Muntho Dhalo, Kukarthang, Jubar and Khalubar in the Batalik sub-sector, that jolted the Pakistanis out of their stupor. By then, the earlier methodology of massing the units and throwing them at Tololing, Pt 4700 complex or Tiger Hill, had ceased. Instead, proper arming, acclimatization, familiarity with the nature of operations, rehearsals, and building up the all forbidding artillery firing units had commenced with zeal. Thereafter, every attack that went in, brought instant success, and were replete with instances of collective and individual bravery.

On balance, it must be understood that there were a few major constraints in accomplishing what the Indian troops achieved during this conflict. To name a few: one, the term of reference that LoC would not be crossed to conduct military operations (resultantly, our troops adopted multi-directional attacks against the enemy positions to capture them); two, the sudden diversion of troops from different areas where they were performing different set of tasks (a case in point is 8 Mountain Division, which was intensely involved in counter-insurgency (CI) operations in the Valley when it was diverted to participate in the ongoing conflict in extreme high-altitude areas); three, the mind-set of the troops from tasks in CI operations to extreme high altitude warfare against an enemy holding dominating heights; four, lack of basic information about the enemy strength, and intentions; five; lack of most suited weapon systems, equipment and clothing; six, inadequate logistics to begin with; and seven; the need to complete operations with a sense of urgency. Yet, the Indian soldiers and their leaders deserve all the appreciation for fighting with a resolve and determination to achieve their objectives.

Aerial reconnaissance played a major part in deciphering the layout and the extent of enemy lodgements. Brigade Commanders made full use of helicopters to configure the enemy's exact dispositions and thereafter formulate battle-winning plans. In a short while, the Artillery commanders devised direct firing from BOFORS, 130 mm Medium guns, and even the 122 mm multi-barrel rocket launcher (MBRL). This preponderance of effective firing that had a shattering effect on the Pakistani forces made the way to the top peaks easier for the attacks being launched by infantry. Infact, it was no surprise that Pt 4875 has been designated as the "Artillery Hill". The commanding officers were well forward with their troops to launch reserves on time and instruct mid-course corrections during the assaults.

Collective and individual bravery was the norm in all battles. At crucial junctures where the situation was so precarious and tilting back to the enemy, heroes like, Rifleman Sanjay Kumar, Lt Col R Vishwanathan, Maj Rajesh Adhikari, Sub Yogendra Singh Yadav,

Maj Vivek Gupta, Capt Vikram Batra, Capt N Kenguruse, Lt Manoj Kumar Pandey, Lt KC Nonkrum, Lt Balwan Singh, Capt Haneef Uddin, Maj Pandropani Acharya, Naik Digendra Kumar, Capt Saurav Kalia, Capt Anuj Nayyar, Capt Jintu Gogoi, Sepoy Imli Akum Ao, and so many more, in just one stroke of raw courage, reversed the situations into Indian hands.

"The Nation will remain the land of the free so long as it is the home of the brave"

– *Elmer Davis*

NOTES

1. While running hasty backward marathons in their hours of defeat, such heavy weaponry, which included mortars, machine guns, anti-aircraft guns, and shoulder-fired Stinger and Anza missiles, fell into the hands of the Indian Army.
2. AS Daulat, *KASHMIR: The Vajpayee Days*, New Delhi: HarperCollins Publisher India, 2015.
3. Gen VP Malik. *Kargil: From Surprise To Victory* New Delhi: HarperCollins Publisher India, 2006.
4. *Laxman Rekha* refers to the LoC which is a sanctified line which is expected to be mutually accepted.
5. Lt Gen YM Bammi Kargil 1999: Conquering The Impregnable Noida: Gorkha Publishers, 2003.
6. Harinder Baweja, *A Soldier's Diary: Kargil The Inside Story* New Delhi: Books Today, 2000.
7. Lt Gen Mohinder Puri, *Kargil: Turning The Tide (New Delhi: Lancer Publishers, 2016)*
8. Harinder Baweja, *A Soldier's Diary: Kargil The Inside Story* New Delhi: Books Today, 2000.
9. Ibid.
10. Lt Gen Puri.op. cit
11. "Point" refers to the height of the feature in metres.
12. A point of interest was that the then Chief of Army Staff, Gen VP Malik, had been a previous GOC of 8 Mountain Division. It was he who was instrumental in entrusting Major General Mohinder Puri, who was the then GOC, and task him to carry out the eviction operations in the Kargil region. It is noteworthy to bring out that it was under the dynamic leadership of this GOC that India gained her first victory over the Pakistani troops in this mountainous region.
13. Baweja, op. cit
14. Only the preceding day, the battalion had moved forward at night, unobserved, to the area of their fire base.
15. A high mountainous feature that dominates the area across the LoC, right up to Gultari on the enemy's side
16. An interesting aspect of this was that their team leader was Maj Sudhir Kumar, who had been an ADC of Gen VP Malik, COAS, till just 7 days ago.
17. Baweja, op. cit

Image 7: Front page of 'The Free Press Journal' dated 26 July, 1999.

THE TIMES OF INDIA

Mumbai, Monday, July 12, 1999   Bennett, Coleman & Co., Ltd.   56 pages including Bombay Times, Ascent & Education Times * Invitation Price Rs. 2

Pakistan pulls out forces, India ends Kargil offensive

By Mehendra Ved
The Times of India News Service

Nawaz Sharif says his decision has averted a war

ISLAMABAD:

Sharif to address nation today

ISLAMABAD:

EC unfolds five-stage LS election schedule

■ Polls from Sept. 4–Oct. 1 ■ 2-day elections in Maharashtra
■ Simultaneous assembly polls in Andhra, Sikkim, Karnataka

The Times of India News Service
NEW DELHI:

EC may consider assembly polls too for Maharashtra

NEW DELHI:

Pakistan sends envoy to Delhi to restore high-level contacts

ISLAMABAD:

Dilip Kumar won't return Pak award

The Times of India News Service
NEW DELHI:

Bofors guns, made in India, will shoot down buying cost

By Mehendra Ved
The Times of India News Service
NEW DELHI:

Image 8: Front page of 'The Times of India' *dated 12 July, 1999.*

PART II
SYNERGY TO VICTORY

Air War in Kargil: A Revisit

Air Marshal Anil Chopra

The Kargil War was fought between India and Pakistan on the high mountains in Kargil District of Jammu and Kashmir, and elsewhere along the Line of Control (LoC) between 03 May and 26 July 1999. Code named "Operation Vijay" ended with a decisive victory for Indian forces and India regained possession of territory occupied by Pakistani intruders, who initially claimed to be Kashmiri insurgents. This war was one of the most recent examples of high-altitude warfare. It was also the first direct conventional war between two nuclear states. The high mountains posed great operational and logistics challenges. Indian Air Force (IAF) was first approached to provide air support on 11 May 1999 with the use of helicopters. The full-scale air operations that began on 26 May were codenamed "Operation Safed Sagar".[1] After a few initial aircraft losses, IAF had to revisit its employment philosophy and commenced high-altitude bombing using precision weapons. Successful strikes by Mirage 2000 aircraft with Laser Guided Bombs (LGBs) not only helped turn the tide of war and hastened the recapture of high mountain peaks, but also greatly reduced Indian Army casualties.

Kargil was among the highest battle field in the world, with outposts on the ridges generally around 5,000 m (16,000 ft) high,[2] and a few as high as 5,485 m (18,000 ft). While the Indian Army had an uphill task to evict the intruders, the IAF had never practiced weapon delivery at these altitudes. No aircraft in the world had been designed to operate in a Kargil-like environment. There is a severe degradation of aircraft and weapon performance at these altitudes. Due to rarified atmosphere, weapons do not perform as per sea-level specifications. Variations in air temperature and density alter drag indices and a host of other factors (never been computed by any manufacturer for these type of altitudes) cause weapons to go off their mark. Notwithstanding the eventual success, there were hits and misses and IAF had lessons to learn. IAF carried out a review of its tactics, choice of weapons employed and weapon delivery techniques, and even technical specifications for future acquisitions of various aerial platforms and weapons. Twenty years after the Kargil War, it is time to take stock and see if all lessons have been imbibed and amends made to fight a future air war with greater finesse and accuracy.

Major Lessons from the Ground War

Many lessons were learnt by the Indian Army from the Kargil War. This included failure to monitor intrusion – need for better Intelligence and reconnaissance. The infiltrators, apart from being equipped with small arms and grenade launcher, were also armed with mortars, artillery and anti-aircraft weapons. Many posts were also heavily mined. This happened undetected. Vulnerability of NH1 at some points close to the LoC highlighted need for alternative and more wider roads. More modern logistics support was needed in mountains. Pakistan had carried out reconnaissance using unmanned aerial vehicles (UAVs). India had to build up a UAV force. Indian Army had to use artillery guns to target the posts that were in the line-of-sight. The Bofors FH-77B field Howitzer played a vital role.[3] Artillery was very effective. Since daylight attack could be suicidal, all the advances had to be made under the cover of darkness, withstanding high wind chill factor, and the risk of freezing. The Indian army launched its final attacks in co-ordination with relentless attacks by the IAF, both by day and night, and it greatly reduced casualties. It was clear that India required greater preparation for high-altitude war.

Operation Safed Sagar: Initial Losses

The IAF began Electronic intelligence (ELINT), photo and aerial reconnaissance in early May. On 21 May 1999, a Canberra PR57 on a reconnaissance mission was hit by a Chinese-made Anza infrared surface-to-air missile. The plane returned on one engine and landed safely. Air strikes on enemy positions began on 26 May 99. Ground attack aircraft MiG-21s, MiG-23s, MiG 27s, Jaguars and helicopter gunships were employed initially and struck intruder positions.

Initially the effectiveness was limited. The MiG-21 was built mainly for air interception with a secondary role of ground attack. IAF's ageing fleet of MiG-21s and MiG-27s operated without modern navigation equipment and pilots strapped GPS gadgets to their thighs or held them in hand. 1000-kg "dumb" bombs were dropped at Army designated bomb impact points which would snowball into landslides or avalanches. The aim was to cut off Pakistan line of communication to such an extent that even the wounded could not be evacuated.

On 27 May 1999, the IAF lost a MiG-27 strike aircraft which was later attributed to an engine failure caused by disturbance of airflow at the engine air inlet during high-altitude rocket firing. An Air Force officer tried to trace the downed MiG-27, despite the potent threat, in the form of enemy Surface-to-Air Missiles (SAM), but his plane was shot down by a Stinger shoulder fired missile in the Batalik Sector. The following day, a Mi-17 was hit by three Stinger missiles while on an offensive sortie in the Tololing sector. The aircraft did not have serviceable IR flares dispenser. These losses forced the Indian Air Force to reassess its strategy. The helicopters were immediately withdrawn from offensive roles.

Mirage 2000 H and LGBs

At this stage, IAF decided to induct the Mirage 2000H and to begin high-altitude bombing using LGBs with high accuracy to destroy well-entrenched positions of the Pakistani forces. The first Mirage 2000 mission was launched on 30 May. Armed initially with Spanish 250 kg "dumb" iron bombs, No. 7 Squadron struck for 3 days infiltrator positions in Muntho Dhalo, Tiger Hill and Point 4388 in the Dras Sector. As the war progressed, the IAF aircrew had to modify aiming indices and firing techniques, increasing its effectiveness in high-altitude weapon delivery. There was no opposition by the Pakistani Air Force (PAF), leaving the IAF free to carry out its attacks with impunity. However, IAF pilots could not ignore the presence of PAF fighters operating regularly within Pakistan occupied Kashmir (PoK). Also, the restriction of not crossing the LoC put limitations of choices of attack directions on the pilots.

The French Atlis II Laser Designation Pod (LDP) and 1000 kg LGBs which came to India with the Mirage 2000 were not suited for targets in the Kargil sector. They were ideally suited for targeting Command and Control and recessed sites requiring deep penetration. The IAF had cheaper US Paveway II LGBs for use with the Israeli Litening LDPs. However, some parts of the Paveway kit were not available, as they were placed under embargo by the US as a consequence of the nuclear test performed by India. Consequently, IAF had to modify and manufacture these parts in order to make the Paveway serviceable for use. Also, the Litening pods required manual alteration as they were not compatible with Mirage computer. Fuzes were not available for the 1000 lb bombs, so pistol fuzes were modified and proved effective. Wing pylon clearance for carrying old 1000 lb bombs was done at Gwalior – the home base of Mirage 2000.

Dumb bombs proved to be highly effective. The first IAF LGB mission, was carried out on 24 June 1999 and destroyed the Pakistani command and control bunkers on Tiger Hill. The first night LGB mission was flown with a time over target (Tiger Hill) of 2.30 am (IST) on 28 June 1999. Achieving a direct hit as reported by the Army, this mission was considered instrumental in paving the way for ground forces to capture Tiger Hill. Pakistani primary supply depot at Muntho Dhalo in the Batalik sector and the large logistics camp at Pt 4388 in Mushkoh Nallah were completed destroyed by Mirage 2000 bombing.

Air Operation Summary

After initial losses, all aircraft operated at an altitude of 10,000 m (33,000 ft above sea level), diving when required and pulling out well out of Man-portable AD Systems (MANPAD) range. The lesser number of airstrips in the Kashmir region extended the revisit time of the attacks. Yet hundreds of sorties were flown enabling a gradual takeover of the mountain posts by Indian Army troops.

Wake-Up Call

Kargil conflict came as a wake-up call for IAF to upgrade the ageing fleets of aircraft for better mountain air operations. IAF acquired and later co-developed the Sukhoi Su-30 MKI large fighters with Russia. The process of acquiring Medium Multi-role Combat Aircraft (MMRCA) was initiated in 2001, a process after which the Rafale aircraft was selected in January 2012. However, due to contractual issues, only

36 could be ordered, and the same will physically arrive in India in 2020.

Reminiscences of the Air Chief[4]

Air Chief Marshal AY Tipnis was the Air Chief during the Kargil war. Many years later, in October 2006, in an interview to the defence magazine "Force", he recalled about Operation Safed Sagar. He thought it was time to talk, because General Ved Malik's book *Kargil: From Surprise to Victory* had just been published; Jaswant Singh had written *A Call to Honour: In Service of Emergent India,* and General Musharraf, the villain of Kargil had published *In the Line of Fire: A Memoir.* All three had been major players in the Kargil Conflict. It was thus time for the Air Chief to put his views in the public domain.

By 10 May, IAF was getting informal information on some hyperactivity in Kargil but when Army Vice Chief was approached to check if all was well, he said that the army could handle the situation. However, the Northern Command had asked IAF elements attached with them for fire-support from Mi 25/35 attack helicopters, and armed Mi-17s for evicting some intruders. IAF elements in J&K responded that terrain at those altitudes was beyond the operating envelope of the gunships. Northern Command and Army HQ had made no such requests at higher levels but were upset that request at lower level had been rejected by IAF. The Army Chief was on a visit abroad. Finally, when the Army Vice Chief met the IAF Chief on 14 May, he was told that IAF required Government of India (GoI) clearance. Also, he was told that the Army must spell out the requirement, but the type of fire support will be decided by the IAF. Notwithstanding, IAF launched reconnaissance missions by Canberras and Jaguars.

It was made clear to the Army at all levels that helicopter gunships were unsuited for the operations. Meanwhile, HQ Western Air Command (WAC) started preparing contingency plans. IAF sought an emergency meeting of Chiefs of Staff Committee on a Sunday. On Monday, 17 May, the RM chaired a high-level meeting with NSA, with Principal Secretary to PM also present. Air Chief briefed on the escalation dynamics of air power; weapon limitations at those heights; risk of crossing LoC; risk of fratricide by own troops; and that helicopter survivability would be low. On 18 May, a CCS meeting was chaired by the PM. The escalation dynamics were discussed. IAF sought permission to use fighter aircraft without restrictions. The general consensus and final direction at the end of meeting was not to use IAF for the moment. But IAF continued to prepare and train.

IAF had believed that often returns from attacking small, close air support targets were low and aircraft vulnerabilities were high. Air power has much more devastating effect when applied to logistics dumps and lines of supply. IAF continued to accelerate the logistics air support to the Army, and flying air defence, photo and electronic reconnaissance missions awaiting further GoI orders for offensive action. Since the Army Chief had been on extended visit abroad, IAF chief wrote a detailed letter on operational issues to the Army Chief for him to read on return. Immediately on return, the Army Chief held a meeting with the other two Chiefs on 23 May and suggested that the services approach the CCS to seek IAF participation. The CCS cleared the use of fighter aircraft on 25 May, but made it clear that there was no crossing the LoC despite IAF explaining the importance. Finally, IAF air strikes during the conflict played a great role. It helped reduce Indian Army casualties and hastened the end of war. Clearly, the Indian Army was the lead service in the operations, and IAF was mainly in support role, the Air Chief acknowledged.

The KRC and GoM Report Status

The Kargil Review Committee[5] (KRC) was set up by the GoI on 29 July 1999, three days after the official end of Kargil War. It was chaired by eminent strategic affairs analyst K. Subrahmanyam. The report was completed on 15 December 1999. The KRC noted that the role of the IAF in support of the Army in Kargil was a significant development with far-reaching consequences for the Pakistani intruders, albeit, the IAF was committed into action after considerable delay. A Group of Ministers (GoM) and task forces were set up thereafter. The GoM findings clearly stated that the intrusion came as a surprise to the Indian government. The report highlighted the role of RAW, IB and the military intelligence just prior to the war, and the lack of inter-agency coordination. RAW's Human intelligence was found to be weak. The report discussed possible Siachenisation of Kargil, meaning full-time manning of all posts. The same has since been done.

GoM suggested thorough review of entire national security system covering National Security Council, intelligence, counter-terrorist operations, border management, defence budget and modernisation, apex decision making, nuclear policy, media relations and information technology, and civil-military liaison.

Based on the report, a full-time National Security Advisor (NSA) has been instituted. Improved aerial surveillance using Indian RISAT satellites and UAVs and EMISAT have been put in place. A centralised communication and electronic intelligence agency, the National Technical Research Organisation (NTRO) was set up in 2004. The Defence Intelligence Agency (DIA) has been set up. Think tanks such as Centre for Joint Warfare Studies (CENJOWS) were set up. Some recommendations have still not been fully implemented due to unresolved differences between the Army, Navy and IAF and the unwillingness of the political class to enact the binding legislation. GoM had recommended the formation of the post of a Chief of Defence Staff and was accepted by the CCS, but has not been implemented till now. Based on recommendations, Integrated Defence Staff (IDS), the Andaman and Nicobar Command, the Nuclear Command Authority, the Strategic Forces Command, the Department of Ex-Servicemen welfare, the Defence Technical Council, and the Defence Acquisition Council were set up. Among the recommendation not fully implemented is entrusting Internal Security (IS)/Counter Insurgency (CI) duties entirely to Central Para Military Forces and the Rashtriya Rifles, thus de-inducting the Army from these duties, wherever possible. The Naresh Chandra Task Force was set up in 2007 for follow-up on the KRC recommendations, and they submitted report on 23 May 2012. Two key action points were having a permanent Chairman of the Chiefs of Staff Committee (COSC), and formal integration of service HQs with MoD with cross-postings. Both of these are still to be implemented.

An Air warrior Assessment

Defence analyst, retired Air Marshal BD Jayal[6] feel that the political, bureaucratic, military and intelligence establishments appear to have developed a vested interest in the status quo. The Chiefs of Staff Committee should have conducted its own classified in-house review of the operations, lessons learnt and individual/institutional failures, but same did not seem to happen. In an age where air power is driving strategic and tactical options, ignoring the role of the Air Force in managing a hostile LoC in peacetime, and relegating it to the side lines, he felt, indicates a national security mindset that remains frozen in the 1962 era. Tactical and armed reconnaissance can be handled better by IAF with Tac R equipment optimised for such missions. The fact that the Pakistani Army intruded against the so-called understandable mindset of its foes only goes to show their tactical shrewdness, and studying their adversary's weaknesses and exploiting them with surprise. The IAF, despite having conducted a major exercise in this sector only a month before the crisis, lost two fighters and one helicopter before even finding its feet. This was not a professional beginning. The interservice rivalries seem to be dissipating scarce energy. The archaic higher security organisation must carry a large share of blame, he says.

Independent Foreign Assessment on Air Power in Kargil

Benjamin Lambath published a book *Airpower at 18,000: The Indian Air Force in the Kargil War*,[7] in September 2012. The Kargil conflict was a milestone event in Indian military history and one that represents a telling prototype of India's most likely type of future combat challenge, he wrote. It took many days of heated discussions between IAF and the Indian Army to decide what role each service would have in repelling the Pakistanis, and the boundaries remained hazy throughout the conflict. There were gaping holes in India's real-time intelligence, surveillance, and reconnaissance capability that had allowed the incursion to go undetected for many days.

The IAF had not trained sufficiently for combat operations in the extraordinary high altitudes as faced in Kargil. Targets were uncommonly hard to spot, and weapons systems behaved differently than at lower altitudes. The IAF pilots creatively used air strikes to create avalanches or rockslides to block Pakistani supply lines. Within a few weeks, the IAF was able to leverage advances in navigation, surveillance, and targeting technology and successfully adapted its more advanced Mirage 2000 aircraft to the conflict to force a Pakistani retreat. *Jugaad* (frugal engineering) and adaptability were the hallmarks.

Aircraft System Testing Establishment (ASTE) in Bangalore helped integrate Israeli-made Litening electro-optical targeting pods onto the Mirage 2000H and Jaguar fighters, and also modify the Mirage 2000H's centerline weapons station to carry 1,000-pound U.S. made Paveway II LGBs.

Significant asymmetry with IAF's far-superior numbers dissuaded PAF from any attempt to challenge its air superiority. Beyond the visible combat capabilities, a lot was achieved in managing intra-theater airlift. IAF fighters were driven to employ target attack tactics using ingress and egress headings that were not optimal. Had the IAF been permitted to cross the LoC, it could have spared the Indian Army the need for its costly frontal assault by attacking their source of resupply in Pakistani-occupied Kashmir. That, however, would have risked escalation to a wider war, perhaps one involving the PAF. Nearly invisible humans well dug into hideouts did not make a good target from the air. As such, close air support paid less dividends than hitting logistic nodes. After every mission, the army gave the IAF the results of the attack. In about 70% of the missions, IAF was told "bombs on target". Pakistan did not expect the combat involvement of Indian airpower.

Criticality of IR flares as an active counter-measure against any enemy infrared-guided missiles was learnt the hard way after a helicopter was lost. In all, enemy forces fired more than 100 surface-to-air missiles at IAF aircraft throughout the conflict. Yet no further aircraft were lost or sustained battle damage. Kargil conflict demonstrated that airpower could be potentially very effective in mountain warfare at high altitudes. It will become more so in context of China. Kargil also provided insights into the IAF's capabilities, limitations, and relations with its sister services. It highlighted areas requiring improvements.

This was the first and only serious clash between two nuclear powers that had a clear winner. PM Vajpayee's directive not to cross the LoC did prevent escalation. Kargil War also demonstrated that nuclear deterrence is not a panacea. Pakistan should think twice about the limits of their nuclear deterrent. The possibility of future, sharp, intense, brief and for limited stakes conventional wars with Pakistan and China exists and India must plan and prepare accordingly. Immediately after Kargil began significant process to convert the IAF from a sub-continental tactical to intercontinental strategic aerospace power with 4th-generation fighters force-extending tankers, airborne warning and control system capability, inter-theater airlifters, UAVs, and the beginnings of a military space surveillance capability. India's intelligence, surveillance, and reconnaissance deficiency has since been substantially improved with indigenous reconnaissance satellites with sub–one-meter resolution, and space-based synthetic aperture radar capability. Indian Army's constant vigil using Israeli Searcher and Heron UAVs and deploying five times larger number of troops permanently in the Kargil sector has made a difference.

Kargil Air War Lessons: Way Ahead

Immediately after the war, IAF began significant acquisition process. It acquired large number SU-30 MKI and upgraded its MiG 29 and Mirage 2000 aircraft. It acquired aerial tankers, Airborne Early Warning and Control (AEW&C) capability, inter-theater airlifters, UAVs, and the beginnings of a military space surveillance capability. A key requirement of the IAF was modern fighter aircraft to maintain clear superiority over Pakistan Air Force (PAF). IAF is also ensuring that all aerial platforms being acquired are capable of high-altitude warfare, including attack helicopters, and fighters are fit to operate at 6 km plus. The new attack helicopters would by armed with reasonable stand-off weapons. PGMs are critical weapon for modern aerial weapon delivery. Dumb bombs used with ingenuity can be devastating especially for HQs, logistic nodes and other interdiction targets. IAF needs at least five AEW&C aircraft of A-50 Phalcon class and 10 of DRDO "Netra" class. India must also accelerate the *Advanced Medium Combat Aircraft* (AMCA) fifth-generation fighter development by allocating all resources on priority.

SAM threats have to be factored in. MANPADS can be moved to high mountain tops. IR flares and Electronic Counter Measures (ECMs) are critical during operations. IAF requires training in high-altitude firing ranges. The situation on this count hasn't changed much. Air reconnaissance and battle damage assessment are crucial for air operations to plan subsequent attacks. Such ability exists. Interdiction pays greater dividends as opposed to Battlefield Air Strikes (BAS). BAS is also risky as there are many AD weapons with all the Armies. Airborne Forward Air Controllers (FACs) in Cheetah helicopters were of great help for air attacks. *Air Power made a great difference to* the ground operations, as acknowledged by field commanders of the Indian Army. It greatly helped reduce ground casualties and compress victory timelines. Operational and technical ingenuity and imagination find solutions to problems discovered during war time uncertainties. These have invariably won wars. Air defence escorts and area Combat Air Patrolling by day and night proved an effective deterrent which ensured total air superiority. At times, PAF F-16s orbited just 15 km (on their own side of the LoC) from IAF strike formations attacking Pakistani targets were kept at bay by our own air defence fighters flying a protective pattern above the strike.

One of the valuable lessons that emerged from the Kargil War was the need for closer joint army–air force planning and consultations from the very beginning. The army must seek IAF support more readily. Intelligence assets like UAVs can be operated in coordination with each other. *Field-level close* IAF–Army coordination was clearly visible as the operations unfolded. More joint operational training in real sense is required. Each service must get the others onboard at the highest level at the earliest. MoD–Service HQ integration is a critical recommendation which is yet to be implemented. "Could a creation of the position of the Chief of the Defense Staff (CDS) have overseen and adjudicate inter-service differences when it comes to the apportionment of military roles and resources?", is being asked. Service HQs must use the services of Think-Tanks to generate approach papers.

The issue of nuclear overhang on a conventional conflict had been well-settled after Kargil. India can expect and must train for future short conventional wars in the mountains with Pakistan and China. Lessons from this high-altitude Kargil War would be applicable to all the world's Air Forces, for it is the first time in the history of military aviation that such an air operation took place in such an environment where conventional long-accepted air power theories no longer held good.

NOTES

1. IAF Official Site.
2. 1999 Kargil Conflict. https://www.globalsecurity.org/military/world/war/kargil-99.htm.

3.   Bofors power proved in Kargil War. https://www.indiatoday.in/india/story/kargil-winning-the-battle-with-bofors-331307-2016-07-25

4.   Air Chief Marshal AY Tipnis interview, *Force Magazine*, Vol. 4, No. 2, October 2006.

5.   Report of the Kargil Review Committee: An Appraisal. https://www.claws.in/images/journals_doc/1400824637Report%20of%2the%20Kargil%20Review%20Committee%20%20 CJ%20SSummer%202009.pdf.

6.   The Kargil Review Committee Report By Air Marshal BD Jayal. https://www.satp.org/satporgtp/publication/idr/vol_15(2)/air_marshal_bd_ jayal_retd.htm.

7.   Airpower at 18,000': The Indian Air Force in the Kargil War, by Benjamin Lambeth. https://carnegieendowment.org/2012/09/20/airpower-at-18-000-indian-air-force-in-kargil-war-pub-49421.

Artillery in Op Vijay: Perspective of a Commanding Officer

Major General Alok Deb

Background

A review of the prelude to each war/conflict between India and Pakistan often gives rise to divergent views about how much warning or actionable intelligence was received from the concerned agencies, before the commencement of the war/conflict. Operation Vijay is no exception to such debate. With hindsight, many from India's strategic community have conceded that while broad indicators of "something in the offing" were available, these were not subjected to a holistic analysis at the national level, resulting in only routine warnings percolating down to troops manning the Line of Control (LoC) on the ground.

During the 90s, for the young Commanding Officers (COs) serving South of the Zoji La in Jammu and Kashmir, the operational focus was either on fighting insurgency or preserving the sanctity of the LoC, or sometimes both. In Ladakh, the LoC was rocky, glaciated in places and deemed to be inaccessible by many, resulting in it being manned only at three locations lying astride old trade routes. Nevertheless, the potential of Pakistan's Force Command Northern Areas (FCNA) to create a serious imbalance in the region seems to have been well appreciated by a few in India, as demonstrated in a plan by a bold Red Land commander during a wargame in Badami Bagh in April 1999, where shallow offensives South of the LoC in Ladakh were planned. While this plan does not seem to have received the consideration that it merited on that occasion, by an unholy coincidence, an operation on similar lines in the same area was under execution by Pakistan, to erupt into the open after just one month. Though stray inputs of Pakistani activity had been received through aerial reconnaissance and inputs from nomads and circulated downwards, there was overall a feeling of mild incredulity as news of the intrusions and patrol clashes began to filter in. This sense was accentuated by the unfamiliar geography of the region – this author was party to an interaction in the initial phases, with two officers from Leh, who on driving down to Dras and seeing the surrounding terrain (probably for the first time), appeared quite overawed by the situation.

Preparing for Battle

Op Vijay unfolded as a series of tactical battles in a high-altitude arena. Precluding the classical employment of mechanised forces, the major role was shouldered by infantry and artillery, supported by all other elements. It is important to recount their state of preparedness, as troops initially inducted were elements of 8 Mountain Division, thrust into conventional operations after moving up from the Kashmir Valley. As this Division was being previously employed for counter-insurgency operations, it had reduced holdings of warlike stores vis-à-vis its authorisation (which is lesser as compared to an infantry division in plains), which led to the situation requiring innovative solutions. Integral unit transport was deficient in large numbers. Consequently, transport of the entire artillery brigade of 8 Mountain Division was pooled in under personal supervision of the Commander to induct the first regiment with ammunition into the theatre, for supporting operations at Dras. Almost all other warlike stores including battalion support weapons were in short supply. Many radio sets were without secrecy devices. Holding of cable for field telephones was again short of authorisation. Camouflage net colours were essentially meant for concealment in wooded terrain, and unsuitable for Ladakh. Most important was the information void. Many maps held with units showed empty spaces North of the LoC. The LoC itself had to be physically marked across talc sheets using chinagraph pencils or OHP marker pens, with reconciliation of such alignments on maps at various headquarters, thereby testing the patience of the staff officers (unlike maps issued by the Survey of Pakistan, which were relatively more detailed, with the Pakistani version of the LoC printed on each sheet). Information on the current dispositions of the enemy on the LoC remained elusive. As regards information of areas immediately in the enemy's depth, units had to rely on data circulated in earlier updates by the Divisional Headquarters from its Valley days. Though ongoing aerial reconnaissance by Army Aviation was able to fill in some gaps in information, much of it still remained. This was the state at the commencement of operations.

Artillery faced peculiar issues. Given the priority that the Dras sub-sector then enjoyed, known gun areas including contingency positions were few. Certain contingency gun positions had been rendered untenable by enemy shelling, with the ammunition reserves stocked in the vicinity blowing up at regular intervals. Thanks to earlier induction of one field regiment from the Corps Artillery Brigade, and headquarters of a Bofors regiment en route to Siachen which had been ordered to delay its move, some artillery liaison was available for incoming units. Considering the appreciated terrain features, layout of defences taken up by the intruders and envisaged progress of operations, technically suitable gun areas to cater for all of these had to be found, which also needed to be accessible for towed guns. With most of the open areas already engaged by enemy artillery, choices were few. Having alternative positions to move into, when under shelling, turned out to be an option available only to some. Planning also had to be carried out for deploying the rest of the artillery brigade which was sure to follow up shortly. In short, notwithstanding textbook teaching, most of the artillery once deployed remained restricted to its particular gun areas, until moved out of the area.

At the commencement of operations, communication, both on radio and cable, was erratic. Manpack radio sets with short whip antennae turned out to be the most reliable means, though subject to interception, since the secrecy devices were not mounted on all sets. This resulted in communication being carried out clearly during operations, with frequent interception by the enemy, resulting in some exchanges that were not parliamentary. For all communication-less fire orders, the COs and individual officers made attempts to camouflage identities by discarding authorised call signs and resorting to local nick names, sometimes causing confusion. Cables had to be frequently re-laid by regimental and divisional signallers, due to their getting cut during enemy shelling. However, as the operations progressed, divisional signallers came into their own command. The Signal Officer of the Artillery Brigade deserves special mention, for establishing foolproof communication on the Brigade Fire Order Net, connecting the Commanding Officer (CO) of a direct support regiment on a hilltop through cable and radio, enabling coordination fires for an ongoing brigade attack, with the entire formation.

Another *sine qua non* for Gunners is accurate survey. Ideally, the divisional and corps artillery are required to be on a common "grid" to shoot together. With even updated maps in short supply, what was available was a single Bearing Picquet (a reference point whose coordinates are known to an acceptable degree of accuracy, which can then be used for obtaining coordinates of other locations at the same level of accuracy, by carrying forward survey processes) in the vicinity of Pandras. This was the start point for regimental survey parties in the Dras sub-sector, with survey data being laboriously built up and shared with incoming units. This effort, however, remained confined to the guns; locations of artillery observers and the targets that they planned to engage were derived solely from the map-reading skills of individual officers, using maps and prismatic compasses. Freshly printed and updated maps started making their appearance from the end of June 1999 onwards.

Execution of Fires

Three brigade-level fire plans incorporating all artillery in Dras were prepared during the operations. Registration of targets for these was carried out by live firing. As accurate locations of enemy were still not available, terrain features were divided into smaller bits and each portion was registered with a different set of batteries. A glaring fact which emerged at the Fire Direction Centres during their execution was the dichotomy between the planned allocation of fire support (carried out as per the teaching in schools of instruction), and the actual allotment when responding to calls for fire, once covering fire had lifted and the layout of enemy dispositions became clearer. Far more centralised and hands-on control of fire than ever envisaged became necessary, to provide guaranteed fire for all – quite distinct from the teachings on "superimposed artillery" (a term familiar to officers who have undergone the Junior Command Course, and a hallowed tenet for gunners steeped in the Commonwealth tradition). Such control was made possible by having at least two officers always present in the Fire Direction Centres, and being in constant communication with their CO, who, since he was physically observing the attacks going in, could reconcile or overrule conflicting requirements. Artillery was also employed in some unique situations. The gaps in information have been discussed earlier. During the initial period, one rifle company whose location was known only approximately was pinned down by enemy fire. In the late evening, with an ice wall in front and being fired upon from other sides, there was no place for the company to fall back. As a last resort, direct support artillery was used to bring down prophylactic fire on the flanks, with the hope that enemy in the vicinity would be suppressed temporarily to permit the company to move to a safer location.

Direct firing by Bofors, the exclusive brainchild of the Commander, 8 Mountain Artillery Brigade, in the operations, was very effective and has been written about extensively. What is less known is another proof of its efficacy – the fire plan prepared for the capture of one objective (Rocky Knob, on the same ridgeline and east of Pt 5140) was not required to be fired because of the accurate direct fire of two 155-mm guns from two different medium regiments. Each bunker on the objective was pointed out by the CO of the battalion providing the firm base. Fire from the guns (150 rounds of High-Explosive Extended Range shells) was directed by Commander Infantry Brigade and CO Field Regiment. Direct shooting using other equipment was not so successful. 75/24 howitzers were dismantled and hauled manpack up the hillsides to engage enemy bunkers, but met with limited success.

Inter Arm/Service Cooperation

All arms and services of the Formation worked together in close cooperation. In particular, mention must be made of the synergy between infantry and artillery, a noteworthy take away from Operation Vijay which was instrumental in achieving success. While joint planning remained the preserve of the higher headquarters, there was almost minute-to-minute coordination at infantry brigade and artillery regiment level and below. Joint reconnaissance by infantry and artillery COs of routes and staging areas, coordination of details such as common names for landmarks, objectives and other targets ensured that no confusion arose at any level, culminating in the production of simple and workable outline fire plans to support attacks. The battle of Tololing witnessed the ultimate synergy between these two arms, when, on the death of a company commander during the assault, the Observation Post (OP) officer from the direct support field regiment held the company together, pressing home the attack till relieved by the CO of the battalion.

As in all wars, OP officers remained a much sought after commodity. The extent of the intrusions and the need to cover these by observation and observed fire necessitated deployment of many more OPs, which were made up from additional units inducted into Dras, and deploying Junior Commissioned Officers (JCOs) in this role. More difficult to manage was the issue of providing such parties for the battalions going in for attack, with some OPs inevitably being recycled, due to non-availability of reliefs as also the time required for acclimatisation and induction – one OP officer uncomplainingly went in for three attacks, with different companies of two battalions, as operations progressed. Another OP officer was requested for by name by the battalion with which he had carried out operations earlier, for another major attack – a stellar example of good faith born out of successful inter-arm cooperation.

Logistic planning and management was a major success story. Once the initial hiccups had settled, the services ensured that supplies of rations, fuel, oils and lubricants (FOL) and ammunition were seamless, thereby ensuring that tendencies of some troops to commandeer ammunition vehicles and unload them at will were curbed. Logistic installations and convoys worked under heavy time and space constraints as did others, while being equally vulnerable to enemy shelling. Their laudable performance does not seem to have been highlighted to the extent that it deserves. Engineers, commencing with the Divisional engineers and later supplemented by others, worked tirelessly, executing all types of engineer close support tasks, including improving entrances to gun areas wherever required. With the enemy retreating after each successful attack, track construction commenced to facilitate preparation of defences, buildup and stocking.

Pakistan Artillery's Performance

A word about Pakistani artillery would not be out of place. Enemy guns, though much lesser in numbers (as was gauged from the number of rounds landing) remained active throughout operations, delivering quick and fairly accurate responses to our own fire – attributable possibly to the holding of Fire finder radars then held with Pakistan. The credit for not incurring more casualties due to enemy counter bombardment must go to the Seconds-in-Command of respective regiments whose efforts resulted in extremely well-sited gun positions (though a sense of the destructive power of artillery can be obtained through details gleaned by researchers from Military Hospital Leh, where it was learnt that 50.5% of all casualties brought into that hospital were due to splinter injuries).[1] Pakistani artillery also proved adept at harnessing fire, deploying guns in ones and twos, to open up at odd times on our locations. Chief amongst these was a mortar, which remained active till the end of operations, which the Indian artillery could not silence for long. A mention must also be made of the illumination shells fired by one 5.5-inch gun, which proved very effective in lighting up the landscape almost down to the National Highway.

Reflections and Crystal Gazing

Despite initially having been put on the defensive, the Indian Army achieved success in Operation Vijay due to the resilience of the Indian soldier and resolute leadership at all levels. All ranks quickly acclimatised to the ground situation and started from the basics to execute assigned tasks. Staff at all levels worked as "servants of troops", ensuring documentation of casualties, transferring battalion support weapons and special high-altitude clothing from units coming down after an operation to others going in for attack, tailoring logistics, and the issue of innovative dry meals (under guidance of Corps HQ) en masse, being an example. Though computers had been introduced in units, these were used as typewriters and preparing stand-alone databases. There was no Intelligence Preparation of the Battlefield (IPB) or Military Decision-Making Process (MDMP). Neither were there any power point presentations. Heli-lift capability and ground-air defence means were limited. Precision munitions (laser-guided bombs) for the

IAF were just under introduction. Information updates to enhance situational awareness were sporadic. Considering the availability of resources and that operations were being conducted on foot, at heights of 15000 feet, there was very limited scope for that much desired "manoeuvre in mountains". It was quintessential mountain warfare, something that the Indian Army has traditionally been known for.

Twenty years down the line, it is interesting to revisit Op Vijay and discuss how this series of tactical battles would have played out in the present day – without venturing into discussions on limited wars, war aims and strategy. Thanks to implementation of the recommendations of various review committees and induction of specialist equipment, surveillance through satellites, airborne warning and control system (AWACS) and unmanned aerial vehicles (UAVs) would have confirmed or dispelled suspicions about enemy intentions, thus providing clarity for decision making. Employment of the IAF across the LoC could become more of a possibility. Larger numbers of Precision-Guided Munitions (PGMs) and inventory of aircraft available for delivering these would result in effective interdiction of enemy lines of communication, logistics infrastructure and destruction of defences. Light Combat Helicopters and their Weapon System Integrated variants (along with the just inducted Apaches) would provide other options for destroying the enemy. Deterring enemy aircraft would be more effective due to improved air defence by IAF. Infantry's larger inventory of weapons, including latest generation small arms, would increase its combat power manifold, offering various options for engaging and destroying the enemy at close quarters. With improved heli-lift capability (Chinooks being also available now), manoeuvre in mountains would become possible, using regular infantry. Avenues for employment of Special Forces too would increase, to create unforeseen asymmetries. Induction of the M777 howitzer into difficult areas would overcome lack of fire support. Artillery would have more options to shoot and scoot, deploy single guns with accurate survey, and track enemy artillery with precision using the Swathi locating radar. OP officers would monitor and engage targets by day and night using Long-Range Optical Systems (LORROS) and Integrated Observation Devices with laser range finders. BrahMos, Pinaka and SMERCH (and later, Dhanush) would contribute towards shifting the war further into the kinetic, non-contact areas. This would no longer be a war fought by infantry and artillery in the forefront as earlier, but a joint, more integrated all-arms battle, coupled with elements of the hybrid warfare. Most importantly, the war would not be fought just in the two domains of land and air. This time, India's nascent capabilities in Space, Cyber and Electronic Warfare could provide the basis for non-kinetic, non-contact options as well.

---

1. Maj Gen Ashok Kalyan Verma, AVSM , *Kargil: Blood on the Snow, Tactical Victory Strategic Failure,* Manohar Publishers, 2002, p. 108.

Keeping The Enemy Air At Bay

Brigadier Akhelesh Bhargava

Introduction

An interesting part of the book written by then COAS Gen V P Malik on Kargil War, is that on the cover page there is a photograph of a Zu Gun of a Light Air Defence Regiment (Composite) (Lt AD Regt (Comp)) deployed at Mattayan for providing Air Defence protection to NH 1A. It set me thinking about the important role that Army Air Defence (AAD) played in the Kargil War.

In the months of April-May 1999, the Pakistani intruders crossed the Line of Control (LoC) and occupied heights in Kargil and neighbouring sectors. The intrusions went on undetected for quite some time, by when the enemy had well entrenched themselves and consolidated their positions. It took some time before it became known that something is amiss, and action has to be initiated against the intruders. At that point in time I was a Major, performing duties of a Battery Commander at Kota.

Just a couple of years back, in 1996-97; a number of Army Air Defence (AAD) Zu guns were pooled from various Army AD units in other commands and were provided to the Infantry Battalions deployed on LoC. They were to be used unconventionally in direct firing role. My unit (a Light AD Regiment (Self Propelled)) had deployed two of them in Keren Sector and I was the first officer to be there with the detachment in February 1997. In response to Pakistani firing, the guns had been very effective, especially in destroying Pakistani vehicles carrying maintenance stores to their posts on LoC including those in Kargil heights and adjacent sectors. Their firing forced Pakistan to abandon movement on the Lower and Upper Neelam Valley Road. They constructed a new road, outside the range of the guns on the leeward side of the mountain there. The effectiveness of the AD guns was put in full use thereafter including during Kargil war.

Situation Prior to Kargil

A decade prior, the Indian Army had been involved in counter insurgency (CI) operations in J&K, and Army AD role as an arm became low on priority. However, the moment own and enemy air activity started during Kargil, in fourth week of May 1999, Army AD was tasked to operate in both AD and ground firing role. However, there were limited AD resources, which had to be deployed as individual weapon platforms.

The Army AD had limited resources in the Northern Command, which comprised just a brigade with three units. The smallest component for deployment in Army AD is a troop and they just totaled two dozen at that point in time. These were just enough to provide AD cover to a limited number of vulnerable areas / vulnerable points identified in the theatre.

Zu-23 twin barrel, light weight guns were deployed all along the LoC in ground firing role since end of 1996 with great effectiveness. The Zu gun had a very high rate of fire and being mounted on a platform, was capable of providing very accurate support fire in ground role, to the assaulting troops, with devastating effect on the enemy. These guns could be disassembled into small parts and lugged up to the mountain tops. The Igla-1M man portable Surface to Air Missile (SAM) could be deployed on any mountain top with ease and they were very effective in air ambush role. The L/70 40 mm medium air defence guns with their vintage towers crossed the Zoji La Pass for the first time. These were basically meant for airfields and assets at lower heights.

Kargil War

When the Air Force took to air on 26 May 1999, it was clear that the Army AD will have a greater role to play. Rightfully so, the Northern Command Air Defence Brigade received its mobilisation orders on 26 May to be ready in designated locations by end May. The Army AD unit located at Leh, part of the Northern Command Air Defence Brigade was the first one to be activated. Initially this Light AD Regt (Comp) was responsible for the entire stretch from Dras to Siachen Glacier.

Later, more Army AD assets were bid for and the same was agreed to. Three Igla troops of a Lt AD Regt (Comp), part of an Air Defence Brigade, were moved from Gwalior into the Sector both by road and air in first week of June. An AD Regiment, part of an Air Defence Brigade were moved from Suratgarh into the sector. Surveillance radars of an Air Defence Group were also deployed to thicken up the surveillance in the area. When additional Bofors units were required to be inducted into the Kargil sector; Bofors units from formations in the plains too received their orders to mobilise. My troop being the affiliated troop with one such unit was also put on standby for providing close air defence support. However, the order to mobilise did not fructify as the 'air war' remained limited to own side of LoC.

A conscious decision was taken by the political hierarchy for the IAF aircrafts not to cross LoC. Pakistanis too ensured that none of their aircraft crossed the LoC, though plenty of air activity was seen on radar in airspace over Gilgit-Skardu. The helicopter activity was high on both sides of LoC, but within the confines of respective territory.

The moment news trickled in about the enemy intrusions, few guns from Lt AD Regt (Comp) located at Leh, were immediately mobilised from Leh to Dras and were deployed in Dras, Kaksar, Kargil and Batalik sectors. The guns were so sited that they could provide both air defence protection as also provide close fire support to assaulting troops. One SAM troop was deployed in Siachen Glacier and another in Leh Airfeild. The one at Leh was relieved later later by L/70 AD guns, so that the Igla dets could be deployed on various heights along with Infantry. Other Igla dets were abinito deployed in air ambush role with Infantry on various mountain heights.

The Lt AD Regt (Comp) ex an AD Brigade, received its mobilization order on 31 May 1999. The unit moved in two parts, one by road and other by air. Igla Sections (Sec) under Maj Manjit were deployed at Thoise Airfield. Igla Sec under Capt Sareen were deployed as independent detachments (dets) in air ambush role on the heights of Batalik Sub-sector. The unit had on number of occasion tryst with enemy. On 14 June, troops deployed at Turtuk Igla det location (along with Infantry), under Lt Deepak came under heavy shelling and many soldiers were injured. On 16 June 1999, at Chorbat La during attack by infantry at Pt 5660 on a Pakistani post, Capt Sareen acted as an OP officer and took effective shoot of 81 mm mortar on Masjid Complex (PoK). Fuel dump was set on fire and few Pakistani soldiers were killed. On 05 July, a Puma Helicopter (Heptr) was sighted opposite Pt 5114, carrying out maintenance of Pakistani Posts. Naik Arvind Kumar fired a SAM at it. The helicopter went behind a hill feature. A second missile was readied and after sometime, when the helicopter reappeared, it was engaged again. The missile followed the helicopter and again tried to go behind a hill. An explosion was heard but hit was not confirmed by intelligence sources. The ceasefire was declared on 26 July at the behest of Pakistan, but in Turtuk Sub-sector they had not vacated certain posts and hence the action continued till end August. On 10 August, SAM was used in a ground role. A detachnment, deployed with an Infantry Company, fired at Pakistani Nusrat extension gun position. The SAM being a heat seeker missile got locked on to the hot barrel of the enemy machine gun. Missile entered the bunker loophole and exploded. The gun was destroyed; ammunition set on fire and few Pak soldiers were killed. On 19 August, at Pt 5440, a SAM operator while performing air sentry duty in anticipation of Pak Helicopter activity, became a target of Pakistani Rocket Propelled Grenade (RPG), which hit him on chest. He was declared dead by RMO of an Infantry Unit. The Regt was de-inducted with effect from 28 September.

The AD Regiment deployed in the Rajasthan Sector received orders on 17 June to move for Kargil Operations. The unit had a tough time travelling across Zoji La Pass, but somehow they managed to get across. An AD Battery was deployed in valley itself at Khunmuh and Sharifabad helicopter (heptr) base. AD troops across Zojila were deployed at Mughalpur (Dras), Kargil helipad, Leh airfield and Thoise airfield. The AD troops at Leh and Thoise basically relieved Lt AD troops for deployment on heights in Turtuk and Chorbatla Sub-sector. The unit was fully ready at all locations by 26 June. The Kargil helipad came under heavy shelling. A Pakistani UAV was sighted and engaged and as a result it scooted back behind the mountains.

Post Kargil

In 2011–2012, I as Colonel AD at Headquarters Northern Command was functioning as Head of Arm (HoA). I made the most of it, by visiting the AD gun locations on LoC and various tasks in the border areas in all three Corps Zones in the theatre. During the visit to 14 Corps Zone, I had the first hand experience of the icy heights firstly in Batalik, Chalunka and Turtuk Sector and later in the Kargil Sector. From NH 1A, the various heights (Tiger Hill, Tololing, and others) look as if they are just there. Once you start climbing them only then do you realize their degree of difficulty. The Kargil War Memorial is a true tribute to our Martyrs.

Any war in present environment is likely to commence with an air campaign. So far little eminence was given to AD in the mountainous terrain. The air activity during Kargil clearly reflected that AD allocation has to be catered for abinito. It becomes imperative that the AD resources of our army and that with air force should be given due importance and urgent acquisition needs to be carried out to ensure its augmentation to meet the current air threat. Pooling it from other sectors will be at cost of denuding those sectors.

Recommendations

The air surveillance resources were non-existent in the conflict zone prior to Kargil war; it would have been a big setback had a full scale participation of Air Force taken place from both sides. As of now, sufficient numbers of Low Level Light Weight Radars have been allocated in the Northern Command, both by Army AD and IAF. The long range surveillance radars of the IAF too have been upgraded.

A large number of SAM troops were broken down into dets and individual missile launchers were deployed in an air ambush role across the sectors. This, though not the best way, made up for the shortfall in Army AD resources in the Kargil war. The use of heat seeking SAM being used against an enemy machine gun bunker at such high altitude in an unconventional way, was innovative and yielded result.

The Igla 1M, SAM have now outlived their life by years and needs an urgent replacement. The procurement process has been on for more than a decade and it is yet to see the light of day. Besides these, IAF being the elder partner in ensuring AD of a sector should cater for adequate quantum of air effort for providing Combat Air Patrol (CAP). However, for that to happen, the strength of IAF too needs to be beefed up for it to fructify. Area AD equipment, such as S-400, currently under acquisition, or its alternative should also be allocated when such operations takes place.

AD is all about electronics and sustained deployment in very low temperatures, is likely to cause degradation of the missiles, ammunition and equipment. The ammunition and missile storage has to be done in temperature controlled environment and accordingly sufficient air conditioned storage facility has to be constructed in formation located in high altitude. Similarly, sufficient air controlled shelters have to be made for equipment storage also.

Conclusion

The Army AD role was limited in Kargil war due to political decision in containing Air Force participation. No Pakistani aircraft or helicopter crossed the LoC in the presence of IAF and Army AD warriors. The contribution of Army AD in ground role was immense and significant and it translated in form of many awards and unit citation.

Record Missions in Support: Army Aviation

Lieutenant General BS Pawar

During a career spanning 40 plus years I had the privilege of spending 16 years in flying both in the erstwhile Air Observation Post (OP) and subsequently the Army Aviation Corps at different stages of service. In my 4000 hours of flying accumulated during this period, the most daunting and challenging experience was flying in High Altitude Areas – almost 2500 of these 4000 hours were flown in mountainous and high-altitude terrain. The first experience in such flying was as early as 1975-76 while heading a Cheetah Helicopter detachment in Leh-Ladakh area. Flying in high altitudes requires special skills and knowledge both regards to the different types of terrain and weather conditions prevailing in these areas at different times of the day. It is to the professional credit and dedication of these pilots who continue to operate in the high-altitude terrains, as also the highest battlefield of the world – the Siachen Glacier.

The Army Aviation was the third eye of the Kargil War. They were in a constant state of alert where man defied machine and the helicopter machine defied and challenged every mission. Together, both the magnificent men in their flying machines gave the attacking Indian army the much needed looks into the enemy extent, layout and weapon locations while braving all odds against being hit by missiles, rocket attacks and machine gun fire. Having observed the enemy targeting the helicopters, these dare devil pilots resorted to evasive tactics, with very limited availability of power (lift component) in their machines, due to the extreme high altitudes and rarefied atmosphere. It was an excellent example of the pilots testing their machines to their extreme limits. Such was their brash bravery and guts, that the then General

Officer Commanding the ground attacking forces of 8 Mountain Division (8 Mtn Div) had to say:

> 'I was witness to the performance of the aviators, who unhesitatingly took to the skies even on short notice to extricate a patrol, evacuate casualties, look and report beyond the ridgelines of enemy positions, direct artillery fire accurately onto targets and even deliver ammunition or food to the ground troops. These aviators displayed acrobatic skills in the most treacherous land terrain, braved all sorts of Pakistani weaponry fired on them. I still recall as to how they landed me on just a matchbox sized space at Tololing'.

The aviators gave the ground planners the vision of the enemy on the other side of the hill. Flying operations along the areas of intrusion were extremely challenging at altitudes of 17,000 feet or more. These men actually mapped the full extent of Pakistani ingress in vital areas of Turtuk, Chorbat La, Khalubar, Jubar, Kaksar, Tololing, Tiger Hill and all mountainous heights such as Muntho Dhalo, Point 4100, Point 5284, Kukarthang, Point 5285, Point 4927 and so on. The extent of intrusion into Indian territory varied from 4-8 Kms Coexistence of Pakistani regular troops from the Northern Light Infantry (NLI) and Special Service Group (SSG) was also witnessed. On an average, each major ridgeline was held by 30 to 40 soldiers under command of an officer. These soldiers were dressed in local attire to pass off as Kashmiri freedom fighters.

Weaponry held by them was heavy and medium machine guns, rocket launchers, automatic grenade launchers, mortar, shoulder fired missiles and even anti-aircraft guns.

News about the disappearance of Captain Saurav Kalia and his men during a patrol in Kaksar region was conveyed to the Aviation unit. In no time was a helicopter airborne to patrol this area and on flying close to the ridgelines started spotting human presence. One pilot reported being fired upon and subsequent confirmatory air reconnaissance confirmed the presence of intruders on numerous ridgelines well inside Indian territory. On 09 May 1999, Capt Satinder while flying a Ranjit helicopter even engaged an intruded position on Tololing. On 13 May 1999, another helicopter pilot, Maj PN Prasad picked up a new trail climbing upto Tololing feature near Dras. Dropping in height to get a clear picture, his machine came under rocket fire. Soon a Pakistani Puma helicopter joined the firing. Sheer skill combined with good luck allowed the pilot to extricate from being downed. Yet, undaunted he radioed for Artillery fire which resulted in the first casualties in the Pakistani camp.

Given the extreme difficult terrain and weather conditions, the army aviation pilots remained fully conscious of doing that extra bit to raise the motivation and morale of the combat troops and logistic organisations. The sheer magnitude of the Army Aviation effort during the Kargil War amounted to at least 2500 missions. Infact an average of 50 missions progressed each day. Despite the major constraint of a high altitude on the pay load capacity, and also a limited capacity to ferry one or two passengers in a Cheetah helicopter, they achieved the unique distinction of evacuating a number of casualties from the forward most locations – in contact battle. Thus, Operation Vijay was truly the aviator's finest hour, wherein the relentless sound of the whirring rotors truly brought hope, cheer and lifted the high morale of our advancing forces. For this exceptional and exemplary valour and grit in heroic battles in Kargil, the Chief of the Army Staff honoured two Reconnaissance and Observation Squadrons of the Army Aviation with special award of Unit Citations.

Army aviation continues to remain the arm of the future. With the increased employment of unarmed aerial systems (UAS)/remotely piloted aircrafts (RPA) at both tactical and strategic levels needs no emphasis, army aviation's role has increased manifold.. With swarm miniaturised drones being increasingly employed, there is a need to graduate to Manned Unmanned Teaming (MUM-T). Technologies like AI and advanced Human Machine Interface (HMI) need to be imbibed in order to manage MUM-T missions. Also, for effect-based operations, concentrated employment of aviation resources should become the norm. Although a number of operations were undertaken, irrespective of the time and weather conditions, with improvements in avionics, the Army Aviation Corps has focused to further enhance its night operational capabilities to support 24/7 operations. Army aviators are remembered by every soldier of the Kargil conflict for their bold and offensive actions, and the intimate support to the units operating on the ground.

Sappers: Turning the Tide

Colonel Madhusudan Dave

Introduction

I spent a large part of my childhood at Kirkee, amidst the environs of one of the Centres of the Corps of Engineers, or Sappers, as they are more commonly known. Surrounded by their numerous accomplishments, both in war and peace, opting for the Engineers on commissioning, came easy. At the Academy, military history intrigued me, tales of the Sappers being of particular interest. Their exploits on a wide range of tasks, including on many occasions, the infantry role, were inspiring. The Burma campaign was where the Sappers had flourished, providing support across the spectrum, while the 1971 operation on the Eastern front was commonly termed the "Sappers War". I was fortunate to have met numerous Engineer personnel who recounted their memories of the 1971 operations, wherein floating bridges, dry gap bridges, track work, demolitions, mine laying and breaching, water supply, helipad construction, etc., had been undertaken under the most adverse conditions. The contribution of the Sappers in field and peace, provision of Engineer support whether in an insurgency environment, or in high altitude, or whether providing aid to civil authorities during calamities and disasters, was also phenomenal. Their motto, in fact, says it all, *"Sarvatra"*, or, "everywhere". The operations in Kargil in 1999 provided yet another challenge to the Sappers.

The background to the operations in the general area of Kargil in 1999, termed Operation Vijay, is well known. Various aspects have been covered earlier in this book. The difficult and harsh mountainous region, the effect of high altitude on personnel and equipment, and the effects of cold weather are but a few of the problems which confronted troops deployed in the region. For the Sappers, these formed the main issues as they set about addressing the various engineer tasks in support of the infantry, artillery and other troops who had been hurriedly inducted into the Sector.

A number of engineer units and sub-units had moved in for operations from Leh and the Kashmir Valley, while others were moved in from their peace locations. The immensity of the tasks which faced them, the undeveloped and harsh terrain, the inhospitable conditions and the timeframe available to complete them were some of the challenges successfully addressed by the Sappers. The engineer regiments and various engineer sub-units which were deployed rendered yeoman service to the fighting and administrative troops – efforts which were well recognised and acknowledged both during and after the operations. A variety of tasks such as mine laying and breaching, track construction, demolitions, water supply, construction of bridges and crossings, provision of habitat, etc., were undertaken in the area. Engineer troops also operated side by side with their infantry counterparts providing close support during the battle. Overall, Kargil would stretch the Sappers in more ways than one, but where, despite the terrain, weather and hostile conditions, the Sappers would prevail, and once again prove their worth to the Nation.

Terrain

Though terrain has been adequately covered in an earlier chapter, for the Sappers the problems are quite different from those faced by others. With one basic adage being to provide mobility to own forces while denying the same to the enemy, and another being survivability, the Sappers had their task cut out. Certain peculiarities of the terrain which would have an adverse effect on engineer support are brought out in brief:

- The area of operations extended approximately over 160 km along the Line of Control, spreading engineer resources thin.
- The area is bifurcated by the Zanskar Range, and on the East extended up to Turtok. Well-defined valleys and ridge lines impacted side-stepping and switching of engineer resources.
- The region was grossly under-developed. Very little infrastructure existed, and roads and tracks, except for the main Srinagar-Leh Highway and a few other subsidiary roads in the

vicinity of military camps, were characterised by their absence. Local resources were conspicuous by their nonexistence.

- Acclimatisation of troops was a must, for rapid deployment of those inducting from lower altitudes. All equipment and stores were required to be inducted via the Valley, procured from factories and depots mainly located in Punjab and beyond. The lines of communication were over long distances and tenuous in nature.

- Area was characterised by necessitating extensive earthwork.

Situation Prior to Kargil Operations

Broadly, 15 Corps Zone in 1999 extended from Ladakh in the East to the Kashmir Valley in the West. The Engineer troops in the Corps Zone comprised integral engineer regiments with the divisions, or those affiliated to the Corps. There were also some engineer task forces which were planned to be deployed in the working season on selected tasks to beef up the engineer strength. 15 Corps had some detachments from Bomb disposal Company and Engineer Plant Unit. The area also had a large presence of Border Roads units, and to a limited extent Military Engineer Services, some of whose resources could be deployed in support of operations, especially in the rear areas, should the need arise.

The Sappers, prior to the summers of 1999, were deployed either in the counter-insurgency grid, or on the Line of Control, engaged in various engineer tasks. The onset of the summers in the Valley and in Ladakh is always a cause for intense engineer activity as it is the commencement of the rather limited working season available to achieve targets. Preparation for the move and induction of engineer stores to forward areas as a prelude to the melting of snows and the consequent opening of roads and tracks in forward areas was also in progress. In addition, Sappers in the Valley were deployed on the counter-insurgency grid on tasks such as road opening, detection and disposal of improvised explosive devices, habitat development, etc. Other Sapper units were deployed for road and track opening in forward areas, construction of roads and tracks for move of guns and meeting logistics requirements, construction and development of new defences and strengthening of existing ones. Relocation of garrisons at

Tangdhar and Kargil was also in progress, while important passes such as Nastachun and Razdhan were also required to be kept open. In addition, the standard operational work tasks and civic action jobs continued at various places in the Corps Zone. The Ladakh Sector had its own peculiarities and saw engineer troops providing support in similar activities as their counterparts in the Valley region, but which now included pipelines, aerial ropeways and operation of snow vehicles in the glacier region. The heavy commitment of engineers also took its toll on training. A few regiments saw their annual Combat Engineer Training Camps being dispensed with and most others struggling to maintain yearly operational work targets could pay only lip service to training. Heavy commitments in the counter-insurgency grid and the Line of Control environment also affected training.

An important distinction from the norm, dictated by terrain, deployment, tasking and requirement, was that the Sappers were deployed in small parties over a widespread area, rather than in concentrated fashion as would be preferable. However, lesser snowfall in the winter of 1998-99, saw the Border Roads opening the Zoji La and Rohtang axes in an earlier timeframe in 1999 allowing repair and rehabilitation of the two axes ahead of the normal schedule, eventually allowing faster buildup of resources to the area.

Engineer Resources

Engineer troops invariably, always fall short in terms of quantum available vis-à-vis the tasks faced. As such, challenges for the Sappers abound. Operation Vijay proved no different, and as the operations built up, as additional infantry and artillery was inducted, so were the engineers. Induction of engineer troops took place over a period of time, which stretched beyond the ceasefire on 12 July 1999. Primarily the post-war induction addressed the need of undertaking various tasks which invariably follow a battle, or war. Details of the tasks are covered subsequently in this chapter.

Engineer resources available initially with 15 Corps essentially comprised the integral engineer regiment of the infantry divisions, the Corps engineer regiment and some resources of Northern Command. Subsequently, additional engineer resources were inducted as operations developed.

Engineer Tasks and Salient Issues during Operation Vijay: Pre-Ceasefire Phase (Offensive by Indian Forces)

A rapidly evolving ground situation, difficulties in communication, as well as the challenges constituted by terrain posed difficulties in intelligence assessments and inputs to commanders. However, brigades had been strengthened by affiliating additional infantry battalions, but corresponding increase in engineers was in a gradual manner did not occur. The major types of tasks undertaken were close support tasks, construction of roads and tracks, construction of defences, fortifications and essential field dugouts such as command posts, advanced dressing stations, development of infrastructure for inducting troops, etc. A number of tasks were undertaken which have been described subsequently.

Close Support Tasks. Initially only limited close support tasks could be carried out due to a mismatch in troops to task. The main tasks undertaken were bunker bursting, mine breaching and track construction. Mine breaching at treacherous heights and in inclement conditions was difficult but ensured without casualties. Novel methods were adopted by the Sappers to address the adversities faced in these tasks to ensure early completion.

Construction of Roads and Tracks. The area of operations lacked significant roads and tracks for progressing offensive operations. Any progress forward in operations was incumbent on the buildup of ammunition and logistics, which through manpower on foot tracks was not possible in the desired quantities. As such, construction of roads and tracks assumed great significance for such buildup. Most roads and tracks being constructed during the offensive phase of Operation Vijay were along alignments which were dominated by the enemy both by fire and observation, resulting in maximum work being undertaken during hours of darkness, or low visibility. A variety of engineer plant equipment comprising dozers, excavator loaders, compressors, rock drills and other engineer equipment was employed along the various selected alignments which varied in length depending on the requirement. June and July 1999 saw feverish activity by the Sappers and saw the birth of new tracks in the area.

Miscellaneous Tasks. A number of other engineer tasks carried out during this period were construction of operations rooms for formations, advanced dressing stations, bunkers, fortifications, artillery gun posts and ammunition points. To facilitate movement of commanders and troops and to facilitate casualty evacuation and logistics resupply by air, new helipads were constructed. In addition, a number of other places were levelled, which could, in an emergency, allow helicopters to land. Water was another requirement which had to be catered for to sustain troops and equipment during operations. All brigade headquarters, along with the Main and Rear Headquarters of 8 Mountain Division, were provided water points. In addition, minimum electrification using medium and man-portable generator sets was provided to formation headquarters and the field surgical centre.

With additional troops being continuously inducted to Kargil, the requirement of transit infrastructure along lines of communication, and around Kargil, became imperative. Engineer troops developed basic facilities for the same along the Rohtang-Leh and the Srinagar-Leh axes.

A major and very critical concern for the staff at the Northern Command Headquarters was the completion of advance winter stocking for troops deployed beyond Zoji La. The onset of operations and the requirement of road space for inducting formations for operations had considerably magnified the requirement of such stocks. Further, in June and July 1999, the duration of the war could not be predicted with surety and every passing day reduced the available window for stocking. With approximately 50% of the advance winter stocking comprising fuel, oil and lubricants, a feasibility study was undertaken by the Sappers for laying of a pipeline across Zoji La, up to Dras, to pump fuel for winter stocking.

Salient Issues Forthcoming from the Offensive Operations

General. A number of factors contributed to the initial hiccups in undertaking operations in Kargil. Firstly, Pakistan's actions were unexpected, their presence in Indian territory a complete surprise and the defences created by them further exacerbating the situation. Initial appreciations of the enemy, as widely reported in the national media, were grossly wrong. Resultantly, engineer resources were moved into the operational area in a relative hurry. The urgency of the situation resulted in a large number of troops being inadequately acclimatised and equipped for the forthcoming operations.

Reactive Nature of Engineer Actions. Initial actions by the engineers were based entirely as a reaction to enemy action due to inadequacy of information and intelligence, of the enemy and his intent. This led to inadequate or deficient deployment of engineers initially, while the operational picture was yet unclear. However, the Sappers during this period proposed that available troops be deployed for improving and developing selected tracks, which was adopted.

Importance of Zoji La Axis. Its interdiction due to the large-scale occupation of Indian territory was a major worry for commanders and staff. A few close misses of enemy artillery on this road kept the worry continuously alive. The engineers undertook reconnaissance for alternate bridging sites along the road axis and prepared them for undertaking bridge construction in case of any contingency. In some places, bridging stores were moved and placed on important bridge sites like Harka Bahadur and Iqbal bridges to address contingencies, should they arise.

Limited Engineer Troops for Assault. The attacker's ratio vis-à-vis the defender having been reworked, each assaulting brigade was beefed up by additional infantry battalions. With a corresponding increase in engineer troops not forthcoming, the availability of engineers for the assault was grossly inadequate and tasks undertaken were limited to essential close support tasks. Further, no bids for additional Sappers were put in because of the faulty assessment of the enemy having hastily prepared defences which were manned by irregulars.

Inadequacy of Equipment. The Sappers lacked certain critical equipment which was essential for operations. Prodders, compressors, rock drills and mine shoes were not held. Some equipment held with units were obsolete but had been retained due to lack of options. Equipment was, however, made up in an emergent fashion. Items procured included Atlas Copco rock drills and Chicago pneumatic compressors. Though procured initially without accessories, these were soon obtained from operational works funds. Some rock drills of 1962 vintage lying in the Engineer Theatre Stores Reserve were also issued, though they proved ineffective being vintage and not in use for a long period.

Requirement of Additional Plant. Though engineer regiments were holding various types of engineer plant, a few of them were under repairs. A timely assessment that these would prove inadequate for the task resulted in early induction of additional engineer plant to Kargil from the Northern Command resources, primarily the engineer plant unit, then based at Nagrota. Eventually, the additional plant contributed considerably towards timely completion of engineer tasks.

Engineer Tasks during Operation Vijay: Post-Ceasefire Phase (Withdrawal of Pakistani Troops)

General. The Sappers are the one "Arm" for whom it is said, "First into battle, and, last to return". Nowhere was this proved more correct than the high altitudes of the Line of Control in Kargil and its neighbouring sectors. The first battle for the Sappers was during the offensive phase of operations, while the second battle commenced once the enemy withdrew (post ceasefire) and the consolidation by Indian forces started. The decision to redeploy 8 Mountain Division in the general area of Kargil was taken in order to consolidate and strengthen Indian presence in the region and to obviate recurrence of a similar situation in future. The earlier formation at Kargil was an independent infantry brigade, and the additional infrastructure required, whether for fighting or living, was immense. In addition, there was a need to sanitise the area, including defended areas for the remnants of war, mainly mines and unexploded ordnance. The additional demand for engineer troops had been worked out and catered for the offensive as well as the post-ceasefire phases. The overall buildup of Sappers finally amounted to about 24 field companies, from the initial 7. Very few engineer tasks can be undertaken without suitable and adequate engineer equipment and stores, and so, a large number of engineer plant, rock drills, bailey bridges, etc. were inducted to ensure that the pace of engineer support was maintained.

Mine Breaching and Area Sanitisation The sanitisation of the areas vacated by the enemy was the immediate and prime concern of the

Sappers after the withdrawal of the enemy. However, this was a tiring and time-consuming task, rendered all the more tedious since the enemy had probably laid additional mines in the days prior to their withdrawal. A number of mines were also booby trapped, or fitted with anti-lifting devices, thus rendering the task fraught with danger. The types of mines and improvised explosive devices recovered included the following:

- Mine Anti Personnel P2 Mark II
- Mine Anti Personnel P4 Mark I
- Claymore Mines
- Pakistan Ordnance Factory – manufactured explosive devices.

The mine breaching and sanitisation was revealing, for it showed that the enemy had not always followed a set pattern for the laying, with a number of mines strewn indiscriminatingly, or randomly. Mines were also found in various likely deployment areas, hidden by earth and stones. Prodders, mine detectors and mine shoes were found ineffective: first, due to the rocky terrain; second, because of false signatures emitted by the numerous metal splinters and other metallic debris of battle scattered in the area; and last, because they were heavy and cumbersome to use at those heights. At places, the enemy also mined, or booby trapped the dead. Large number of mines were breached during Operation Vijay.

Construction of Roads and Tracks. As brought out earlier, the area of operations lacked communications, with a marked absence of roads and tracks. A number of tracks were planned: both operational tracks capable of taking vehicles and gun movement, and animal tracks for move of mules and ponies. A large number of these, during operations, were constructed under enemy's observation and heavy shelling. A majority of the earth-moving plant in the Sector was deployed on such track construction. Sappers undertook track construction tasks with distinction.

The track construction and improvement undertaken during and after operations brought out quite a few lessons for the Sappers. Some were new, while others reinforced earlier experiences. Multiple attack points, heli-lifting and forward deployment of dozers, larger requirement of rock drills along with higher requirement of explosive in rocky terrain, requirement of a safe working zone, necessity of constructing animal transport tracks along gradients suitable for subsequent upgradation to Class 5 or 9 operational tracks were some of the salient points brought out.

Helipad Construction. In the post-ceasefire phase, another important requirement was the need to have a helipad at each post to allow casualty evacuation and forward winter maintenance. However, terrain constraints, mainly steep slopes and sharp ridges, prevented such construction at forward posts. Instead, helipads were provided at or near each company and battalion headquarter. Some isolated posts, where the terrain permitted, were also provided helipads. In order to cater for snow in winters, fibre reinforced panel helipads were also catered for. Many helipads or mounting bases were constructed to cater for Mi-17 and Cheetah helicopters. Today, they also handle Dhruv sorties. Problems faced mainly related to surfacing requirements in snow, dust proofing of surface. Where Mi-26 helicopters had to operate, only Pierced Steel Plate surface was suitable, though much greater anchorage needed to be affixed to the helipad surface.

Habitat. Catering for an entire division habitat in the short period of 4 months before winters set in was an onerous task. However, keeping various factors in mind, availability of operational works funds, the time available for procurement and construction, and the engineer troops available, only 50% of the requirement was targeted for the year. The urgency of the requirement was palpable for a division need to be billeted before the winters. Over 50 vendors were contacted for supply of stores. Increase of the supply base ensured rapid procurement, especially of Fibre Reinforced Panel module shelters with inbuilt polyurethane foam insulation for the higher altitude posts. Many such shelters (or equivalent) of various types were constructed in a short period of 3 months through ingenuity, tenacity and dedication by the Sappers deployed at the various posts. A simultaneous requirement was the construction of steel permanent defences, other fibre-based shelters, tubular shelters for animal transport, hangars, field surgical centres, advanced dressing station, operations room, etc. The work was mammoth for stores had to be carted or heli-lifted to the higher reaches, and construction involved levelling of work sites in rocky terrain. Actual construction took place in just over 3 months before the winters set in, with the first month having been utilised for initial procurement and move of stores. The achievement of the Sappers at Kargil is stupendous and can be gauged from the fact that equivalent construction undertaken on an emergent basis elsewhere in the Valley earlier had taken approximately 3 years, employing approximately an equivalent number of troops. The only difference was that some of the shelters in the Valley were of a different design, though not affecting the construction time materially.

Engineer Casualties and Awards

All wars have casualties, and Kargil was no exception. The Sappers had their share of casualties, despite the best efforts of the commanding officers to avoid them. The war also showed Sappers exhibiting acts of gallantry and devotion to duty which were duly recognised and rewarded. However, it must be kept in mind that for every act rewarded, there are many others which go unnoticed in the fog of the battlefield, and selfless acts sometimes remain unrewarded. Nevertheless, the very nature of battle brings forth its visible heroes and the Sappers were no exception. Engineer units too, performed exceptionally in the battlefield, as well as after hostilities ended; ensuring all tasks were completed within the laid down timelines. Their performance too was recognised through the award of battle and theatre honours and unit citations at various levels.

Challenges Faced by Sappers during Operations

The Sappers very rarely have an ideal, or near ideal situation for provision of combat engineer support during operations. In fact, more often than not, the Sappers are faced with daunting odds and difficult circumstances whether in battle, or in field conditions. Kargil was no different, and everything seemed lined up against the Sappers. And as usual, the odds were faced fearlessly and with elan. No unit or individual was found wanting. Shortage of manpower, equipment, stores and other resources never stopped, or deterred either the unit, sub-unit, detachment or individual from achieving and completing their tasks in time. Shortages and deficiencies were made up through improvisation, problems addressed through ingenuity and resourcefulness and typical Sapper "Jugaad". When all else didn't seem to work, a smile on the dusty, tired and exhausted face of the willing and able Sapper ensured that the task still got done! No wonder most Sapper units of the Indian Army proudly and prominently display the following, or equivalent words, in their units – *"the difficult, we have done, the impossible is being done, for miracles, we need just a little more time"*.

The Sappers at Kargil faced a number of challenges. Some of the one's worth mentioning are covered in subsequent paragraphs.

Command and Control. Under normal circumstances, the Commanding Officer of the Division Engineer Regiment is responsible for advising the formation commander and coordinating the employment of the integral engineer regiment. He is also capable of taking on the responsibility of some additional engineer resources placed under command, or in support. However, such additional engineer resources would normally not exceed three to four engineer field companies or say a regiment plus. However, with additional Engineer regiments being provided to 8 Mountain Division, the task of management of engineer resources was beyond the capability of the Commanding Officer of the integral Engineer regiment. This strength of engineers in the Division was the equivalent of approximately two engineer brigades and had its own peculiar problems. As such, a number of aspects such as planning, coordination, move of stores and tasking were centrally controlled by the Engineers Branch at Headquarters 15 Corps. However, possibly, in such cases where operations are limited to a particular area, it may be worthwhile to consider induction of an Engineer brigade headquarter for the purpose.

Communications. The communications to the forward areas from the Corps Headquarters was tenuous and inadequate. The dedicated engineer radio net could also not be established due to the distances involved. A definite need exists to improve this aspect through provision of reliable line communication supplemented by holding of adequate, secure high-frequency radio sets with regiments. In addition, a larger reserve of satellite communication equipment needs to be maintained centrally at Corps level for issue in such contingencies.

Engineer Intelligence. There was inadequate information and intelligence about engineer intelligence requirements such as topography, obstacles and communications on both sides of the Line of Control. A more pragmatic approach towards gathering, collating, storing and disseminating engineer intelligence as actionable updates is necessary, as is the need to move from the theory of "Geographical Information Systems", and lip service accorded to it, to its actual ground implementation and usage towards practical and existing requirements.

Equipment Issued by Depots. Equipment which was issued by depots from old stocks was found to be not up to the standards. One of the main reasons was their vintage and long storage time at depots. A definite need exists to ensure a closer watch on inventories at depots, their regular turnover, and in-depot maintenance and replenishment systems based on usage pattern. A standardised smooth and workable system for emergent procurement during selected contingencies must be laid down and diligently observed without getting mired in red-tapism.

Inadequacy of Engineer Equipment and Resources. Major deficiencies existed in first line authorisation such as vehicles, rock drills, water supply pumps, compressors and generators. Where held, these were of old vintage and incapable of performing at high altitudes. Pumping sets could not provide water at such altitudes and a large number of them did not have accessories and parts due to non-availability with depots, or obsolescence of equipment. A revamp of systems is necessary to ensure a "push" system for making up deficiencies of equipment and accessories in units. Further authorised equipment held needs to be reassessed, and effective modern systems procured/authorised. At the same time, there is a need to ensure its ruggedness to be handled under trying field conditions. Adequate reserve stock is also required to be held at depots.

Troops to Task. Most brigades had been built up to six to eight infantry battalions. However, the corresponding increase of Sappers for close support tasks was not done, which led to non-availability of Sappers for many requirements. A brick system for incremental increase in engineers from the formation of the inducting infantry battalions during such operations could be explored. In such cases, additional infantry battalions could ab initio move with the specified engineer strength itself. Alternately, additional engineers should be earmarked from specified formations to move during such contingencies, akin somewhat to the present concept of dual tasked formations.

Training. The large deployment on operational works prior to operations found Sappers ill-equipped initially to convert from an operational works mind-set to a battlefield environment. Though adjustment was fast, certain aspects of training which had been compromised because of prolonged deployment in a counter-insurgency or operational works environment were badly affected. Troops were found ill-equipped to handle enemy mines and enemy mine-laying tactics. A number of engineer units could not train adequately on Sapper tasks due to heavy involvement in other tasks and curtailment/cancellation of the annual training camps. A relook towards practical, though formalised engineer training in units is necessary. It can take into account the employment of the unit but should lay down certain inviolable training guidelines to be observed by the formation commanders. Lip service towards training needs to be stringently avoided. Also, there is a need to avoid the concept of "on the job training" which is used conveniently by many commanders, including senior engineer officers to do away with formalised engineer training methodology.

Vulnerability of Roads and Bridges. Roads in mountains pass through difficult terrain, and any location can become a choke point, if interdicted. Bridges and culverts especially are very susceptible to enemy action, as well as weakening over time due to passage of heavily loaded vehicles and convoys. Further, the alignment of these roads in the Kargil Sector, vis-à-vis the Line of Control makes roads and bridges susceptible to enemy action. Nature and lay of terrain also preclude the creation of diversions or a bypass. A shortage of bridging equipment due to peace time deployment of reserve equipment could also hamper restoration operations at places affected by natural occurrences, or interdiction by enemy. A possible answer lies in procuring adequate stock, and pre-dumping bridging equipment at specified points along roads which will ensure early availability of reserves during contingencies. Over time, widening of areas at selected choke points could also be explored, or where feasible abutments were created at alternate sites for future construction of equipment bridges and culverts. The Zoji La Axis was found to be very vulnerable to interdiction, which would have created a major crisis, had it taken place. A similar vulnerability had existed earlier too, during partition, and subsequently in the 1965 and 1971 operations; however, over time, and a prolonged period of relative, though not complete inactivity, earlier lessons had been overlooked or forgotten.

Operational Work Stores. In the absence of, or delay in adequately revising the War Establishment stores, or the existing dichotomy of standard and mountain modification of engineer regiments vis-à-vis their areas of deployment, a greater reliance must be made on procuring warlike stores through operational work funds. These could include, but not be restricted to snow vehicles, all terrain vehicles with lesser width, lightweight bridges of varying length, pre-fabricated mobile shelters and ancillaries, motorised aerial cableway sets, lightweight mine laying and marking stores, etc. However, a certain degree of standardisation in such procurement, along with suitable trials is a must, lest quality and application suffer.

Availability of Pioneers and Labour. Disbandment of pioneer companies affected their immediate availability and application in the combat zone, or in store dumps. Similarly, such situations warrant immediate hiring of labour, which however, gets caught in myriad red tape with respect to availability of funds and sanction by the competent financial authorities. Suitable mechanism needs to be put in place to address these requirements.

Inadequate Knowledge of Engineer Operations. Other arms and services were not fully aware of the capabilities and limitations of the engineers and could not fully appreciate or gauge the associated problems. Planning parameters and the need to adapt them to actual existential realities was lost sight of, by commanders who demanded much more than was practically possible. Further, a frequent change in planning parameters also resulted in delays and avoidable confusion. Commanders need to familiarise themselves with the intricacies of engineer operations as concerning the command level, especially with regard to employment, and constraints which exist from situation to situation affecting engineer output

The Years that Followed Kargil

The conduct of Operation Vijay and the manner in which combat engineer support was provided to the troops deployed for operations and those being inducted along the lines of communication brought out a lot of valuable and essential lessons. Various studies were subsequently carried out, both by the Indian Army and the Corps of Engineers, to analyse and review the engineer support rendered during operations. The aspects studied included, but were not limited to command and control, engineer intelligence and the exploitation of geographical information systems, mobilisation procedures, deployment aspects, battle drills, construction drills and methodology, equipment modernisation and holdings, inventory management, review of authorisation, procure and build-up suitable and adequate reserves of engineer equipment within theatres to ensure a ready availability during contingencies. A number of issues relevant to the Army in general with respect to improvement of staging and induction facilities, forward dumping of equipment and stores, etc., have also been addressed. A large number of these have already been affected on ground, with visible improvements in all aspects being noticed. Today's Sappers are definitely better poised for the future.

However, though a lot has been achieved in the years that followed Kargil, it is essential that the lessons learnt are not lost sight of, or forgotten, as time passes. History tends to have a long memory, and an unforgiving nature. The progress and gains made in the last 20 years need to be carried forward further. It is also true that certain aspects related to engineer unit *tartib* and training is at times being lost sight of, and equipment not measuring up to requirements. Though the present priorities, responsibilities and workload could be blamed, as the causal factors, nevertheless, it is unacceptable for the organisation. Compromises cannot be acceptable and should never be permitted, with digression reflecting directly upon the commanders in chain as a failure to exercise their command and authority.

However, the silver lining is that the Engineers are better equipped and trained today to meet the challenges which may arise in years to come. The strides and advances towards improvement have borne fruit and need to be carried forward methodically through a planned effort, in order to provide a desired end point.

Conclusion

Operation Vijay demonstrated the capability of the Engineers to perform under adverse and trying conditions with a mix of modern and outdated equipment, shortages and inadequate training in certain aspects of engineer support. Lest this be accepted by the environment as a benchmark, that the Sappers will always deliver despite lack of training and shortages in holding of equipment and stores, there is a need to suitably sensitise the environment with regard to the minimum requirements of the Engineers during battle. We have come a long way since Kargil; much has improved in all spheres, especially equipment and stores. However, the commitments of the Sappers both during peace and field continue to impinge and affect formalised training. Further, the concept of "on the job training" appears to have again been accepted by the environment as a natural and intrinsic part of the Sapper's working environment. Lest it again become an existential reality and affect the Sapper's efficiency, the Indian Army needs to be clear on what constitutes acceptable training for war. In the meantime, as the Sapper's have always maintained, despite the odds, "All will be done; though miracles will take just a little time".

Communications:
The Battle Winning Factor

Colonel Narjit Singh

"Sartaj over"

"Sartaj over"

(A crisp message was received on the radio at the Brigade HQ)

"Say Again over"

"I say again, Sartaj over"

The signal operator in the Brigade HQ rushed to check the list of revised code words.

"OH MY GOD!!, Sartaj stood for Tiger Hill, Tiger Hill has been captured", exclaimed the operator.

There was jubilation on receiving the radio message conveying the capture of Tiger Hill by 18 GRANADIERS.

SIGNALS were fully baptised into the Battle.

From an intense counter-insurgency environment in the Kashmir Valley, 8 Mountain Division Signal Regiment on 29 May 1999 moved with a sense of urgency and commitment to create and provide the necessary communication support to the combat units that would be operating on the icy heights of Kargil. There was both a sense of anxiety and enthusiasm amongst all ranks. The Regiment under the command of Colonel S Bhatnagar was made responsible for all communication requirements for operations in the Dras Sector, with the Divisional Headquarters at Matayan. However, just as soon the Matayan communication complex became unusable due to accurate and heavy enemy shelling and was relocated Mughalpura. Secure communication to all Brigades was engineered on Radio Relay and as backup also on line and Radio. Braving enemy shelling, Lance Naik KE Chaitram, Singalman MR Sahoo and Signalman Vinod Kumar were the first of the many who were martyred while establishing communication in the Dras sector due to artillery shelling.

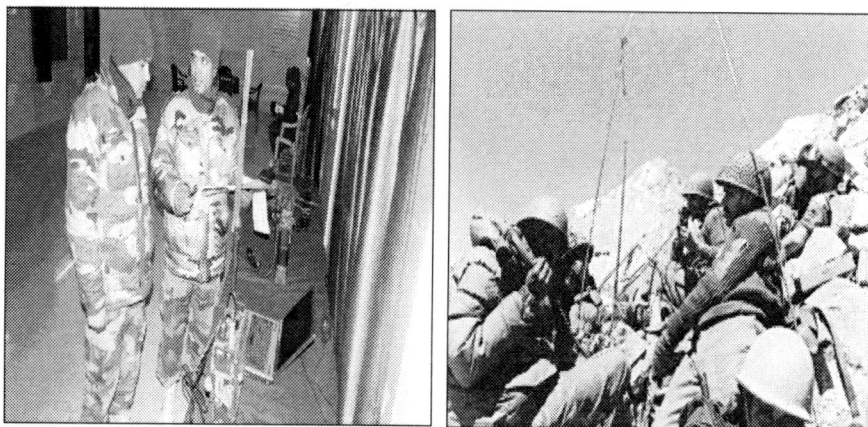

Establishing Communications at Mughalpura

192 Mountain Brigade and 56 Mountain Brigade were also inducted into Dras to establish additional communications required between Mughalpura and Dras as the number of units inducted in the area of responsibility (AoR) of 8 Mountain Division doubled with the induction of the PARA Brigade and 192 Mountain Brigade. Infantry battalions and the artillery regiments were under command HQ 8 Mountain Division by mid-June. The already stretched resources of the Regiment were stretched far beyond the designed capability; the resources with brigade signal companies were also augmented in terms of officers, men and equipment from the Regiment to cater for additional requirement for offensive operations. Secure-line communications were ensured till the forward-most base of the battalions undertaking operations as radio communications were prone to interference and jamming.

To overcome the limitations of terrestrial communication systems, satellite-based communication systems were introduced during Op VIJAY. The challenge of training, establishment and handling of these systems was overcome, and reliable communications established for both operational use and used extensively for welfare of the troops by the provision of STD facility.

Correct appreciation of the fast-changing tactical situation by the Commanding Officer, dynamic junior leadership and unflinching devotion to duty of troops provided secure and reliable forward communications from the Divisions HQs to the formations under command.

Line Communication to other units

One of the many challenges that came to the unit was provision of communication to the PARA Brigade. The PARA Brigade was deployed in the Mushkoh Valley after induction into Op VIJAY and put under command of 8 Mtn Division. Due to technical and terrain difficulties a direct link from forward posts to the brigade could not be established. To provide secure reliable communications, it was planned to lay a new communication cable from Mountain Brigade HQ to PARA HQ. It was decided to lay cable WD instead of cable CQ as time was at premium and the load of CQ drums being unwieldy for carriage on mules would have delayed provision of line columns to the formation. Further, all movements beyond the loading point at the road end were permitted only after last light. On 27 June 99 at 6 pm, the line party commenced line laying on manpack. All along the route, it was pitch dark; intense firing of enemy artillery shells and automatic weapons could be heard. The line party knew of the existing danger in the Mushkoh Valley but carried on with the task with determination and courage, unmindful of their personal safety.

Even while laying, the line snapped a number of times due to enemy artillery shelling. The speech strength on the laid line was not very good, because the cable distance was large. Therefore, the line party was once again entrusted with the task of laying a second pair by combining the two lines and thereby reducing the line loss and improving the speech strength.

The maintenance of the lines was also a difficult and a challenging task. Line men were placed at Bakharwal, Munthung and Batugul and worked under enemy shelling to ensure uninterrupted communication.

Local Radio Extension at Tiger Hill

Tiger Hill by virtue of its name and tactical significance had become the focus of entire nation. The pressure to capture Tiger Hill was being felt by 8 Mountain Division. Tiger Hill Top was at an approximate height of 5100 m and approx 8-9 km from NH-1A, and Dras Valley dominated them by observations. The two battalions tasked to capture Tiger Hill were 18 GRENADIERS and 8 SIKH and commenced their attack on the night of 02/03 July 1999.

The Tiger Hill Top is itself very steep and the approaches were well fortified and covered by the enemy. Lines needed to be laid to the base of the Battalions but intense shelling in the area kept damaging the cables. Lt Udayan Acharjya, a young and enthusiastic officer of the Regt, was entrusted with the responsibility to establish two-way secure radios at the base. Sub M Sebastian, a tough and motivated JCO, meanwhile was to establish the same at 18 GRENADIERS.

The two-way radio dets team started climbing at about 12 noon on 03 July. The base station of Radio System was placed at Dras for direct communications with the battalions during the attack.

At night shelling intensified along with a slight drizzle but the Radio Local Extn team reached the base of 8 SIKH and had established the vital necessary communications with Dras. These communication dets continued to provide crucial communication to both the battalions for next 6 days of operations amidst heavy shelling in the area.

Communication for Capture of Tololing Ridge

8 Mountain Division took over the responsibility of Dras sub-sector on 01 June 99. It was decided to clear Tololing Ridge first. On 07 June 99, the Unit moved to establish an officer-manned VHF Radio Anchor Station to overcome the screening of radio communications faced by the assault companies of 18 GARH RIF.

Next day evening, Capt SJS Sandhar along with two operators and two combat porters started the climb. The party took 8 hours to reach their destination as it was directly visible to the enemy and on several occasions, they invited automatic fire and fire by rocket-propelled grenades that injured one of the porters.

Soon after, they established the Anchor Station and were through to the Brigade as well as the forward elements of the battalion. Although line communications were also engineered for the battalion, these were disrupted frequently due to enemy shelling and the Anchor Station proved vital for passage of operation information to the Brigade HQ. Over the next 6 days, heavy enemy shelling continued in the area, but the communications of radio remained through with the activation of the Anchor Station.

The Anchor Station relayed all messages and was the mainstay of communications during the operations till Tololing Top was captured by own forces.

In the coming days too, the Anchor Radio Station was deployed for a number of operations. The Anchor Station was once again proved to be very effective and instrumental in providing real-time secure and reliable communications for the attack on the Black Tooth and "Pt 4700".

The Signalers drew a great sense of satisfaction and pride in providing effective, secure, timely operational communications much beyond their capability under extremely hostile conditions.

Op Vijay: Logistics Support in Testing Times

Colonel Sushil Chander

"Tiger Hill was the Greatest Victory of the Kargil War"

Gen VP Malik, PVSM, AVSM (then Army Chief)

Long snake lines of local mules, ponies and army mules made daily trips carrying precious loads of ammunition, rations, K-oil and drinking water towards the fighting echelons. These saviours trudged unmindful of dangers of war on narrow foot tracks amidst the noise of battle at night to ensure unbroken supplies. The doctors and personnel of the Remount and Veterinary Corps (RVC) were also geared to treat many sick and wounded animals and braved the war conditions well forward. Their handlers also deserve a special mention to have kept their animals in marching shape throughout the operation, without any breakdowns in hauling tons of loads at various troop locations.

War in mountains is said to be a "logistician's nightmare". Logistics for operations in mountains is a herculean task that demands forethought, detailed planning, inherent flexibility coupled with practicality to cater for all inevitable contingencies, and meticulous execution to support the Field Army and facilitate delivery of a devastating punch to the enemy.

In the summer of 1999, sinister designs of Pakistan lay fully exposed, when the intrusions by troops of Pakistan Northern Light Infantry (NLI) were detected in Ladakh, along the Line of Control (LoC). Ladakh, the Northern Division of the state of Jammu & Kashmir (J&K), is divided into Kargil and Leh Sector. The 434-km long National Highway-1 (NH-1, now NH-1D), running from Srinagar to Ladakh is the region's only link to Kashmir Valley.

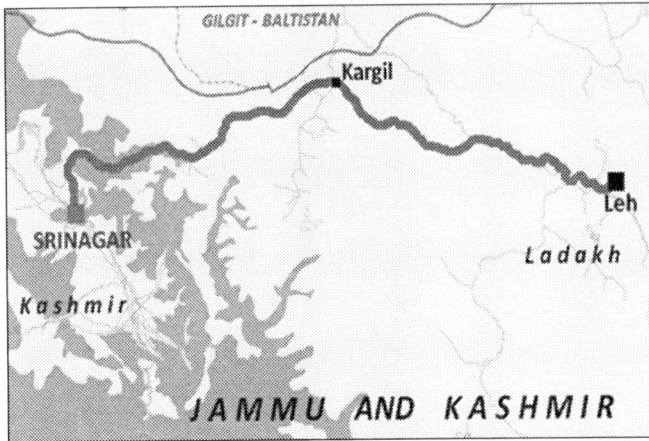

Alignment of the National Highway-1 (NH-1) [1]

This situation made Ladakh vulnerable to isolation, most susceptible near the town of Kargil, as NH-1 passes close to the LoC in the Kargil District. The road passes through Zoji La Pass, a checkpoint at 11,600 ft near the town of Dras. The occupation of main heights along the national highway would have resulted in domination of this lifeline, virtually cutting off Ladakh region from the Kashmir Valley.

Mountainous Terrain: Impact on Logistics

When the offensive operations were planned by the Indian Army, to re-capture the peaks in the most inhospitable conditions, with some features at heights of above 18000 ft above mean seal level (MSL), the offensive field formations were invariably assured of the availability of intimate and effective logistics support. The planned offensives in the Batalic Sub-Sector and Turtok Range threw up numerous logistics challenges. The seasoned Indian military commanders were well aware that the deadly combination of extreme cold weather, rugged mountains and rarefied air has a dramatic adverse impact on both the men and material. The rugged mountains were not only difficult to climb because of rocky face and steep gradient, but also the extra-ordinary heights of peaks, between 15000 and 18000 ft and more, meant that the oxygen was scarce which turned even breathing into a laborious exercise. Reduced oxygen levels in rarefied atmosphere led to numerous physical health issues. While steep slopes hinder movement, the extreme cold conditions act as catalyst to demoralise and incapacitate the soldiers, and have severe adverse impact on the performance of equipment, both in terms of accuracy and range.

Ladakh is an arid region with very less rainfall and little vegetation. The extremely low temperatures and heavy snowfall during previous winters had led to formation of large tracts of glaciated terrain with sub- zero temperatures, amply exhibiting the hostile nature of geographical area in the Kargil Sector. The ridgelines are treeless, vast and barren with loose rocks strewn all over. The snow on the peaks begins to melt rapidly with the onset of summers. Dras, a sub-sector of Kargil, is commonly considered as the second coldest place in the world, after Siberia. The barren land with sub-zero temperatures is called as the 'Cold Desert', in reference to it being highly inhospitable for human beings. The weather and terrain in mountains proved almost as formidable a challenge as the enemy and multiplied the unique and complex logistical problems manifold. The Himalayan conditions and topography demanded an extremely effective logistics support, as prolonged exposure of soldiers to extreme weather conditions could have severely degraded their ability to fight.

Logistics Concept

Forward stocking of ammunition, assemblies and components of weapons and equipment, rations and fuel down to brigade level and in certain cases, even to battalion level played a crucial role in meeting immediate requirements for accretion of forces in the Kargil Sector. Shortfall was made up by moving stocks from other Sectors.

The Movement

The geographical conditions had serious and adverse implications for the conduct of offensive operations and movement of the logistics required for supporting them. The limited availability of roads and tracks made the logistics support, a very challenging task. While the mountainous terrain, rocky, narrow and winding roads severely hampered the vehicular movement, active Pakistani shelling made it a dangerous endeavour.

During the initial movements of men and materials by the Indian Army, the Pakistani troops interfered by firing that caused considerable harassment, which also affected the supply of fuel and rations. The movement of artillery guns, mortars, other weapons/equipment and ammunition was carried out on war footing. Movement of these guns and weapon systems to their areas of deployment was a daunting task. Heavy artillery guns were moved with difficulty over rough and rugged trails to their designated gun positions. The movement of stores (including Engineer stores) and clothing was expanded to a very high magnitude. As the field formations moved swiftly for offensive action, the stocks had to be built up expeditiously to meet exponential rise in demands. However, the task was completed well in time. The experiences of the past wars gave the frontline commanders and men a reassurance of the way the logistics support services had geared up to meet the surge in wartime requirements.

Ammunition Support

The phenomenon of rarefied atmosphere implies that an artillery shell fired at a target located at a range of 1 km hits 70 inches higher than at sea level. The range increases significantly but the accuracy suffers adversely. The artillery shells and mortar bombs fired at enemy bunkers, located at peaks, would tend to land on reverse slopes. The folds of undulating and mountainous ground provided natural hides for the enemy troops from ground and aerial observation. The masking of fire necessitates higher expenditure of ammunition to support attacks in mountains. The estimated ammunition expenditure due to extremely unfavourable, rugged and rocky geographical disposition exceeded far more than that of normal estimates. Expenditure of small arms' ammunition, mortar rounds and artillery shells went up exponentially. Large quantities of ammunition of various types, major share being artillery ammunition, were moved by road transport, mainly consisting of Army's 3rd Line transport and civil hired trucks (CHTs). The Army Service Corps (ASC) personnel worked tirelessly and innovatively to move ammunition and warlike stores from the Ammunition and Ordnance Depots, respectively, to the frontline troops, ensuring replenishment of stocks within strict timelines. A well-coordinated effort under the Ordinance Services (OS) Directorate in close coordination with logistics staff officers at Army Headquarters and various formation headquarters ensured that the unexpected heavy requirements of ammunition for artillery guns, mortars and small arms was met in time.

Mortars were fired at high rates to make up for inaccuracies, and ammunition was expended quickly. Massive artillery barrages preceded assaults by infantry to inflict severe punishment on the enemy. Positions on the forward slopes were destroyed by the direct fire of Artillery guns and heavy supportive fire continued till the final assaults. The Bofors Guns, supported by mortars and other artillery weapon systems, played a crucial role in providing an intimate, accurate, responsive and overwhelming fire support to the attacking troops in various "fiercely fought" battles. The inaccuracies caused by erratic behaviour of projectiles were overcome by concentrated firepower that preceded all ground attacks.

Large quantities of ammunition for infantry troops which included missiles, rockets, grenades, ammunition for medium and light machine guns, sniper rifles, 81 mm and 51 mm Mortars were moved by surface transport to road heads, from where porters and ponies carried them to the forward troops. The ammunition of all types was adequately supplied and never allowed to fall short.

Rations & Fuel

In May 1999, when the operations commenced, the situation in terms of rations and fuels for existing strength of troops was well in control. Besides, the logistics support system was already well established. For the accretion forces, expeditious stocking was carried out. The aviation fuel was also stocked within the initial three days to enable full exploitation of Army Aviation helicopters. While limited quantity of fresh rations was already available, additional requirements were supplied from Jammu.

In the adverse weather conditions, it is absolutely necessary that the troops be provided with high-calorie rations. Meals ready to eat (MRE) came to good use as freshly cooked food was not feasible to be carried to frontline troops operating on the mountains. In addition, composite meals (that cater for up to 20 men) were extensively provided to troops. Besides, special high-altitude rations were also provided. The units carried out their own improvisations for survival rations provided to the troops. Efforts were made to provide hot meals before attack and during lull in the operations, to boost their morale.

As the operations were carried out during summers, the snow on peaks had melted by June 1999 end, and water became a scarce commodity. At places, where snow had not fully melted, it was not found fit for human consumption due to contamination by explosives. Water consumption during steep climb was high, leading to emptying of personal water bottles carried by troops. The units then came up with improvised techniques to ferry water to troops. Air Transportation of water was also resorted to, at times.

Clothing

The large number of troops which were inducted into the Kargil Sector from Kashmir Valley and other lower regions/plains needed to be provided with special clothing and equipment, as it was not readily available with the units. Hence, special clothing was side stepped from Leh and Siachen Glacier and available reserves released to meet the surge in requirement. Even the part-worn serviceable (PWS) stocks of clothing were utilised to meet the emergent requirement.

Role of Porters and Ponies

The foot movement in mountains is calculated in time and not in distance. The uphill climb is limited by foot trails and ridgelines with additional 1 hour allotted for every 300 meters of ascent or 600 meters of descent. Porters and ponies became the primary means of logistics, where vehicles could not pass. The availability of porters and ponies during initial phases of build-up was a problem, as much of the local population had left the area due to persistent Pakistani shelling. The issue was resolved by entrusting the task to The Ladakh Scouts to arrange local porters and ponies. Being from local areas, the porters and ponies proved their worth in providing close logistics support by supplying ammunition and rations on foot trails, in hail of enemy fire, between supply points and the Infantry units.

Mules were extensively used to carry the mortars, medium machine guns and ammunition on the hilly routes, up to trans-shipment points, from where the porters carried the loads on gruelling uphill climb. On an average, the porters could complete barely one trip a day due to severe terrain and altitude restrictions. Porters were also required to carry water.

Air Maintenance

Air Maintenance by Indian Air Force (IAF) was put into effect, in addition to the surface transport efforts, especially for Chorbat-La ridge and other difficult areas. Troops from Chandigarh, Agra and Bareilly, and air defence (AD) equipment were moved by using IAF transport aircrafts. The transport aircrafts, namely. IL-76, AN-32 and Mi-17 lifted required stores to the Sector for dumping at designated areas and specially constructed forward helipads.[2] Even Cheetah helicopters of the Army Aviation Corps lifted troops and materials during emergency situations. At times, even ammunition for forward infantry troops was replenished by the helicopters.

Medical Support

The extremely adverse ground conditions dictated that troops undertake steep uphill climb and frontal assaults, which, in spite of detailed planning and meticulous execution, at times resulted in heavy casualties. Rapid climb to high-altitude areas without due acclimatisation, during initial stages of operation, got many troops afflicted with acute mountain sickness (AMS) leading to symptoms like muscular weakness, fatigue and/or loss of appetite. The sudden increase of altitude also adversely affected the eating and sleeping patterns of troops. The cold weather and freezing conditions inflicted incapacitating injuries on many troops. In spite of best efforts and provision of special clothing post-transfer from other sectors, limited cold weather casualties due to frostbite and chilblains were reported throughout the duration of war.

The casualties, however, did not deter the Indian troops from superhuman heroics that have become a part of the local folklore. In the operation, both India and Pakistan faced many casualties. In many instances, the Pakistan Army refused to accept that the killed Pak troops were indeed from their ranks, i.e. mainly from the Northern Light Infantry (NLI) Regiment. Such absurd reaction from Pakistan Army was irrefutable evidence of cowardice. The indifference, displayed by the Pakistan's hierarchy for their own fallen soldiers, contributed significantly in lowering morale of their troops which, in turn, precipitated their early defeat as the Indian Army units undertook bold and fierce offensive action against Pakistani intruders and eliminated the enemy piece-meal.

For effective medical support, the medical set up of Trishul Division included field ambulances (now designated as field hospitals), Regimental Aid Posts (RAPs) and Advance Dressing Stations (ADS). Later, few more field ambulances were also moved and deployed at Dras. The doctors and paramedical personnel in hospitals, Regimental and Mobile Aid Posts, detachments and Advance Dressing Stations worked tirelessly to provide the most intimate medical support to field units and saved precious lives of the wounded troops.

Barring initial hiccups, air evacuation of casualties in the midst of heavy shelling and enemy small arms fire proved a morale booster for the Indian Armed Forces. The two squadrons of Army Aviation flew more than 2500 missions, logging over 2700 hours of flying from makeshift helipads under extremely hazardous conditions. The daring actions by the Army Aviation Squadrons enabled heli-evacuation of the battle casualties to the Military Hospitals in the Northern theatre, leading to an early medical attention.

Air Evacuation of Injured Troops, in the face of enemy fire,
was a daunting task.

The efforts to provide medical support stood out and many battle casualties rejoined their units in the conflict zone, post recovery.

Contribution of Individual Service

Army Service Corps (ASC)

The ASC Battalions of the two divisions and other ASC sub-units were inducted for the duration of operation. These units and their detachments supplied rations and fuel under strenuous conditions and heavy enemy fire, especially in the Dras sub-sector. The newly inducted animal transport (AT) unit, distinguished itself by giving a heroic account of transportation by mules under very tough conditions, that made a strong case for retention of AT units, some of which were otherwise disbanded or placed under suspended animation.

ASC mules carrying arms and ammunition to the front

Long treks from road heads to forward troops, carrying ammunition boxes and rations over rugged and slippery slopes, tested the commitment of mule drivers and animals, alike. The ammunition carried by ASC mules and local ponies enabled sufficient availability with troops and at gun areas to provide close fire support to the assaulting troops. The air maintenance battalions at Chandigarh also played a significant role in ensuring effective air maintenance of fighting formations.

Army Ordnance Corps (AOC)

The Ammunition and Ordnance units of AOC played a crucial role in provision of ammunition, clothing and spares; notwithstanding exponential rise in demands due to accretion of forces, during the entire duration of war. Regional Ammunition Depots (RADs) in the Northern Theatre played pivotal role in ensuring that the ammunition is speedily pushed forward to the Ammunition Points (APs) and gun areas. The special trains carrying ammunition form Central Ammunition Depot and certain RADs based in other theatres that were dormant, were unloaded at designated intermediate locations, from where CHTs carried the ammunition direct to forward areas.

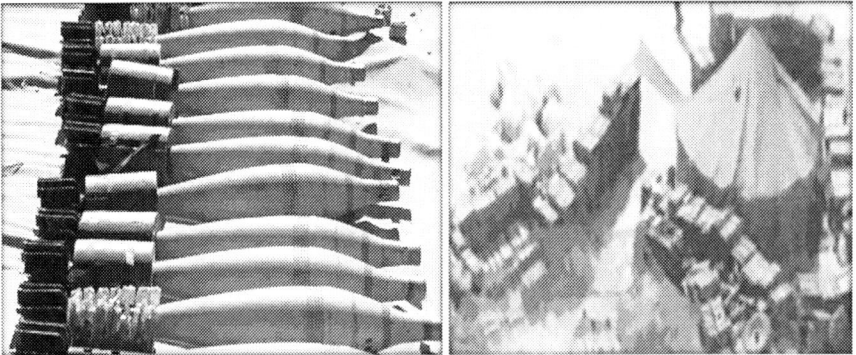

AOC ensured that the ammunition was always available

The Guns, mortars and rocket launchers carried out concentrated fire to cause a devastating effect on enemy, as the ammunition was always made available. The Ordnance Maintenance Parks (OMP) and Divisional Ordnance Units (DOUs) also played their roles with dedication; as personal clothing, equipment and spares for weapons/equipment were provided timely and complete Ordnance logistics support ensured. The Regional Ordnance Depots (RODs) worked tirelessly to provide a wide range and depth of components, assemblies, clothing, arms and equipment for field formations during the entire duration of operations. The Field Ordnance Depots (FODs) received large quantum of stores that included newly introduced weapons, namely, flame throwers, automatic grenade launchers (AGL), radio sets, INSAS rifles, night vision devices (NVDs) and binoculars; and vigorously pushed these forward to the field units. The depot also got two old 75/24 Pounder Guns overhauled and dispatched to operational area for employment in the direct firing role. All the AOC units, thus, gave a great account of themselves during Operation Vijay.

Electronics and Mechanical Engineers (EME)

The EME Battalions and other repair echelons contributed very well by ensuring that the helicopters, guns and vehicles remained in serviceable state in spite of continuous and extensive employment during the operations. While the AOC readily provided necessary engines, major assemblies and components, the EME personnel swiftly moved to repair the vehicles and equipment, a fine example of synergy between the two services. Repair and recover detachments gave an excellent account of themselves. In situ repairs were carried out and equipment/vehicle downtime was kept to the minimum. The EME workshops and detachments recovered over 650 vehicles, replaced 200 engine assemblies and carried out numerous repairs. Modifications, where required, were carried out to ensure that maximum weapons and equipment remain functional and optimal efficiency maintained.

EME personnel in action in the forward area

To the credit of EME personnel, their extensive repairs including improvisation and cannibalisation kept the Bofors guns functional and firing during the entire duration of operation.

Army Medical Corps (AMC)

AMC gave a noteworthy account of its services to the nation. Establishment of Forward Surgical Centres (FSC), Advance Dressing

Stations (ADS), Medical Aid Posts (MAPs) and Regimental Aid Posts (RAPs) was carried out in the forward areas, to provide immediate treatment to the wounded troops. The Army doctors, nurses and paramedical personnel worked round the clock with scarce regard for their own personal safety. Some of the medical teams performed over a dozen operations every day. One of the ADS in Batalik sub-sector was entirely officered by three women-officers. Therefore, a clear message was given to the countrymen that, the Indian Army takes good care of its gallant troops.

Emergency medical aid in the forward area

The prompt medical aid and speedy evacuation to hospitals acted as a massive booster for the morale of brave Indian troops.

Remount and Veterinary Corps (RVC)

Employment of 2000 mules, including 300 local ponies, was carried out during the operation. Movement of mules at night resulted in heavy strain on the mule drivers and animals. However, effective care by the RVC personnel ensured that not a single mule was lost due to illness, a commendable feat indeed.

Corps of Military Police (CMP)

The CMP controlled the move of civilian and military traffic and also facilitated planned recovery of vehicles.

Army Postal Service (APS)

A great amount of surge was noticed in the quantum of letters received for forward troops. This additional workload was handled very efficiently by the APS personnel. Many postal detachments were also established in the forward areas.

Support of Local Population and Civilian Administration

A very interesting and encouraging aspect, which came to light, was the overwhelming support offered by the local population of the Kargil Town and adjoining areas. The local men offered to carry rations, ammunition and essential stores for the Army units, free of charge, in those circumstances and conditions where grave threat existed to their life and limb. These volunteers who were from the local population worked tirelessly to support the attacking troops, immensely boosting their *josh*. It is estimated that on an average, at least one male member of every house in Ladakh served as a porter. Besides, the local civil administration gave complete support to the Defence Forces. The civil-military relationship was indeed at its best.

Takeaways

The logistics support provided to the field units and front-line troops during the entire duration of Operation Vijay was commendable and speaks volumes about the inherent flexibility, coordination and immense effectiveness of the existing system. The operation, however, also attracted significant attention to certain deficiencies and inadequacies as discussed under:

- The dependence on import was an aspect that exposed chinks in the Indian armour. The Indian Army was required to import ammunition for certain weapons from friendly foreign countries. Even the coffins for transportation of mortal remains of martyred soldiers had to be imported.

- Some of the Ambulance and Stretcher Bearer Companies (of AMC) and Animal Transport units (ATUs, of ASC) had been disbanded or placed in suspended animation earlier. Evacuation of causalities posed a challenge due to shortage of stretcher bearers. This put additional workload on the fighting troops and depleted their strength.

- Dedicated air evacuation resources were limited. As the operations progressed, Army Aviation helicopters were pressed for casualty evacuation from forward areas to Logistics Support Area (LSA) from where the Air Force Mi-17 helicopters lifted causalities to the military hospitals. The evacuation was generally during daylight.

- The availability of vehicles in units was less than the authorisation. Besides, in addition to the deficiency, the serviceability of vehicles was not satisfactory. The shortages were, however, made up by employing the civil hired transport (CHTs).

- One of the divisions, prior to induction into operational area, was employed for counter insurgency operations in the Kashmir Valley. The emphasis was, therefore, on serviceability and usage of small arms and ammunition. Over a period of time, certain deficiencies had crept in, which affected the availability of weapons, equipments and radio sets. These deficiencies were however, made up expeditiously for the operations.

- The ammunition dumping was carried out at high speed with vehicles carrying ammunition directly to Gun Areas and Ammunition Points (APs). This led to overstocking at certain Gun Areas and Ammunition points, and also created accounting problems.

- Transportation of large quantities of artillery and infantry weapons' ammunition was carried out to meet the sudden surge in requirements. Such large-scale movements of ammunition could have been avoided by accurate forecast, planning and placement. Adequate and well-dispersed stocks of necessary range of munitions and vital components/assemblies must always be maintained to successfully cater to unforeseen spurt in requirements during operations/war.

- Water scarcity became visible by the month of June 1999; the restriction on water consumption was imposed, limiting it to 1 litre per day due to problems faced in transportation of water by tankers.

- Availability of local ponies on commencement of operations was a problem. The problem was resolved to an extent by arranging local porters and ponies. The remaining deficiency was made up by the induction of AT Battalion of ASC. However, the carrying capacity of mules had got reduced significantly due to high altitude and extreme cold conditions.

- INSAS rifles, new radio sets and binoculars were issued to units just before the operations, for which repair and maintenance expertise was not available. However, for repair and maintenance of INSAS rifles, additional trained personnel from factories were attached to the field units.

- Other issues included holding of old, vintage weapons and equipment by the Army units. These issues were adequately highlighted by the Kargil Review Committee (KRC) in its report and remedial measures suggested.

Op Vijay enabled the Indian Army to analyse the problems encountered during the operation, take remedial measures and be ready with progressive improvement in both operational and logistics preparedness. A very positive outcome, which resulted from the in-depth study and deliberate analysis of the logistics preparedness for Operation Vijay, was the Government's decision to open the doors for 100% participation of domestic private industry in the Defence Sector in May 2001.[3] The initiative also included limited (26%) participation in Defence Sector by the foreign vendors through the Foreign Direct Investment (FDI) route. Participation of both the private industry and the FDI by foreign vendors was subject to grant of industrial license by the Ministry of Commerce & Industry. This historic step led to a series of policy changes and developments and consequently a great leap has been taken by the country towards indigenisation and self-reliance in the Defence Sector.

Conclusion

Operation Vijay was, in fact, more than a rousing victory for India. The decisive victories by the Indian Armed Forces, duly assisted by the most intimate and effective logistics support provided wholeheartedly by all the services, ensured that Pakistan lost its credibility and face, both nationally and internationally. The image of the Indian Army, including all Arms and Services, was greatly enhanced as the sanctity of the LoC was restored to the pre-intrusion state. It is to the credit of all services and the logistics staff at the Army Headquarters and various Formation Headquarters that in spite of existent constraints, all necessary requirements of ammunitions, clothing, rations and fuel were met in time. The services were well geared up and never let the frontline troops look back, over their shoulders for ammunition or weapons to fight the adversary. In the extremely inhospitable terrain, that has no parallel in the history, all units of AOC, ASC, AMC, RVC, EME and other services exhibited marvellous synergy to support the operation most effectively and met the aspirations of the field units to a large extent. The timely and assured logistics support to the frontline forces proved the age old saying, *"Logistics is the Unseen Hand that Shapes the Army's Punch"*.

NOTES

1. Image: Courtesy Google Maps
2. Colonel Gurmeet Kanwal, "Logistics Support", in *Heroes of Kargil*, Army Headquarters, New Delhi, pp. 147-148.
3. Department of Defence Production (DDP)/MoD, Industrial Licensing Policy in Defence Sector, available at http://www.makeinindiadefence.gov.in/IndustrialLicensingpolicyinde- fence.pdf; accessed on 06 May 2019.

The Indian Navy:
The Silent Response

Raghunandan M C and Shreya Das Barman

Although the Operations by Indian Army and Indian Air Force are known to the general public, much has not been discussed about the role of Indian Navy. From the first briefing of the Kargil situation to the Chief of Naval Staff (CNS) in early May, the naval responses were systematic, graduated, and in consonance with the progress of land operations. Although the increased presence of the battleships was not to escalate the conflict, the Navy ensured that it was ready to mobilise in case the conflict escalates to a full-scale war.[1]

Blocking the sea: Operation TALWAR

It was a known fact that major trade flows for Pakistan, especially oil, took place from the Karachi Port. This made it crucial for Pakistan to secure its sea-lanes on communications, to maintain flow of oil from the Gulf region.

Under "Operation TALWAR", over thirty Indian Naval ships were parked outside the Karachi port, just 13 nautical miles from the harbour, in the contiguous waters. This gradual increase of the Indian Naval fleet, along the western coast, was seen as a viable deterrence against Pakistan.

(Indian Navy celebrates its silent Kargil victory, published in DNA)

Under "Operation TALWAR" by the Indian Navy (IN), the Western Naval Command was immediately ordered to enhance the surveillance of the Gujarat and Saurashtra coast. IN satellites, reconnaissance planes, and other modes of gathering intelligence were enabled with immediate effect to monitor the moves of the Pakistani Navy (PN). To further enhance the missiles and gun densities of the naval ships, the Eastern fleet was moved to the western coast. Move of the flotilla was detected by the media and published in Gulf papers, which also sent the desired signals to Pakistan. It was reported in *The Saudi Gazette* that the IN was prepared for, if necessary, a naval blockade against Pakistan, to force withdrawal from Kargil.

Jointness in Operation

Tri-service cooperation had many facets during the Kargil operations, and the Navy was able to chip in where needed. The Navy's squadron of specially equipped electronic warfare aircraft operated extensively along the Line of Control in support of land operations. Specialist hydrographic survey teams of the Navy were also conjoined with the Army's artillery batteries to pinpoint gun locations.

(Admiral Sushil Kumar, Chief of Naval Staff during Operation Talwar)

From 28 May, the Indian Coast Guard also came under command of the Navy, which led to greater sea and aerial surveillance. The Naval fleets carried out aggressive patrolling in the Arabian Sea to send a strong message to Pakistan. Such strong measures had the Pakistan Navy on their defensive best, resulting in them directing their own '(un)battle-worthiness' to keep well clear off the Indian Navy and not to go in the near vicinity of the Indian ships. It lay in wait in the North Arabian Sea posing a strategic deterrent to Pakistan.[2] Incidentally, INS VIRAT, which was the only aircraft carrier in 1999, was under refit. Yet, undeterred by any such handicap, the Navy undertook trials of using the deck of a container ship for take-offs and landings for their Sea Harrier aircraft.[3]

Ready to impose a naval blockade

The Navy's maritime aircraft went on reconnaissance missions over international waters, its versatile Sea Harriers took to air, and its destroyers fired surface-to-air missiles with a 120-km range, whilst the submarines travelled deep in the sea.

(The Kargil War by Ashok Krishna)

As of mid-June, ground operations were gradually progressing. Therefore, as per a scaled response, the Navy, on 12 June, ordered arming of Torpedoes and commenced escorting of oil tankers, which had a tremendous psychological impact on the Pakistani fleet. In due course, this also had their DGMO enquire as to why the Indian Navy had deployed their marine might against Pakistan.

Pakistani Navy flew its maritime aircraft, and after the realisation of the scale of Indian Naval deployment, it went into a defensive mode, warning its vessels to steer clear of the IN. They actually began escorting their tankers that were heading towards Karachi. In a state of evidently visible panic, the Pakistani forces also terminated their ongoing courses at their Air Force Academy and War College, and recalled retired personnel on duty.[4]

Ready to meet a nuclear threat: CNS

During the course of the Kargil conflict, Pakistan had tried to blackmail India with the nuclear threat. To this, the Chief of Naval Staff, Admiral Sushil Kumar, responded that IN was prepared to meet any threat including a nuclear one. The reference was to nuclear, biological and chemical defensive measures.

(Maj Gen Ashok K Mehta, The Silent Sentinel, 5 August, 1999)

Thus, by executing a well-conceived and deliberate plan, by mid-July, the Indian Navy had seized the initiative at sea. Therefore, Kargil conflict saw the integration of Tri-services where IN was a effective strategic deterrent to Pakistan. Apart from a deterrent, the former Prime Minister Nawaz Sharief later disclosed that Pakistan was left with just 6 days of fuel to sustain itself if a full-fledged war broke out[5]. "Operation TALWAR" was the first instance of the Navy supporting land operations in a predominantly territorial war. This highlighted the effectiveness of Naval deterance in such conflicts.

Kargil conflict was a timely reminder that the troublesome neighbour could never be taken for granted. For the Indian Army, it was a period of trial, but despite the irreplaceable human losses, it turned out to be a glorious chapter in its history. The Navy acquitted itself with honour during the operations. It was swift in its reaction; prompt in formulating plans and displayed great clarity on the nature and conduct of operations. The IN lived up to its name of being the silent service.

NOTES

1.   Lt Gen YM Bammi Kargil 1999: Conquering The Impregnable (Noida: Gorkha Publishers, 2003.)

2. Ashok K Mehta, The Silent Sentinel, August 5, 1999, available at https://www.rediff.com/news/1999/aug/05ashok.htm

3. Lt Gen YM Bammi Kargil 1999: Conquering The Impregnable (Noida: Gorkha Publishers, 2003.)

4. Ibid.

5. Vice Admiral GM Hiranandani (Retd.), "Chapter 9: Operation Talwar during the Kargil War in 1999." In Transitions to Guardianship: The Indian Navy 1991-2000. Ministry of Defense (Navy), Naval Headquarters, New Delhi (2009).

BOFORS IN ACTION

OPERATIONS AND LOGISTICS

REJUVENATING FOR THE ACTION

SIGNALS

THE COMBAT TEAM

PART III
PERCEPTIONS AND OPINIONS

Military Strategy in Kargil War

General VP Malik

Introduction

Kargil war, forced on India 20 years ago, will always be remembered for (a) its strategic and tactical surprise; (b) the self-imposed national strategy of restraint, thus keeping the war limited to the Kargil-Siachen sector; (c) military strategy and planning in keeping with the political mandate; and for the (d) dedication, determination, and daring junior leadership at the tactical level. In a fiercely fought combat action, on the most difficult terrain that gave immense advantage to the enemy holding the mountain tops, we were able to evict Pakistani troops from most of their surreptitiously occupied positions. Pakistani leadership was forced to sue for the ceasefire and seek withdrawal of its troops from the remaining areas. A blend of determined political, military and diplomatic actions enabled us to transform an adverse situation into a military and diplomatic victory.

A lot has already been written about this war, particularly its political, tactical and exceptional human resource efforts. My aim in this chapter is to narrate the lesser known military strategy and linked operational details of the war.

Geo-strategic Backdrop

India and Pakistan both tested their nuclear weapons in May 1998. With a new sense of responsibility and with much fanfare, the Prime Ministers of both India and Pakistan signed the Lahore Declaration on February 20-21, 1999, for a peaceful and cooperative relationship in future. A part of this Declaration was a Memorandum of Understanding (MoU) for the two nations "to engage in bilateral consultations on security concepts and nuclear doctrines with a view to developing measures for confidence building in the nuclear and conventional fields aimed at avoidance of conflict".

After the Lahore Declaration, our political leaders expected that cross-border infiltration and militants' activities in Jammu and Kashmir (J&K) would taper off. The Army Headquarters' assessment of the ground situation was different: it indicated "no change in the ground situation; there could in fact be some escalation in the proxy war in the immediate future due to Pakistan's internal compulsions and its politico-military situation." This was conveyed in the review meetings in the Ministry of Defence (MoD) and the Cabinet Committee on Security (CCS). While addressing Army Commanders in April 1999, I had stated, "This diplomatic initiative has definitely opened the door for improving relations. But, unless Pakistan translates it into ground realities, and stops sponsoring the proxy war, these Confidence Building Measures (CBMs) cannot be expected to fructify. Pakistan's military has been and in the foreseeable future is likely to remain negatively Indo-centric."

On May 2, 1999, I gave an interview to a journalist and stated, "Recent Lahore Declaration has not in any way changed the ground situation in Kashmir. If anything, the Pakistan Army and ISI are still active in aiding and abetting terrorism in the state."

As we later learnt, just when political preparations for the Lahore meeting had been going on, Pakistan Army was busy planning and carrying out reconnaissance to initiate intrusion into the Kargil-Siachen sector with a view to:

- Altering the alignment of the Line of Control (LoC) east of the Zoji La and denying the use of the Srinagar–Kargil–Leh highway (NH-1A, renamed later as NH-1D) to India.
- Reviving Jihadi militancy and terrorism in J&K.
- Capturing Turtuk, a strategically important village located on the southern bank of Shyok River in Ladakh, through which an ancient trade route cuts through the Ladakh Range into Northern Area of Pakistan.
- Highlighting the Indo–Pak dispute over J&K to the international community.

Why did Pakistan Army initiate this operation in the midst of ongoing political bonhomie? The possible reasons could be as follows:

- Pakistan Army, over the years, has developed a negative Indo-centric view and vested interest in maintaining tension with India. Senior Pakistan Army officers had started believing that a stable nuclear balance between India and Pakistan permitted offensive actions to take place with impunity in Kashmir.

- Pakistan military planners expected that India would not undertake an all-out offensive against Pakistan and run the risk of ending the conflict in a state of stalemate.

- India's pre-emption on Siachen Glacier in 1984 continued to hurt the Pakistan Army like a thorn in its flesh. It was a psychological drain for the Pakistan Army Chief General Pervez Musharraf who had failed many times earlier to get some Siachen posts vacated.

- There was a growing concern that the Kashmir issue was losing its international salience. The waning militancy in J&K needed to be rejuvenated.

Gaps Between Own Deployment in the Kargil Sector

During 1980s and 1990s, due to very poor communications and climatic conditions, the LoC, beyond Zoji La, was considered a low-priority area. Large-scale movement of forces was not expected. Few possible approaches were held as per military appreciation. Most of the posts along the LoC had large gaps, ranging from 9 to 36 km. A similar pattern of defences with large gaps was adopted on both sides of the LoC.

Intelligence Failure and Wrong Identity of Intruders

Prior to the sighting of a few armed personnel wearing black salwar kameez identified initially in the Batalik sub-sector in the first week of May 1999, there were no intelligence or ground surveillance reports regarding possibility of large-scale infiltration or preparations of war by the Pakistan Army. Thereafter, for many weeks, both civil and military intelligence kept harping on the situation as "militants' intrusion." Pakistan made effective use of radio communications for deception purposes to indicate that the intruders were Jihadi militants.

In an article, Air Vice Marshal Manmohan Bahadur, VM (then a staff officer with the Chief of Air Staff) had written, "There were many lessons to be learnt from Kargil, the foremost being that 'Eternal vigilance is the price of liberty.'" Too many people who were supposed to monitor the frontier didn't do their job. Much has been written about the failure of intelligence agencies (both military and civilian) and the turf wars and lack of coordination between them, but surely, how could our spymasters have missed activities like the one at Skardu? Air Commodore (retd) Kaiser Tufail, Pakistan Air Force, who was director of operations of Pakistan Air Force in 1991 has written, "Helicopter flying activity was feverishly high as Army Aviation's Mi-17s were busy moving artillery guns and ammunition to the mountain tops. Troops in battle gear were to be seen all over the city. Interestingly, messes were abuzz with war chatter amongst young officers. In retrospect, one wonders how Indian intelligence agencies failed to read any such signs, many weeks before the operation unfolded."

On 19 May 1999, the Vice Chief of the Army Staff (VCOAS) visited Srinagar to get an update on the situation. The same day, GOC 15 Corps told the Daily Excelsior, "A local counter-insurgency operation ... jihadi militants in Kargil backed by the Pakistani Army want to revive the defeated proxy war and to internationalize the situation by building up a war hysteria ... the local situation is to be dealt with locally.... It will be a time-consuming operation for which no specific timetable could be given. Media reports about use of helicopters, gun ships and aircraft by India were not correct. Hopeful that all groups (of infiltrators) would be eliminated in a few days ... they were on a 'suicidal mission!'"

Lack of intelligence, surveillance and inability to identify intruders for several days cost us heavily in early operations. This issue was raised by me in the CCS to convince its members that we were facing Pakistan Army and not Jihadi militants.

COSC Briefing on 21 May

On 20 May 1999, I returned from an official visit to Poland and Czech Republic. Salient aspects of my briefing done that night and in the Chiefs of Staff Committee (COSC) next day were as follows:

- Exact number of intruders, their identity and precise locations were not clear.

- NH-1A was partially cut off.
- The extent of intrusion from Mushkoh to Turtuk, the intensity of artillery fire and some helicopter movements indicated that the Pakistan Army could be involved.
- As per my orders given before leaving from Czech Republic to India, some troops had been moved to the Kargil-Dras sector.

An early lesson in my professional career, "First situation report and assessment of any event is seldom balanced. It is either over-optimistic or over-pessimistic. Based on inputs; every commander must make his own appraisal, preferably by visiting the ground."

Assessment of Situation: My Thoughts

I visited Udhampur and Srinagar on 22 May 1999. Due to bad weather, I could not fly to Kargil. My assessment of the situation after briefings at both locations was:

- So far, ground-level reaction had been only in the form of "counter-militancy operations." Local commanders followed anti-militancy "Rules of Engagement." Movement of additional units and sub-units had been done in haste; neither adequate strength nor logistic support was ensured. Operational missions by Kargil brigade were being given in an ad hoc manner without proper planning. There was an urgent need to establish exact identity, strength and precise locations of the intruders at the earliest, as also for deliberate planning, in view of the nature of terrain and entrenched enemy on mountain tops with a long field of vision/fire.

- Overall, the situation appeared to be much worse than what had been conveyed to me till then. The intrusion had been deliberately planned and executed. The Pakistan Army was definitely involved. It had taken initiative, achieved tactical surprise leading to penetration from Mushkoh to Southern Glacier (Siachen). A division plus level effort to handle the situation was not sufficient.

- Pakistan's political or military objectives were not clear. We needed more information in that context. Meanwhile, Pakistan

Army had to be stopped and deterred from making further moves into Kargil and elsewhere.

- It was essential to be prepared for all contingencies that may arise, either due to enemy action or to achieve our own political and military aims under changed circumstances. The situation demanded much greater military effort to create a strategic asymmetry along entire Indo–Pak front and to achieve an escalation dominance.

- The CCS was exercising restraint. It had denied the use of air power in the CCS meeting held on 18 May 1999 fearing that it would escalate the conflict.

Working on Military Strategy: Relevant Questions

It was clear that we needed much greater forces on the western front to prevent Pakistan from doing any more damage and to undo the present situation. There were many aspects to be considered:

- What political objectives will be given to us? Will the government be prepared to declare a war and go the whole hog? Will the CCS allow conflict escalation and full participation of other two services?

- How will escalation dominance work in the Indo–Pak nuclear environment?

- After nuclear tests in May 1998, India had become a nuclear nation. Several sanctions had been imposed. How will the government handle the international opinion?

- Unless political leadership declares a war, how do we achieve mobilization without causing alarm in the country and abroad?

- How soon can we launch a counter offensive? How will the climate (Jun-Jul) impact our war effort?

- There was a need to take immediate stock of our inventories and review our capabilities for offensive and defensive operations.

COSC Meeting for Joint Military Strategy

The COSC met on 23 May 1999. All the three Chiefs agreed that we should participate in the conflict jointly and work on a joint strategy.

We must employ all our resources optimally, in an integrated manner. Allocation of exact missions would be a matter of detailed coordination, keeping in view characteristics and capabilities of assets available with each service.

As Chairman, COSC, I had to brief the CCS on the assessment of the situation and an outline of military strategy. We took a unanimous decision to work on and recommend a joint military strategy including use of naval as well as air power.

On 24 May 1999, I briefed the CCS on the situation and our responses till that date. I told them that we had to be prepared for war escalation either by Pakistan or by us, if necessary. In such a situation, all three services would have to be prepared and act cohesively. I also informed them about our discussions held earlier and emphasized the need for a joint military strategy, as well as to take initiative to facilitate operations of 15 Corps and Northern Command. With that, I sought permission for the use of air power and Navy. The CCS agreed to that but gave a rider that we should not cross the LoC or the international border. In outline, the political and joint military strategy to be followed was as follows:

Political: India has been a victim of intrusion; yet it is exercising restraint. It will take all measures, including military, to ensure that intruded area is vacated. The armed forces will not cross the LoC or the International Border.

Joint Military: A military posture to prevent Pakistan from reinforcing its military forces opposite Kargil; threaten and maintain pressure on Pakistan throughout land, air and sea border; try and create strategic imbalance for Pakistan armed forces; be prepared to launch forces across the border or LoC at short notice; retain balance on borders with China and Bangladesh.

Joint Military Strategy

The COSC came to the conclusion that we must adopt an aggressive posture in the air, on the seas, and all along the LoC/international border to prevent Pakistan from focusing on Kargil only. We should be prepared to undertake both offensive and defensive operations. Why?

Even though we were politically mandated not to cross the border or the LoC, in a dynamic situation like war, one has to consider all possible contingencies. In this situation, further escalation of the war could not be ruled out, either due to Pakistani action, or by us to achieve the given objective. The directions to the army, therefore, were that our forces should be deployed in such a state of readiness so that at a short notice, we should be able to launch an offensive anywhere across the LoC and the international border. This deployment was to be achieved with maximum security and minimum disturbance to normal air, rail and road traffic and other civilian activities along the border.

The COSC decided to abide by the political terms of reference but to keep our military options open; and to some extent, make it visible to Pakistan. The crux was (a) If Pakistan pumped in more troops in Kargil-Siachen sector to strengthen its position, or took initiative elsewhere, we would retaliate and cross the border. (b) If we could not evict Pakistan from Kargil by the end of monsoon season, we should be prepared to cross the International Border (IB). This matter was explained to the Prime Minister by me separately. He saw the rationale. However, it required the COSC to seek permission from the CCS, if such an action was considered necessary.

Implementation of Military Strategy

The army implemented the military strategy in two parts, as follows.

Part 1: The intruded areas were divided and prioritized into five sub-sectors: Mushkoh, Dras, Kaksar, Batalik and Southern Glacier. Immediate induction of necessary additional troops was given or approved with a view to stabilizing the situation as early as possible and then to remove all intrusions through deliberate operations. Northern Command was directed to eliminate all direct/indirect interference on Road to Srinagar–Kargil–Leh, and to ensure security of all communications within J&K.

Part 2: Headquarters Northern, Western and Southern Commands were directed to be prepared for offensive operations at a short notice, should that become necessary. Corps-level offensive and defensive operational plans were reviewed by the COAS with all Army and Corps Commanders. After detailed discussions, each Corps Commander was asked to prepare and hand over a copy of the Corps Operations Instructions to the Director General Military Operation (DGMO).

After finalizing and sending operational directions, the COAS visited all formations on the Western border and went to Kargil every week.

Movement of Formations

Movement of major formations/units carried out for the above tasks was as follows:

- Kargil division (two brigades had already moved) to take over operational responsibility of Dras and Mushkoh sub-sectors by 1 June 1999.

- Another division was moved by different routes (Rd Srinagar-Zoji La and Rd Manali-Upshi-Leh) to Baltal and Leh. Tactical HQ was moved by air to Baltal on 26 May 1999.

- Few other divisions were de-inducted from many other operations and were inducted in Kargil and Dras sector.

- Additional 155-mm Bofors artillery regiments and 122-mm MBRL battery were moved.

- Additional AD regiments and helicopter flights were moved into 15 Corps/Kargil-Ladakh.

- Holding/pivot formations deployed along the international border/LoC were tasked to carry out forward deployment and exert pressure through active surveillance and patrolling.

- Strike formation deployed elements along the international border/LoC to monitor enemy activities and liaise with holding formations for offensive operations. Operational logistic requirements of strike formations were re-organised.

- Dual-tasked formations moved to their assigned corps on the Western front and given interim locations nearer to the border.

- Part of amphibious brigade was tasked to move by sea to Goa for any amphibious operation, if required.

- In June 1999, Para Bde was moved to Mushkoh sub-sector to clear its vast, difficult remaining area up to the LoC.

What did it involve?

We had a complex and not a set piece situation as laid down in the War Book. As per War Book, unless "precautionary stage" was declared and financial powers decentralized, large-scale movements of troops and material could not be done. Many activities essential for the preparation of hostilities hinged on other ministries – Railways, Surface Transport, Petroleum and Natural Gas and so on. The preparation process was severely constrained. However, regular CCS meetings enabled us to get over most of the bureaucratic hassles. Movement of combat as well as combat support formations to and within Northern Command was given high priority. Military special trains moved units/formations and logistic requirements from different parts of the country to their destinations on the western front.

Role of The Navy

The Indian Navy had issued instructions for an alert even before the CCS meeting of 24 May. INS Taragiri had been deployed on a barrier patrol off the coast of Dwarka. The Navy added two information warfare Dornier aircraft and deployed INS Veer and INS Nirghat. Instructions were issued by the Government so that our shipping fleet stood warned.

The Navy Chief decided to supplement the Western Naval Fleet with selected units of the Eastern Naval Fleet and moved the latter to the Arabian Sea. This step enabled the Navy to extend the range of its deployment.

Naval staff carried out analysis of Pakistan's oil vulnerability and planned to interdict Pakistani oil tankers. The naval projection of "reach and mobility" had an immediate impact. Pakistan started providing escorts to its oil tankers as they moved out from the Gulf to Karachi.

Role of the Air Force

The Indian Air Force (IAF) had been providing Mi-17 helicopter sorties for airlifting of troops for redeployment. On 21 May 1999, a Canberra on a reconnaissance mission had been hit by enemy fire while flying along the LoC in the Batalik sector. But it was able to return safely. The IAF responded very quickly after the CCS approved employment of air power on our side of the LoC. It launched first close-support air strikes with MIGs and armed Mi-17 helicopters on 26 May 1999. The IAF faced early losses but after reviewing its tactics and employment continued with greater determination.

In the third week of June 1999, the Air Chief sought permission from the CCS for a few fighter aircrafts to cross the LoC while engaging the Pakistani logistic base Muntho Dhalo. But despite recommendation of the COSC, the CCS rejected the request.

Diplomacy: Sartaj Aziz's Visit

Soon after 24 May 1999, diplomatic pressure from Pakistan and international community on India started building up. Initially, Pakistan Prime Minister Nawaz Sharif suggested that air strikes (within our own country) be stopped "as a precondition for talks". When this suggestion was rejected by India, he offered to send Foreign Minister Sartaj Aziz to New Delhi. The Government accepted this offer.

This was worrisome for me. Any attempt to seek a diplomatic solution at this point of time would result in a militarily disadvantageous solution as so far, we had not been able to recapture any tactically significant area from the intruders in the Kargil sector. Such a situation could lead to humiliation, as had happened in 1962.

On 5 June 1999, I decided to address the army through a special log, the gist of which is given below:

- Enemy has violated the Line of Control (LoC) in some areas of Dras, and Batalik. However, we have succeeded in containing the enemy.
- Our plans and preparations are foot, we shall rid our land of intruders at the earliest.

Situation in Early July 1999

By the end of June 1999, our formations were on the roll. They had begun to achieve successes in all sub-sectors. Nawaz Sharif visited China to obtain support for a cease fire. Later, prompted by General Pervez Musharraf himself, he met President Clinton in Washington DC for the same purpose. Meanwhile, positions occupied by the

Pakistan Army fell one after another. We captured many features from 16 June till 07 July 1999 through which our victory was evident.

Nawaz Sharif requested President Clinton to intervene and to persuade India for a ceasefire. Pakistan accepted inviolability of the LoC and now wanted to pull out troops from the remaining locations on our side of the LoC. By 10 July 1999, Pakistani troops had been evicted from 99% of Batalik sub-sector, 95% of Dras sub-sector and areas close to the NH-1 in Kaksar and Mushkoh sub-sectors. Para Brigade was already deployed for mopping-up of the rest of the Mushkoh sub-sector.

Decision to Allow Pakistani Withdrawal

On 08 July 1999, the then Prime Minister Atal Bihari Vajpayee called me to his residence. Only he and the then National Security Advisor (NSA) Brajesh Mishra were present at the meeting in the room where we met. The Prime Minister informed me that Pakistan had sought a cease fire and withdrawal of its forces to their side of the LoC. He wanted to know my reaction. It was apparent that either of the two prime ministers or their interlocutors had discussed this issue before I was summoned. My immediate reaction was that the Indian armed forces would not accept such a withdrawal. We had suffered many casualties and now that the events were swinging in our favour, the troops will ask why we were letting the enemy escape. I told the Prime Minister that I needed to consult my colleagues in the COSC and also the formation commanders on this issue.

A few hours later, the Prime Minister called me again. This time he wanted to know how much more time we would take to clear the remaining Pakistani intrusion. I replied that it might take three weeks, hopefully two weeks, but I needed to keep one week as a reserve. He then said that we had already suffered some casualties. Would we suffer more? I responded by pointing out that we were fighting a war initiated by the enemy. Our effort always was and would be to minimize our casualties. Before I left his house, he reminded me that the country would soon have to go through the elections for the Parliament. The constitutionally specified time was running out.

Meanwhile, my colleagues in the COSC, the Vice Chief of Army Staff (VCOAS) and the DGMO had collected at my residence for an urgently convened meeting. We discussed the Prime Minister's suggestion of allowing the Pakistani troops to withdraw from the pockets still held by them and its implications. The DGMO also spoke to the Northern Army Commander on the classified phone.

The important questions before us were (a) should we accept the withdrawal of the Pakistani forces? If we did, what would be the political and military implications of withdrawal? (b) What methodology should be adopted to allow such withdrawal? (c) How would Pakistani forces conduct themselves during the withdrawal phase? (d) What contingencies could be faced during this period and how should we prepare ourselves to meet them?

There was a perceptible shift in the political situation now. We could carry on with the eviction operations but there was little chance of our being permitted to cross the LoC. If we decided to carry on with military operations up to the LoC, there would be political and diplomatic implications. We could lose the international and domestic support that we had been able to muster so far. One has to bear in mind that a war is fought to achieve a given political aim. If that aim is achieved, it makes little sense to continue with the war. We had also to take into account acute shortage of some arms, ammunition and equipment in our services.

We also had serious doubts about whether the Pakistani forces would actually withdraw. They simply could not be trusted. Our main apprehension was that Pakistani troops could occupy some important features close to the LoC where logistic support for them would be easier to obtain and they could indulge in extensive mine-laying on their withdrawal routes. Implications of escalating the war on the western front with deficient weapons and equipment in the monsoon months ahead were also discussed.

After lengthy discussions among and within the services, we agreed that we could accept a phased withdrawal of the Pakistani forces from sub-sectors to be prioritized by us. We felt that the Pakistan Army and its leadership could not be wholly trusted; their sincerity needed to be tested. We decided that a ceasefire along the entire front should not be agreed to. In the first phase, the withdrawal should be restricted to Kaksar sub-sector. Other sub-sectors could follow thereafter. We also felt that a time frame for withdrawal should be laid down by us so that Pakistani forces would not be able to lay mines or booby traps during withdrawal.

Late in the evening, I went to the Prime Minister's residence once again and conveyed our recommendations as well as reservations. The Prime Minister accepted these views. He instructed that all our recommendations and reservations should be built into the proposed withdrawal plans for the Pakistani forces.

On 10 July 1999, we were informed in the CCS meeting that Pakistan wanted a one-on-one meeting of the DGMOs in Lahore to work out details for the withdrawal of Pakistani forces from rest of the Kargil sector. I agreed with the meeting but objected to sending our DGMO to Lahore. Finally, it was agreed that the meeting would be held on Indian soil, in the Border Security Force (BSF) premises at Attari near Amritsar.

During the Attari Meeting on 11 July 1999, with seized Pakistani documents and marked maps, our DGMO showed proof of Pakistan Army's involvement in the intrusion. Pakistan DGMO agreed to withdraw troops from the remaining areas as per plan given by us. Pakistani withdrawal commenced on 14 July 1999. Three pockets close to LoC were not vacated by them. I informed the Prime Minister. After obtaining his permission, these positions were attacked and recaptured on 23-25 July 1999.

Strategic Lessons

Kargil war broke out within 2 months of the Prime Ministers of both India and Pakistan signing the Lahore Declaration. It proved Admiral J.C. Wylie's first basic assumption in his paper "Military Strategy: A General Theory of Power" that "Despite whatever effort there may be to prevent it, there may be a war." Military history tells us that nations who neglect this historical fact make themselves vulnerable to military surprise and defeat. This assumption, therefore, is a reminder to the strategists to visualize security threats, the possibility and nature of conflict and to always remain prepared.

Another basic assumption for war planning is that "We cannot predict with certainty the pattern of war for which we prepare ourselves." It has seldom been possible to forecast the time, the place, the scope, the intensity, and the general tenor of a conflict. This assumption implies that our security plans should cater for the complete spectrum of conflict. Our military strategies and doctrines, therefore, must be flexible capable of application in any unforeseen circumstances. As military history very often tells us, planning for uncertainty is less dangerous than planning for certitude.

Within days of the conclusion of the war, the Kargil Review Committee (KRC) was set up by the Government which pointed out many weaknesses in our higher defence control organization. A Group of Ministers Committee was set up thereafter to implement recommendations of the KRC. While most of the recommendations were implemented, not entirely in the letter and spirit, some important ones were left out.

Lessons Learnt

Several lessons emerged from this war. Some important lessons were:

- There may be remote chances of a full-scale conventional war between two nuclear weapon states. But as long as there are territory-related disputes – currently we have them with China and Pakistan – the adversary can indulge in a proxy war, a limited border war, or both. A proxy war too can lead to a limited war.

- A major military challenge in India has been the political reluctance to a pro-active grand strategy or engagement. This disadvantage is enhanced manifold because no loss of territory is acceptable to the public and the political authority. This is a strategic handicap and a risk in any war setting, which increases in a limited war scenario. It is, therefore, essential to have credible strategic and tactical intelligence and assessments, and effective surveillance. For commanders, it often leads to a temptation to deploy more forces along the border/LoC at the cost of reserves.

- Information operations are important due to much greater transparency of the battlefield. A military operation requires moral high ground. The adversary have to be exposed and denied any moral justification. This needs a comprehensive media and information strategy.

- Successful outcome of a border war depends upon our ability to react rapidly. The new strategic environment calls for faster decision making, versatile combat organizations, rapid deployment and synergy amongst all elements involved in the war effort, particularly the three services.

- A pro-active grand strategy and capability to wage a successful conventional and nuclear war is a credible deterrent. A conventional war may remain limited because of credible deterrence or escalation dominance, when one side has overwhelming military superiority at every level. Such deterrence may prevent a war; it gives more room for manoeuvre in diplomacy and in conflict. Over the years, we have managed to erode such a deterrence capability.

- Any war in future will require close political oversight and politico-civil-military interaction. It is, therefore, essential to keep the military leadership in the security and strategic decision-making loop.

Conclusion

Kargil war was the first and only serious clash between two powers, after declaring themselves nuclear, that had a clear winner. It has settled the issue of limited conventional war under the nuclear overhang. Indian armed forces with their new high-tech weapons and equipment, organizations, joint and service doctrines can expect and must train for future limited wars with both China and Pakistan.

A Reminiscence:
Kargil 20 Years After

Lieutenant General Mohinder Puri

Twenty years have passed since Pakistan's perfidious actions across the Line of Control (LoC) in the Kargil Sector surprised the military and the nation that nearly brought the two sides on the brink of a war. Although, a general mobilisation had taken place, the operations were restricted to East of Zoji La, with clear restrictions on not crossing the LoC. This by itself was an enormous challenge for the Army and the Air Force, resulting in the termination of hostilities – an easy escape route for the enemy to fight another day. With this one single order, the option for the ground forces to address the opposition from the rear by crossing the LoC and at the end of the war, to take the retreating Pakistan army in our net was regrettably closed. For the Air Force, the option of flying in a south-north direction to effectively engage the enemy was severely restricted. We paid for this with a large number of casualties and perhaps prolonging the war for 50 days. But the decision was political and did earn us international goodwill.

I had the privilege and honour to command 8 Mountain Division (8 Mtn Div) in the Valley, where we were tasked for Counter Insurgency (CI) operations and for a longer period of time during the Kargil war and thereafter. The situation in Kargil in mid May 1999 demanded an urgent response to the Pak army's incursion in the Mushkoh-Dras-Kargil-Batalik sectors. After some deliberations, 8 MtnDiv was tasked to move across Zoji La and assume operational responsibility of Dras-Mushkoh sector by 01 June 1999. 56 Mountain Brigade (56 MtnBde) had been moved in mid-May to respond to the incursion and were deployed in Dras under 3 Infantry Division (3 InfDiv). 79 MtnBde, the Corps reserve brigade, was placed under command of the Division to make up for the loss of 81 Mountain Brigade which was retained in North Kashmir for CI operations. The brigade was given the responsibility of Mushkoh Valley. The third brigade, 192 Mountain Brigade, was in the process of handing over the CI grid to the Rashtriya Rifles prior to their induction into the war zone.

Since the division was operating in CI operations, a quick change to conventional operations was the need of the hour. CI and conventional operations are as different as chalk and cheese. Whereas CI operations required immediate response with rapid planning lest militants played havoc before timely and expeditious response, conventional warfare required deliberation and meticulous coordination not only amongst assaulting troops, but also with a vast array of supporting arms and services including the Air Force. Therefore, the successful transition to conventional warfare configuration in equipment, as also the psyche within a very short time that was available was of utmost importance. We had a short window to complete the orientation before taking on any major task.

The initial assessment on critically analysing the inhospitable terrain, the extreme high altitude at which troops would be operating and the enemy incursions on dominating ground created a great deal of apprehensions in the mind. The first view of the terrain as one crosses Zoji La into Ladakh is awesome and one is struck by the high mountain peaks varying in height from 18000 to 21000 feet (ft) with valleys at an altitude of 10000-11000 ft. The entire area or most of it is devoid of cover with razor sharp ridges and steep peaks which are jagged and extremely difficult to negotiate. The soil is loose with gravel and stones rolling down with each step one takes. The scarcity of vegetation in the summer months combined with the extreme high altitude makes breathing laborious and adds to the fatigue factor, thereby seriously impacting on the physical combat efficiency of the troops.

Under such varied conditions, the conduct of military operations demands proper acclimatisation to prevent incidence of high-altitude sickness besides building up physical capacity of troops, special clothing to survive in the extreme cold climate and extremely high levels of physical fitness. In the initial stages of the war, units which were hurriedly inducted into the battle zone without proper acclimatisation and clothing suffered avoidable heavy casualties. The effect of high altitude coupled with limited availability of roads and tracks with a few laterals made movement slow, tiresome and tedious and time consuming. Consequently, building up a viable military force backed by sustainable logistics became extremely cumbersome. The movement or shifting heavy equipment including guns and ammunition from one location to another became equally difficult.

Tactically, the terrain favoured the defender enormously and put the attacker to serious disadvantages. In a terrain devoid of vegetation, with approaches of attack being narrow, restricted and arduous, the attacking troops were likely to suffer heavy casualties. Notwithstanding the tactically favourable impact of the terrain on the defender (enemy) coupled with inhospitable weather conditions, the division took up the challenges and displayed courage and bravery beyond the call of military duty and pushed the Pakistan army back to where they belonged.

On assuming command of the Dras-Mushkoh sector on 01 June 1999, I realized that the information of the enemy was fairly scanty, particularly their detailed deployment on ground on various heights. While we did make an assessment of their overall deployment and the likely force level they could have employed, the details, unfortunately, left us in the dark. One of the surest methods of acquiring information in the battlefield, I daresay, is by physically launching patrols which can confirm information acquired from other sources. Air photos are an invaluable asset, but again in this case, in the air photos supplied to us by Research and Analysis Wing (R&AW), there was a total mismatch in the interpretation of the air photos with the maps. This was mainly due to difference in the scale; with the result we could not with accuracy locate the information available on the photos. Our patrols, on whom we were dependent also did not come up to our expectations. I found in some cases there was a reluctance and shyness to close in with the enemy positions to gain vital information. Nevertheless, with time, there was an improvement and the initial hesitation could well be attributed to the process of getting "blooded" into the battle. However, where troops were in contact, we could get a fairly accurate assessment of the enemy strength and dispositions. Slowly and deliberately we put the information together to come to a viable assessment of Pakistani deployment and formulate our course of action.

I had asked for reasonable time to prepare for the first attack and fortunately commanders up the chain of command condescended to my request. During the preparatory period, many activities were taking place and a great deal of issues had to be properly coordinated. Around 10 June 1999 or so, the situation was critical. Since about a month back, starting from the better part of May 1999, there were no tangible results to show that the situation was turning in our favour. We had not met with any success and even the presence of my division did not create any sense of confidence in the environment. We had only conveyed our confidence of retrieving the situation by word of mouth, with no visible achievements to boast about. It was a lonely period for me, filled with anxiety, apprehension of failure, trepidation and worry. By 12 June 1999, a number of artillery units had been placed under my command. The D-Day had finally arrived for which we had been preparing since the last 12 days. All loose ends had been tied up and we awaited the commencement of the attack with a great deal of expectation and I dare say with fleeting moments of apprehensions.

The Tololing feature was representative of the deepest penetration made by Pakistan in Dras. One actually has to stand at Dras and look towards this feature to believe the extent of his domination. From enemy's deployment on this feature, they could dominate the highway both by observation and fire and interdict any move or build-up besides cutting off troops along the valley by direct firing weapons. By holding features on the ridgeline, the enemy had assured a secure route of maintenance for his troops at Tololing. The attack progressed on night of 12-13 June 1999 and by 7 am or so we had overcome the opposition. The capture of this feature by 2 RAJ RIF marked the turning point of the war, and from there onwards we maintained the momentum and captured ridge after ridge with the indomitable courage and bravery of the troops.

If I were to give a couple of reasons for our success in pushing back the Pakistan army and restoring the status of the LoC, it would be the courage, spirit and bravery of our young officers and men who fought against all odds to uphold the highest traditions of the their regiments and the army. Their valour and sacrifice will be a part of folklore, and a source of inspiration for the future generation. The second reason, I would attribute to the high standard of leadership displayed by the brigade commanders, commanding officers (COs) and the young officers by leading from the front with one single order- "follow me". Very few armies of the world can boast of such a high commitment of leadership.

What is therefore the shape and model of the war in future? Are we likely to have an all-out war in a nuclear background on our western borders with Pakistan and China containing us or actively confronting us on the eastern borders in collusion with Pakistan. In my view, future wars are likely to be fought across soft borders or on disputed areas, rather than in areas where the borders are permanent and clearly demarcated. International pressures will ensure that the spectrum of war remains restricted and limited. So against Pakistan, Jammu and Kashmir (J&K) will continue to be a bone of contention, and with China, their so-called claim areas in Ladakh, Uttarakhand and Arunachal Pradesh will continue to remain contentious issues which may well ignite a limited war. The centre of gravity must therefore shift to the LoC, and disputed areas with China from the hitherto emphasis on conventional warfare in the plains and deserts. While it remains essential to maintain a high degree of deterrence in the plains by modernisation of mechanised forces, our focus in procurement of equipment and force levels must shift to the LoC and Line of Actual Control (LAC) environment. Similarly our training manuals, training directives and institutions, which are still heavily weighted in favour of conventional wars, must do a rethink in creating viable responses in the LoC/LAC environment. Sub-conventional wars, proxy wars and low-intensity conflicts (LIC) will overtake the conventional threats and as far as Pakistan is concerned, we should be prepared for them, "to inflict on us a thousand cuts". Thus, there is a need to maintain a strong deterrence force encompassing the three services and a strong military reaction capability in the hill sector of J&K.

It will not be out of context to mention the need to streamline the policy for border management so that incidents along the LAC and the international border can be handled with an effective response. Presently, the LAC is manned by the Indo-Tibetan Border Police (ITBP) under the Ministry of Home Affairs (MHA) while the area of operations falls under the army. This obviously leads to functional, command and control problems. An effective policy would be to place the ITBP and border management under the operational command of the army and the Ministry of Defence (MoD). Similarly, in J&K, the international border presently manned by the Border Security Force (BSF) under MHA needs to be placed operationally under the army and the MoD. Dual responsibility leads to lack of clarity on security issues as well as creates functional problems amongst the various agencies which consequently results in delayed response to border problems.

Lastly, 20 years have passed since the Kargil War and I salute the supreme sacrifice made by the officers, Junior Commissioned Officers (JCOs), and, men for our better tomorrow. My prayers also go to the families who lost their near and dear ones. May 8 Mountain Division continue to live upto their credo *"Forever in Operations"*.

Defining Moments in Kargil Heights: GOC's Perspective

Lieutenant General (Dr) VK Ahluwalia

"It is high time that the country became ruthlessly realistic about its limitations and priorities. First and foremost, Pakistan's survival must precede everything else, including our attachment to the Kashmir cause. Secondly, it has to be understood that our economy is our weakest point and has to be given priority over any other consideration. ..."[1]

Ambassador Shahid M. Amin, Pakistani Foreign Service, 1999

While flying the Cheetah helicopter between Leh and Kargil, as a young air observation pilot (AOP) in 1976-78, I was pretty familiar with the aerial route and alignment of the line of control (LoC) on the ground, the line that delineated the de facto border between India and Pakistan. The erstwhile "Cease Fire Line" was re-designated as LoC following the Simla Agreement, which was signed on 03 July 1972. To my surprise, on 31 December 2005, while driving up to the same sector, now as a newly promoted Major General, to take over the mountain division in Kargil, I realized that every feature on the ground looked so very different. There was a great difference in identifying features on the ground, when flying a helicopter and when moving by vehicle on the same route. The road journey, with innumerable winding bends and loops (*jalebi mods*), would just not come to an end! Soon, we encountered a thick sheet of ice on the road, leading to mild skids by the vehicle, due to the earlier snow falls. Worse, it had started snowing very heavily, and within minutes the visibility reduced to a mere five meters or even less. So much so that we had to halt midway to strap the non-skid chains to the wheels of the vehicles. It appeared to me as if we were the only two light vehicles moving on the road, and that we were not in communication with anyone. Seeing the deteriorating weather condition, we hoped that the liaison officer, a naib subedar, who was travelling in the trailing vehicle, was in communication. Not a soul could be seen anywhere close to the road.

Due to the whiteout conditions, there were moments when there was pin-drop silence in the jeep between the three of us – Captain Vivek Murthy (ADC), driver and me. Months later, the division staff would inform me that not only were they monitoring the move, but there were a few anxious moments as well due to the breakdown in communications and the worsening weather condition. According to the locals, it was the heaviest snow fall in recent years. In retrospect, it was an excellent way to be baptized into the battle zone, where weather and terrain are equally hostile on regular basis. Later, during our long drives to the units and formations, Vivek, a voracious reader, would always narrate his perspective of Op Vijay, and many more stories to keep me amused.

Experience of LoC

Operations on the LoC are unique. The LoC is neither demarcated on the ground nor does it really follow any well-defined geographical features. So, experience helps! Having commanded an infantry brigade on the LoC in Baramulla-Uri Sector (Rampur) in 2001-02 (two years), I had the added advantage of flying helicopters along the entire stretch of LoC in the Valley and Ladakh region while operating from the Srinagar Air Base. Subsequently, the command of a field artillery regiment in Rajouri Sector for a brief spell and tenanting the appointment of Colonel General Staff (Operations) of the Nagrota Corps helped develop an understanding of operations on the LoC. It may be recalled that period 2001-03 was the litmus test for the Indian Army, due to the intense phase of insurgency in the Valley. Concurrently, the ongoing "Operation Parakram" required complete focus on the LoC.

Based on my study of the terrain and Pakistan's strategy in Kargil, as the GOC of the 8 Mountain Division in 2005-06, it has been my endeavour to share my perceptions and thoughts, on the events as they unfolded in 1999, and the way ahead on "Kargil after 20 years".

Apprehensions

Just as one had read "Slender was the Thread" by Lt Gen LP Sen before taking over the infantry brigade in the Valley in January 2001, I had read a few books about the Kargil War (1999), and perused the unclassified parts of "From Surprise to Reckoning: The Kargil Review Committee (KRC) Report and the Group of Ministers' Report". Kargil was a household name by that time in both India and Pakistan, for different reasons though. While the effectiveness of Army's surveillance along the affected areas of intrusion was certainly examined, the role of RAW, IB, military intelligence, and their inputs were also scrutinised in detail. It was the only modern war that was fought exclusively in mountains – in fact, it would be correct to call it in the "extreme high-altitude mountains."

Coming back to the long spell of the very slow drive from Leh to Kargil via Biamah on 31 December 2004, I must be honest to admit that there were certain apprehensions within me, which kept me fully engaged with a number of questions. Perhaps, that was another reason that there was silence within the vehicle. With the bad weather continuing, and the visibility dropping to dangerously low levels, contemplations become one's companion. It triggered several questions that flashed through my mind. A few hard-learnt lessons of the Nagrota Corps in 1996-98 and the infantry brigade on the LoC, in the Valley, during Op Parakram in 2001-02, also started to revisit my memory lane. Of course, a few of these questions were also based on the lessons of the Kargil Conflict and my earlier experience of serving on the LoC:

- Post the Kargil War and given the persistent bad weather conditions, have we actually improved the intelligence, surveillance and reconnaissance (ISR) capabilities along and across the LoC, to have greater transparency and situational awareness? The idea of improvement in the intelligence architecture at the national level did not cross my mind even once – it was not important to me at that point of time.
- Have we taken actions to review our operational concepts for fighting in the mountains, and build our capability by providing advanced weapon systems and state of the art communication equipment?

- How effective has the army aviation been to carry out reconnaissance and surveillance, especially during the winters? What is our vertical envelopment and heliborne capabilities in the mountains?
- Is there a need to discuss the significance of manoeuvre and fire power in the mountains to achieve our objectives with minimum casualties?
- What is our coordination with the flanking formations, for both conventional operations and against proxy war cum infiltration of terrorists from across the LoC to the Valley floor?

These questions notwithstanding, there was an overwhelming sense of pride and confidence in me to be trusted to command the elite Mountain Division, whose motto itself is **Forever in Operations**. Compliments to my predecessors who had given a motto that was most exciting, motivating and inspirational, and now, it was for me to rise to the occasion to prove it. Although I had commanded an infantry brigade in a high-altitude in the Valley, I feel that to define and to understand a high-altitude area, one should visit the Kargil Heights. Every feature, every ridgeline is part of an extreme high-altitude area, and that too in a cold arid desert like conditions; hence, the challenges are enormous. Indian soldier faces them most smilingly!

National Highway NH-1A: The Lifeline

After visiting the units and formations on the ground, analysing the intrusion areas, and studying the Kargil Conflict, my understanding of the importance of national highway (NH-1 Arenamed as NH-1D in 2010) has been further reinforced. It connects Srinagar with Leh, via the Zoji La (La means a mountain pass; altitude of 11575 ft). It needs no further emphasis. It is the lifeline of the region, even though it remains closed for about 5-6 months due to heavy snow fall in the region, thus warranting winter stocking to take place during the summer months.

The alternate route to Leh via Manali-Rohtang Pass had its own set of challenges, which has now improved enormously. The NH-1A is dominated by the Pakistani posts at several stretches of the surface road. Any interdiction of the road could lead to cutting off Kargil and Leh, and any action to control Turtuk in the Partapur sector would have an adverse effect on the operations and maintenance of our troops deployed in the Siachen sector.

Image 1: Snow Cutting at Zoji La

As Generals' clique had served in the FCNA, Pakistan, they had identified the gaps and the area that would be most suitable to dominate the NH-1A. Having studied the activities and profile of deployments of the Indian troops over a few years, they identified Dras sub-sector as a critical vulnerability of India, from where NH-1A could be effectively dominated. There was no alternative surface road connecting Srinagar and Kargil; they visualized no resistance as the prominent ridge lines and the dominating heights like Tiger Hill and Tololing had remained unoccupied. It was also relatively easier to maintain its troops, due to better network of communications and logistics system. Simultaneously, it gave immense advantage to the adversary, as it could effectively interdict any Indian movement along the NH-1A, thus preventing any movement of vehicle bound troops, logistics, and winter stocking for the entire Ladakh region. However, Pakistani soldiers, on seeing no resistance, went on to occupy additional heights in Mushkoh, Kakser, Batalik, Chorbat La and Turtuk sub-sectors. The location of the intrusions is given in Image 2.

Image 2: Areas of intrusion by Pakistan.

B : Bases.

Genesis of Pakistan's Failure

Smarting under repeated defeats in 1947-48, 1965 and 1971, which finally resulted in the dismemberment of Pakistan, our neighbour resorted to a proxy war and cross-border terrorism from the late 1980s. This was done with a view to destabilize India in general and Jammu and Kashmir in particular. In fact, the very idea was conceived by General Muhammad Zia-ul-Haq, President of Pakistan, in mid-eighties, called **Operation Badr**. It may be recalled that a near similar conflict took place between Zoji La and Kargil in May to November 1948, when Indian Army evicted the Pakistani soldiers and opened the road axis up to Leh.[2] After the humiliating defeat in the Indo-Pak War of 1971, Pakistani Army further suffered yet another setback, and a loss of face in front of their populace, when Indian Army pre-empted the occupation of Siachen Glacier on 13 April 1984. Nasim Zehra, the celebrated Pakistani author, justifiably stated in her Book, "For some, the shame and anger had lingered."[3]

Given this background, Pakistani generals' "clique of four",[4] had already decided by mid-October 1998 to launch a cross-LoC operation, called **Operation Koh Paima** (Op KP; Mountaineering Trip). They had all served in the strategically important areas along the LoC. Within hours of taking over as the Army Chief on 7 October 1998, General Musharraf had appointed each one of them to a key position, except Major General Javed Hasan who was retained as Commander, Force Command Northern Areas (FCNA). It is undisputed that General Musharraf was carrying the "cross LoC plan" with him ever since his tenure in the FCNA, and he had then got that opportunity.

Nasim Zehra gives out that the aim of Op KP was to conduct a "limited infiltrate and capture"[5] operation. Pakistan was worried over the weakening of insurgency in J&K, which was detrimental to their long-term proxy war. However, post the nuclear tests in May 1998, the generals believed that with the success of Op KP and a "measure of nuclear blackmail", the world powers would intervene to resolve the unsettled J&K issue in Pakistan's favour.[6] Nasim also highlights that some young officers from within Pakistan's 10 Corps (it is responsible for all areas North of Chenab), fearing that this operation was **"clear suicidal"**, even urged the General (Chief of Staff) to abort the operation. Despite such resistance, the plan was approved, as conceived. Yet again, there was a huge miscalculation on Pakistani generals' part, particularly after the dismal failure of Operation Gulmarg in 1947-48 and Operation Gibraltar in 1965, both of which were launched with a view to annex J&K. This miscalculation was further reinforced by General Musharraf's belief that "the Indians would never fight back." It was concluded by the generals that the military and diplomatic success of operation KP was guaranteed.[7] Otherwise, we may have faced a Kargil-like situation during 1996-98 itself.

According to Nasim Zehra, the soldiers of Northern Light Infantry (NLI) battalions started moving across the LoC, onto the ridges and heights dominating the Dras bowl by end of October 1998 itself. Pakistan failed to appreciate the likely reactions of India in not allowing Pakistan to cut off NH-1A, to pursue its strategy to internationalise the J&K issue, and to increase the tempo of proxy war in the Valley. Also, the generals' clique was dismissive of diplomacy's role in resolving the J&K issue. General Jahangir Karamat, the then Pakistani Army Chief (1996-98), was one of the generals who did not accept the self-proclaimed geopolitical strategist, Lt Gen Aziz Khan's near similar plan to occupy the heights that Indians had vacated during the winters.[8]

Total Secrecy

It was more than evident that Pakistan had laid overwhelming emphasis on maintaining total secrecy about Op KP, while even at the highest political level, the Prime Minister of the country was not informed of the plan and its likely implications, leave aside taking approval. Pakistani Army took several measures to achieve its aim of maintaining secrecy. Even the other two sister services air force and navy were kept in the dark. In 1973, the three regiments (Karakoram Scouts, Northern Scouts and Gilgit Scouts) were formed into NLI, with their regimental Centre at Bunji, near Gilgit. These troops belong to the Northern Areas.[9] Pakistan Army leadership decided to induct them only in local tribal attire with light weapons so as to give it the semblance of mujahideens. They continued to maintain routine military activities and did not induct any additional troops from the hinterland. No military traffic indicating movement of troops was permitted from Rawalpindi to Gilgit and beyond.[10]

While radio transmissions were carried out to show activities of the mujahideens and regular troops as routine activities, ISD and STD facilities were disconnected from the military garrisons and local areas to prevent leakage of information.[11] Strict censorship was imposed on troops' writing letters to their families. Area was isolated as civilians and media were not permitted to move beyond a particular geographical alignment. The Generals' clique gave no indication to the political leadership about their sinister designs even when Indian Prime Minister Mr Atal Bihari Vajpayee had proceeded on a peace mission, by bus, to Lahore in February 1999.

Op Vijay: Brief Analysis

"Our officers are not directing the battle from behind but are right in the front."
— ***George Fernandes, Raksha Mantri, 1999***

Besides the intelligence failure at the national level, we certainly had our inherent fault lines of "inadequate surveillance of the LoC" on the ground to carry out effective surveillance, and of "denial", wherein we denied the scale and magnitude of the intrusion in the initial few days. It was due to piecemeal information from different quarters, and partly due to our belief that the intruders could be pushed back from the local incursions. The intrusion remained a matter of speculation in terms of the numbers, extent of intrusions, regular or irregular troops and the intension of Pakistan.[12] In fact, the inflow of information was so vague that the then Defence Minister had announced that the intruders will be pushed back within 48 hours. And so, did a few senior military officers as well. It merits a mention here that rapid diversion/ induction of 8 Mountain Division, along with other arms and services into the Kargil sector, including Air Force by later part of May, and our build-up followed by offensive actions took the enemy by shock and surprise. They had not foreseen such a rapid response, redeployment and commitment of the Indian troops to fight against all odds. Indian Army ensured logistics too were fully mobilized to support the inducted troops, and the artillery guns by way of transportation of ammunition. It proved its mettle, despite the major constraint of not crossing the LoC and fighting against an entrenched enemy on dominating heights and capturing the icy mountain peaks one after the other. While the induction of Air Force gave a huge psychological advantage to our troops, the last of intrusions in Mushkoh, Dras and Batalik sectors were also evicted by 26 July 1999. Given the details of Op Vijay being so critical a matter of study, especially its famous battles, we decided to cover them in depth in the part titled, "Blood, Guts and Glory" in order to do them justice.

Operation Green Kargil

On driving along the national highway to visit the formations and units, I was intrigued by bold signages suggesting "You are under observation of the enemy." I halted at each of these places to look at the feature that was dominating the road stretch, which was invariably followed by running commentary of Vivek's historical perspective. The answer to my basic question, to the formation commanders and the accompanying staff, of whether we had taken any actions to prevent direct observation of the enemy drew a muted response. To prevent direct observation/domination of the NH-1A, we carried out a survey of the exact extent of the road stretch that was under enemy's observation. We decided to take passive action, as a long-term measure, to prevent direct observation of our movements along and astride the road by planting trees – willows and poplars – in rows on the enemy side of the road. It was indeed a huge challenge to grow trees in a cold arid desert. As it was conceived to give strategic cum ecological advantage, this project was named "Operation Green Curtain", later renamed "Green Kargil". The plantation was done, in selective stretches of road, by employing the civilian labour, under the supervision of the local units in close vicinity. To our utter surprise, Indian Army (8 Mountain Division) was awarded the BNHS National Green Governance Award by our Prime Minister, Mr Manmohan Singh at the Vigyan Bhavan, New Delhi, on 10 November 2005. Much before the announcement of the award, I distinctly remember that Lt Gen Hari Prasad, Army Commander, Northern Command, who had read the concept of Operation Green Curtain, asked me a pointed question during his visit to Dras on the Kargil Diwas, "VK, tell me what prompted you to undertake this venture?" Besides, stating the well-rehearsed strategic-economic-ecological advantages, I said that this action should have been taken in 1947, as the enemy has been dominating the road axis since then. We would have created an effective screen between the dominating heights and the NH-1A.

Diplomatic Initiatives and the Nuclear Bluff

Op Vijay was a stirring victory for India. It was at the same time a loss of face for Pakistan both at the national and international levels. Although Pakistan achieved strategic surprise in Kargil, it finally resulted in a mere tactical success. For Pakistan, it was in fact a political, strategic and diplomatic failure. It clearly established that J&K problem is closely linked to proxy war and cross-border terrorism. However, it also brought out that it cannot be resolved by occupying heights across the LoC. We hope Pakistan has realized that deceit and military muscle power is not the way to resolve the J&K problem – in fact, there is nothing to resolve as it is an integral part of India. Against the backdrop of the nuclear test in May 1998, Pakistan's nuclear capabilities had acquired centrality in all their strategic thoughts. However, Op Vijay, and more recently our surgical strikes both by the ground forces in September 2016 and by the air power in February 2019 have successfully played their "nuclear bluff" and won.

With forceful pro-active political and diplomatic initiatives, India has enjoyed a clear advantage at the international level. Given the degree of difficulty involved in capturing dominating heights at extreme high altitudes, the image of the Indian Armed Forces, the army in particular, was enhanced manifold.

Before proceeding to assume command, I perused the KRC Report again to compare with the prevailing ground situation. Yes, Op Vijay certainly provided vital lessons to improve our operational effectiveness for the future, a few of which were in line with my apprehensions. The recommendations at the national level – intelligence, jointness and integration, appointment of Chief of Defence Staff (CDS), role of media and information, and use of advanced technology – are given in the end notes.[13] To name a few lessons which were of immediate importance to me were:

- Effective intelligence, surveillance and reconnaissance (ISR) capabilities at the operational and tactical levels, and dissemination of information, and to improve secure signal communications with the FDLs; in addition, to analyse the methods to improve winter air surveillance along the LoC.
- Need to discuss and review our war-fighting concept, manoeuvre and fire power in the mountains, creation of reserves, organizations, structures, weapons and equipment to fight effectively in extreme high-altitude areas (HAA); also, to check adequacy and stocking of ammunition in safe positions.
- Need to develop infrastructure, operational tracks, helipads and logistics to support troops deployed close to the LoC; and develop interbattalion and intervalley surface connectivity, for the obvious advantages.
- Post-Kargil, and more importantly, ascertaining the level of motivation, morale and confidence of all ranks was vital.

It clearly stood out that jointness in planning, preparation and execution of operations is vital to fight in an integrated manner. Due to instability in the region and unsettled territorial disputes, we would continue to require our boots on the ground to prevent any Kargil-like intrusions in the future. Therefore, we felt that improving our ISR capabilities, indigenously developed, should be accorded top priority to provide transparency on and across the LoC.

20 Years of Kargil Conflict

With 20 years having gone by, while it is important to rejoice and celebrate the victory, in my view it is expedient to analyse both the changed geo-political environment and the security matrix on the sub-continent. We need to take a stock of the actions taken to improve our preparedness for the future. Now, China and Pakistan share a much closer relationship between them, which is often referred to as "stronger than steel" and "sweeter than honey." With China's investment in China Pakistan Economic Corridor (CPEC) since 2015, as part of Belt and Road Initiative (BRI), China would also have much greater stakes in Pakistan. Presence of PLA security personnel in Gilgit-Baltistan region, in the hinterland, and in areas around Gwadar port would certainly have immense security implications for India. Therefore, India should cater for economic cum strategic impact on India in the long term. This also means that Pakistan–China ties are likely to grow further. China would extend its support in building Pakistan's infrastructure in terms of roads, rails, airfields, ports, energy power grid, establishment of special economic zones; defence industrial base; and in cyber, space and artificial intelligence domains. India should therefore be prepared to deal with a collusive threat to our national security. The changed geo-political reality and the changing regional security matrix and its impact on our security should form an essential part of our national security strategy (NSS). It would be prudent to revisit the NSS periodically to analyse our actions.

In the current and futuristic scenario, "Kargil type of intrusions" are most unlikely to occur. We have set a benchmark wherein all elements of national power were involved to support Op Vijay at multiple levels. From now on, such kind of misadventures may actually result in a total war, the nuclear weapon status of the two countries notwithstanding. Simultaneously, we need to take a stock of our operational readiness to face different forms of complex threats: proxy war and state-sponsored terrorism throughout India, conventional operations and intrusions across the LoC, continued efforts by Pakistan to radicalize the youth in J&K, psychological and propaganda warfare and a wide variety of non-traditional security threats.

It is undisputed that "information and technology" are the drivers of change in the twenty-first century, equally, if not more, in warfare of the future. The vital tools of fighting in the mountainous terrain would be in the realm of Technology, manoeuvre, fire power, self-contained battle groups (light formations/groups), special forces (SF) and scouts; Robust infrastructure, tailor made logistics; Mechanised elements, drones, fire power systems and army aviation as manoeuvre arms; and Mountain warfare-oriented training.[14]

With unsettled territorial disputes and the psyche of the public in India, Pakistan and China, not to lose an inch of territory, the probability of conflicts triggering in the mountainous cum disputed regions remain high. The conflict could then rapidly spill over to a larger region, as it happened in Indo-Pak War, 1965. It is appreciated that the conflicts in the future are expected to be short and intense, combined with sub-conventional operations and information warfare in its full dimension. Even post-Kargil, Pakistan has continued with its policy of proxy war cum cross-border terrorism. Although we have not experienced hybrid warfare in its entirety on the Indian sub-continent so far, but we should be fully prepared to tackle multiple dimensions of hybrid warfare in the future.

Besides protecting the territorial integrity, we would be required to disrupt and destroy adversaries' capabilities and their operating systems, by both kinetic and non-kinetic means. To achieve absolute conflict domination, we will have to confront threats from land, air, space, cyber, electromagnetic and psychological domains.[15] Due to competition among the great powers to dominate strategic space, cyber, outer space, information warfare, and artificial intelligence and its military applications, advanced countries have moved ahead at a rather fast pace. We must ensure that these futuristic technologies and their military applications form a critical part of our NSS. Air power remains a vital component of a war winning strategy, due to which the significance of jointness and integration cannot be overemphasized.

To improve our situational awareness, to fasten our decision making, and to speed up the Observation, Orientation, Decision and Action (OODA) loop, it is operationally expedient to put in place an effective Command, Control, Communications, Computers, Intelligence, Information, Surveillance and Reconnaissance (C4I2SR) on priority. In the Indian context too, battlefields would progressively transcend beyond conventional domains into the world of information and artificial intelligence (AI). It requires the army to be well networked and integrated with the other services to undertake joint operations. Also, to be operationally effective and to minimize logistics requirements, lighter formation would facilitate speedy and sustainable offensive operations in the mountains.

There are a host of other recommendations at various levels, which have been considered in the concluding part "Emerging Challenges and the Way Ahead."

Punitive Actions with Strategic Balance

I have always felt that whenever any such misadventure by Pakistan comes to light, on small or large scale, we should first take punitive military action to impose our strong will on the adversary, rather than first informing the world community. Of course, concurrently, actions should be taken to maintain strategic balance at the national level. When faced with situation such as in Kargil in May 1999, a strong nation must first punish the intruders militarily and then seek world opinion and support. We must raise the cost of such misadventures at multiple levels; this also includes shaping of world opinion from a position of military strength. This can happen only if we achieve effective military deterrence by improving our military capabilities in both conventional and non-conventional war-fighting mechanism, robust infrastructure and logistics, soft power and demonstrated power. Secondly, if our neighbour violates the sanctity of the LoC or the International Boundary (IB) by indulging in intrusions at several places, like it did during Kargil Conflict 1999, then we should not bind ourselves to not to cross the LoC/IB to conduct operations. In such situations, it should be our endeavour to defeat him in detail, with minimum casualties to our troops. This part requires political clarity and political will to enable the armed forces – transformation of defence structures, modernisation and jointness – to give a befitting reply. It is also time to take decision on "theaterisation, jointness and optimum utilisation of limited resources" to move ahead. "Peace through Strength" is an expression used by various leaders like the first American President, George Washington (1793) and Ronald Reagan in the 1980s. It was felt that strong military capabilities could help to preserve peace. It is true even today.

Having discussed the essential aspects, the vital question that comes to mind is whether, over the past 20 years, have we prepared ourselves to face the challenges of the future? The short answer is "No." We have a lot many actions to take at multiple levels, to transform and modernise our armed forces to achieve the desired military deterrence. This aspect, and many other, have been discussed in the last part 'Emerging Challenges & the Way Ahead.'

Conclusion

Indian Armed Forces have consistently proven their worth by their sense of professionalism, commitment and responsibility. It is true that the Indian Army was surprised by the Pakistani soldiers, by occupying ridges and heights over a wide frontage and intrusions as deep as 5-12 km across the LoC. It is also true that, given the constraints of not crossing the LoC and the degree of difficulty of capturing dominating heights occupied by the intruders over a wide frontage, the Armed Forces faced one of the biggest challenges in the recent times. Undeterred, the Indian soldier fought gallantly with a view to achieve victory, in true spirit of Operation Vijay. The Kargil conflict has given us many lessons, which merit actions at different levels: national, strategic, operational and tactical.

Information and technology have become the key elements of warfare. Given the nature of territorial disputes, we are likely to face two types of conflicts in the next one to two decades: One, given the unsettled territorial disputes, the probability of triggering a short and intense conflict in the mountainous terrain, especially in disputed regions remains high, along with induction of irregulars, cross-border terrorism and information warfare in its full dimension; two, a hi-tech conflict in which conventional methods are integrated with non-conventional ones to form a hybrid warfare would be dominant in the Indian context. In the true spirit of Op Vijay – to achieve decisive victory – we should be fully prepared to tackle multiple dimensions of a combination of conventional cum non-conventional threats in the future.

NOTES

1. Shahid M. Amin, "Kargil: The Unanswered Questions II—Time to Shed Illusions." *The Dawn*, 26 July 1999, Accessed on 10 May 2019, https://www.rand.org/content/dam/rand/pubs/monograph_reports/MR1450/MR1450.ch3.pdf

2. Ashok Kalyan Verma, "Blood on the Snow, Tactical Victory Strategic Failure", Manohar Publishers and Distributors, p. 52.

3. Nasim Zehra, "From Kargil to Coup, Events that shook Pakistan", Sang-e-Meel Publications, Lahore, 2018, p. 92.

4. Khaled Ahmed, "Kargil Clique", Newsweek, Oct 12, 2018, & Zehra, ibid. "Clique of Four" comprised the clique's boss, General Parvez Musharraf, Pakistan's Army Chief, Lt. Gen. Aziz Khan, Chief of General Staff (CGS) at the General HQ (GHQ), Lt. Gen. Mahmud Ahmad, the "think tank of the Pakistan Army," and the Director General of Military Intelligence, and perhaps the most important member of the clique was its fourth member, Maj. Gen. Javed Hassan, who presented himself as a "geopolitical strategist and headed the Force Command Northern Areas (FCNA).

5. Zehra, op. cit.

6. Ibid., p. 94.

7. Ibid., p. 18

8. Ibid, p. 91,

9. Amarinder Singh, "A Ridge Too Far, War in the Kargil Heights", Motibagh Palace, Patiala, 2001, p. 40.

10. Ibid.

11. Ibid., p. 41.

12. Verma, op. cit., p. 97. The "no mistake syndrome" in promotion-related matters leads to this attitude of doing just enough to cover your arse (an American expression that says it all), but this is hardly conducive to confidence building and decisiveness in crisis.

13. National Level considerations were: Need for improvement in the intelligence system at all levels, organizational structures, capacity building, technologically advanced intelligence equipment, and integration and coordination; Use of satellites and drones for intelligence gathering; Appointment of Chief of Defence Staff (CDS) and greater focus on jointness to take timely decisions and fight in an integrated manner; Effectiveness of media in contemporary conflicts and shaping the perception at the national and international level; "India's first TV War" and the media aroused the patriotic fervour and brought the nation together to support the armed forces wholeheartedly. In addition, impact on security due to changes in the geo-political and regional security matrix, with a host of other recommendations, is given in Part 5.

14. Seminar, "Changing Contours of Mountain Warfare: Improving Effectiveness in the Indian Subcontinent", December 12, 2018,

Signals: 20 Years After Kargil

Lieutenant General Rajeev Sabherwal

Beyond the icy unforgiving heights, stark jagged edges, rarified atmosphere and bitter cold obtaining in Western Ladakh, there lies *inter alia* the saga of the Indian Army Signaller. It is a tale of grit and innovation, in the face of challenges and inadequacies. Now, 20 years beyond Kargil, the time is opportune to take a peep into this history and trace the evolution to present times.

The definitive memory of the Kargil War, for all future generations of Signallers was that of the Commanding Officer of a frontline Signal Regiment, whose left leg was shattered knee downward when a bomb exploded in front of him. The officer was next to the adhoc Signal Centre near the Tactical Headquarters, when the explosion happened. Indeed, the word "adhoc" is the apt description of the extant communication setup. The war was a litmus test for the Corps of Signals and the Regimental Signallers hailing from all arms and services. There were lessons to be learnt and changes to be made, some of which got captured in the Kargil Review Committee Reports. It is a widely acknowledged fact that the Signallers dealt with the emerging challenges professionally, demonstrating the ability to support unprecedented accretions, with attendant logistic echelons in a barren high altitude area virtually devoid of telecom infrastructure. The Kargil War was for the Corps of Signals, a watershed event which propelled the growth path to uncharted territory. To an extent this was also in sync associated with the growth in the civil telecom segment, the Internet, the IT revolution and the software industry.

An Overview of Communications during Op Vijay

Provision of Signal communications during Op Vijay was severely constrained by terrain imperatives and impacted by enemy action.

During Op Vijay, the Indian Army was still to holistically benefit from the economic liberalization of 1991. The situation in different parts of our borders was a study in contrasts. By May 1999, the communication infrastructure on the Western borders had vastly improved with the commissioning of the forward looking strategic backbone, the Army Static Switched Communication Network (ASCON) and the grid based Army Radio Engineering Network (AREN) for mobile operations. The state on the Northern and Eastern borders was however still far from satisfactory. Signallers who have served in the area would recollect the ubiquitous Permanent Lines more commonly referred as the "PL Routes", miles upon miles of communication cables strung over sturdy World War design metallic poles. The PL Routes were the mainstay of communication during the Kargil War. The PL Routes had different kinds of multiplexing equipment mounted on both ends; which enabled simultaneous voice and tele-printer circuits on the same pair of cable. The PL Routes also served another important function. During snowed out conditions and in the pre GPS era, they served as assured navigation aids for vehicle columns and patrols.

The PL Routes were supplemented by the Radio Relay sets, a robust family of equipment which had a mind of their own. It was a challenge to get them going, even for the most experienced technician. However old-time exponents swear to the hilt about the equipment and tend to brush aside the new generation radio relay sets with disdain. They say that the new sets do not bring out the "true signaller" in you. A few fixed satellite terminals had been commissioned to connect far flung posts. They had huge, unwieldy antenna and the outdoor part of the equipment just stopped working in the sub-zero temperatures. It was not uncommon to see innovations like locally fabricated heat jackets wrapped around the Low Noise Amplifiers, which was the heart of the antenna segment of the satellite terminals. The exchanges were a mix of old magneto exchanges and the newly received auto exchanges. This resulted in some unique situations. The infantry battalions and most of the brigades were on the magneto exchanges which belted out a high current on the cables. At times, due to faulty connections, this high current simply burnt out the circuits in the auto exchanges which were designed differently. The change from the famous magneto phone with the cranking handle to the auto phone with a dial pad/dial ring was in a way the harbinger of things to come. The radio equipment was dominated by the old warhorse – the American design ANPRC-25. Even today, we hear nostalgic stories about the radio set from the veterans. Significantly communication in the mountains was comparatively archaic, hierarchical, and tenuous. The despatch rider was frequently used as a fall back option when all other means of communication failed.

During the war, the Directorate General of Signals acted swiftly to catalyse the release of critical additional signal equipment and stores from the Field Ordnance Depots, coordinate their transfer from other Commands, ensured ramped-up production by DPSUs and expedited procurement ex-import. A variety of Commercial Off The Shelf (COTS) equipment was inducted during the operations to fill up crucial voids. These included equipment like Satellite Phones, hand held walkie talkie sets, mini exchanges and the like.

The Drivers for Change

The primary growth driver for change, post Kargil, was the set of lessons learnt during the war. The key lessons from Op Vijay revolved around the following issues:

- Need to comprehensively improve the mechanism for dissemination of aerial photography and surveillance feeds to users.
- Need for comprehensive reform in provision of regimental communication.
- Necessity for reserve equipment at selected echelons.
- Need to improve upon the back-bone communication infrastructure, both in terms of scales and bandwidth.
- Need to re-examine the repair and recovery philosophy associated with telecom equipment of all origins.

There were other important external growth drivers which have enabled this generation shift.

- **Analog to Digital**. The last two decades saw a complete conversion from analog devices to digital devices. This has not only changed the family of communication equipment, but has changed planning, scaling, organisational structures and procedures in the Corps.

- **Convergence of Communication and IT.** The second driver behind the shift has been the gradual and now almost complete convergence of communication and IT equipment. The reliance on made to a purpose terminal devices, gave way to generic computational devices like laptops and tablets which today also operate as communication devices.

- **Adoption of Commercial Off The Shelf (COTS) technology.** Militaries have traditionally been averse to civil use technologies. However the Corps of Signals has resisted this tendency and uniquely adopted a non-conventional flexible approach of exploiting COTS technology in a big way. This has arguably been the greatest catalyst and the Corps has not been left behind in the cascading growth story in non-military space.

- **Proprietary to Open Standards.** The Corps has also adopted open standards, as opposed to restricted proprietary standards, prevalent till even a decade back. This has ensured our equipment is interoperable with the universal Information and Communication Technology eco-system in both hardware and software. In the realm of the strategic backbone, commercial software standards and networking equipment have been used, with an additional military designed security layer.

Tracing the Path of Evolution 20 years after Kargil War

The Corps of Signals has evolved into the 21st century, technology driven "nerves of steel" of the Indian Army. The Corps has today established a state of the art Army One, a strategic backbone network which hosts numerous services and applications pan India. In addition the Defence Communication Network (DCN), envisaged as an exclusive and a highly secure tri-service communication network has been rolled out. The strategic networks offer a high degree of network assurance to its users, along with a trained team of Signallers who can optimally man and utilize the networks. The strategic backbone networks have almost completely shifted to high capacity Optical Fibre Links. The mobile segment has seen the adoption of versatile and robust solutions like the Mobile Cellular Communication System (MCCS), suitably modified from the commercial space, which now serves vast segments of our Western borders. Similar equipment is also being inducted in other sectors.

The switching and access segments are on the verge of complete shift to a new generation equipment. The Corps of Signals has also adopted satellite based systems in a significant scale and is now poised for an exponential growth path in conjunction with Indian Space Research Organisation (ISRO). The existing family of radio equipment is fully data capable and has the assurance of being made in India. The tactical equipment is mounted on high mobility vehicles which gives the signallers the required reach to support the forward edge of the battlefield. Software based video conferencing and streaming of UAV surveillance feed has been refined. Progress has also been made in realizing better synergy with the IAF in the Tactical Battle Area.

The security of communication and information systems cannot be divorced from each other and the personnel of the Corps are handling the pan India Cyber Security aspects for the Indian Army at the functional level. The Indian Army is now exploring newer frontiers like Artificial Intelligence (AI) and Cyber Electromagnetic Activities (CEMA) – which involves the unification of Electronic Warfare (EW), Spectrum Management and Cyber fields.

Future Trajectory

The future beckons and new vistas are on the verge of being opened. Amongst the clutch of avenues, the following can be identified as the key elements which would be of importance in the future. Military communication has learnt from the growth of the Internet and is adopting the best practices from this all pervasive network. The future networks of the Indian Armed Forces would be aimed at bringing IP data packets seamlessly to the forward cutting edge of the battlefield.

- The reliance on satellites will be another key to the future trajectory. The proliferation of satellite terminals, static, mobile and hand held would increase. The Indian Regional Navigation Satellite System (IRNSS) would be integrated to the next generation satellite systems and other communication devices.
- The Indian Army will shift from a hired circuit model to an

owned circuit model. It is on the verge of shifting over to a completely new Network for Spectrum (NFS), a versatile strategic backbone with features that can lead the Indian Armed Forces towards a truly Network Centric environment.

- The key requirement of delivering high bandwidth data to every user in the tactical battle space, without compromising on security, would be addressed with the induction of high capacity Radios, which is likely to replace the existing family of radios.

Conclusion

The communication segment of the Indian Army is technology driven, and the last two decades have seen new generations of technology being inducted, adopted and superseded. The new technology also required changes in training, employment philosophy and has had a direct bearing on the nature of war fighting. Building on the strong foundations laid by the Signallers of yore, today's Sparrow remains just as passionate and committed. Evolution comes naturally to all Signallers, and the future remains exciting. Being the most pervasive amongst the communicators of the sister services, the Corps of Signals is also poised to be the driver for the much-anticipated tri service integration.

Today, the Corps of Signals is no longer a supporting arm; it has now fully proved to be the enabling arm of Indian Army enhancing its battlefield potential and helping it to achieve operational success both in the 'Kinetic' and Non-Kinetic' operations.

Lessons From Kargil Operations

Major General P K Chakravorty

"There are five essentials for victory:

- He will win, who knows when to fight and when not to fight
- He will win, who knows how to handle both superior and inferior forces.
- He will win, whose Army is animated by the same spirit throughout all its ranks.
- He will win, who prepared himself, waits to take the enemy unprepared.
- He will win who has military capacity and is not interfered with the sovereign."[1]

– Sun Tzu, The Art of War

Background

Kargil conflict took place in 1999. This was preceded by three wars with Pakistan. It is clear that Pakistan is a nation that is deceitful and cannot be trusted. In all conflicts, the war was initiated by Pakistan. In the first war, Pakistan's intent was to capture Jammu and Kashmir, the second war was again on Kashmir, and the third war was the crisis in East Pakistan leading to the creation of Bangladesh. The Kargil war was similar, with the intention to interfere in the Line of Communications from Srinagar-Kargil to Ladakh region. Pakistan always made grand plans, which were difficult to execute. Furthermore, they underestimated the capability of the Indian Armed Forces and this has been their waterloo. Nevertheless, Pakistan continues to fight a "Grey Zone" conflict with India and it devolves on India to continuously read the situation and be ready of Pakistan mischievous thought process.

Why did Kargil happen? Nasim Zehra answers this in the Introductory Chapter of her book, "From Kargil to the Coup, Events that Shook Pakistan". Pakistan named the conflict as Operation "Koh Paima". The aim was to interdict the Srinagar-Zojila-Kargil-Leh highway, NH-1A by setting up posts and pickets on the strategic heights of Dras and Kargil. As per Pakistan, this would successfully choke Leh and Siachen, allowing them to dictate terms for the settlement of Siachen and Kashmir issue.[2]

The planned operation was principally restricted to 80 Infantry Brigade with its Headquarters at Minimarg. 62 Infantry Brigade with its Headquarters at Skardu was involved in reconnaissance for supplementary action. 323 Infantry Brigade located at Siachen was also given incidental tasks. These three formations came under Force Command Northern Army (FCNA) located at Gilgit and 10 Corps located at Rawalpindi. The go-ahead for the operation was given in early October 1998. To maintain security, it was referred as an exercise and most communications were by briefings. According to the plan, the minimum across Line of Control (LoC) incursion would extend to 9 km into Indian-held areas of Dras and Kargil. By end of October, the occupation of posts started. 6 NLI entered Dras and occupied posts vacated by India, for the winter months. Within two months, the FCNA Commander exploited the opportunity to expand the operations further, without bothering about the consequences. The area of operations was expanded from one sector to five sectors due to the absence of Indian Troops. The initial plan to occupy 10 to 12 posts ultimately increased to occupation of 140 posts. The units involved and the areas they were responsible for are as stated below:

- 12 NLI – Tiger Hill.
- 6 NLI – Dras.
- 13 NLI – West of Kaksar.
- 5 NLI – North East of Batalik.
- 7 NLI – Chorbat La.
- 3 NLI – West of Turtuk and Shyok River.

By the end of December 1998, Pakistani forces had infiltrated 7 km deep, from several directions. On 16 January 1999, Operation "Koh Paima" was approved by the Pakistan Military Operations Directorate post a meeting with the Chief of Army Staff.[3] While the troops kept extending their foothold in Indian soil, their logistics plan was difficult to manage. Meanwhile, the Lahore Declaration was signed between the two Prime Ministers on 21 February 1999. Between March and April 1999, the Pakistan troops were fully in position. They occupied the watershed positions across the LoC in Mushkoh, Dras, Kaksar, Batalik and areas West of Turtuk.

It was fortunate for India that 5 PARA operating West of Turtuk spotted unusual movements on 09 February 1999. Further firing took place in March 1999 when Indian troops observed Pakistani troops clearing bunkers in the Chorbat la region. Digging was reported by shepherds in the Batalik Yaldor region in early May 1999. The summer patrolling by Indian troops started in May 1999 and gradually, the truth emerged. The Zoji La pass opened early in May 1999 and Pakistani troops located at Tololing began offensive operations on 03 May 1999. They first attacked a reconnaissance group and then an ammunition dump in Kargil on 09 May 1999.[4] Retaliation by Indian troops started on 04 May 1999. A battalion attacked a post in the Yaldor-Batalik sector.

The truth gradually began to dawn on the Indian side as to the extent of occupation by Pakistan forces. Gradually, the full-scale retaliation started. By 26 May, the Indian Air Force stepped in and there was heavy buildup of artillery and troops. The Pakistani posts with poor logistics began to feel the heat and gradually two issues became prominent for them. First, the lack of artillery and the second was poor logistics replenishment. With induction of additional troops, the Indian Army was able to capture Tololing by the third week of June and Tiger Hill complex by 04 July 1999. Meanwhile, pressure was maintained along other locations. By 05 July, Pakistan started withdrawing its troops and by 07 July, India captured Jubar in Batalik sector. By 26 July 1999, Indian Army announced complete eviction of Pakistani intruders. Like the Razakars in 1947-48, Operation Gibraltar and Operation Grand Slam in 1965, Operation "Koh Paima" failed.

Lessons

Higher Direction of War
It is two decades since the conflict took place, but the lessons are relevant

even today. Pakistan has remained deceitful and untrustworthy ever since it was created. The First War in 1947-48 witnessed the employment of Razakars, the 1965 War witnessed infiltrating columns under Operation Gibraltar followed by a bid to capture Akhnoor as a part of Operation Grand Slam, the 1971 War saw refugees entering India from erstwhile East Pakistan and the Kargil conflict witnessed incursions across the LoC. On all occasions Pakistan has been the initiator and India has been responding. The recent surgical strikes in Uri in 2016 and the Balakot air strike in February 2019 have demonstrated India's capabilities to launch strikes under a nuclear overhang. We must plan strikes into Pakistan in areas of our choosing with Integrated Battle Groups to send a strong signal of our capabilities. Pakistan will learn a lesson, only once its Regular Armed Forces are hurt.

To undertake these operations there is a need for synergy between the three Services. As recommended by the Group of Ministers, there is a need for Chief of Defence Staff to coordinate operations of all the three Services.

Intelligence

The Kargil conflict occurred due to lack of intelligence.[5] As described earlier, Pakistan started the operations in October 1998 and the Indian Army came to know about it in May 1999. In accordance with Government directions, the National Technical Research Organisation (NTRO) has been set up. Electronic Intelligence (ELINT) and Human Intelligence (HUMINT) have been strengthened considerably. At the level of the Armed Forces, satellites and Unmanned Aerial Vehicles (UAVs) are available for real-time surveillance. However, actionable intelligence needs to be provided for better results.

Air

The Indian Air Force flew first operational sortie on 25 May 1999. As the intrusion was only 5-12 km, it was extremely difficult for aircraft to hit the target with free flight bombs without collateral damage. Accordingly, Precision Laser-Guided Bombs were fired by Mirage 2000 at NLI Headquarters at Muntho Dhalo that proved to be extremely effective. Reconnaissance flights were flown by Canberra and Jaguars. The Precision Guided Munitions (PGMs) fired by Mirage 2000 enabled the operations to culminate faster and helped in decimating the infiltrators.[6] There is a need for the Air Force to induct Tejas and Rafale type aircraft to operate in these areas. As demonstrated in Balakot, in February 2019, the Air Force must have sufficient numbers of PGMs. Further our pilots must train extensively on mountains and they should have a high-altitude firing range.

Artillery

The Gunners played a predominant role in the Kargil conflict. The Bofors Gun proved to be the pièce de résistance of the conflict. 105-mm Field Guns, 120-mm and 160-mm Mortars, in conjunction with 122-mm GRAD BM 21 Multi-Barrel Rocket launchers (MBRLs), decimated the enemy and broke their will to fight.[7] It is estimated that 70%-80% of the casualties on both sides of the LoC were caused by Artillery Fire.[8] The important lessons learnt during the conflict are enumerated below:

- Surveillance is an artillery function and in terrain as obtaining in Kargil, this task would be done efficiently by High Altitude Long Endurance (HALE) UAVs. These would give a clear picture of the troops, vehicles and their deployment. Furthermore, they could be used for observation and correction of Artillery Fire. A step in the right direction would be to procure Unmanned Combat Aerial Vehicles (UCAVs), which would enable engagement of targets in addition to provision of Reconnaissance and Post-Strike Damage Assessment.

- The weather in general area around Kargil is unpredictable and changes frequently. The accuracy of the Artillery round is impacted by the weather condition. There is a need for providing accurate Meteorological data. This is possible by equipment like Digicora. The other method is to fire weather rounds. These rounds applicable to datum limits give the corrections for weather which can be applied like datum and witness point corrections.[9]

- For pinpoint accuracy in destruction of enemy emplacements and cause high casualties, Guns must be used in the direct firing role. Positions must be prepared with ammunition for this purpose. This was done during the conflict with great results.

- Counter bombardment is a major task for the Artillery. While UAVs could undertake this task with precision, there is a need for Weapon Locating Radar for the Mountains. The equipment has been developed but needs to be trial tested.

- Ammunition management is the key for the Artillery battle. Ammunition dumps must be located in tunnels in the mountains to avoid being targeted. Ammunition replenishment needs to be carefully planned and practised. Ammunition movement must be on alternate axis. In this case, the alternate axis through Rohtang, Pang, cross Taglangla, Karu, Leh and onwards to Kargil has been developed.

- Artillery has an excellent system for manning Observation Posts in the Siachen Glacier. It would a desirous to extend this to other areas in the Leh theatre to enable them to be available for tasks during crisis.

Engineers

Engineers played an important role particularly in track improvement, construction of emplacements and building the defences to ensure that the posts were not vacated at any time of the year. They utilised plant equipment intelligently to ensure speedy movement of troops, stores, guns and ammunition.

Logistics

Logistically, the Pakistani plan was a strategic blunder. The withdrawal of the NLI was pathetic. They did not even bury their dead comrades. Pakistan all along lost all operations due to its poor logistical planning. On the Indian side, there is a need to adopt the push system and all repairs must be undertaken in the combat zone. There must be a seamless procedure to replenish ammunition and supplies.

Conclusion

The Kargil Conflict was overall a strategic blunder by Pakistan. The posts established in wilderness could not stand the might of the Indian offensive. On India's part there is need to overcome the shortcomings noticed. ELINT and HUMINT need constant upgradation to monitor Pakistan activities along the Line of Control. India should always be prepared to counter reckless actions by Pakistan.

NOTES

1. Sun Tzu, "The Art of War".
2. Nasim Zehra, "From Kargil to the Coup, Chapter 5", Sang-e-Meel Publications, Lahore, Pakistan, 2018, p. 138.
3. Abbas Hasan, "Pakistan's drift into Extremism", published in London, 2005.
4. Gaurav Savant and Muzamil Jaleel, "Pakistan Pounds Srinagar-Leh Highway", *The Indian Express*, June 01, 1999.
5. Lt Gen Mohider Puri, "Intelligence Failure Led to Kargil War", *The Economic Times*, January 14, 2019, www.economictimes.indiatimes.com, accessed on May 18, 2019.
6. Maj Gen Jagjit Singh, "Kargil War: Role Played by the Indian Air Force", *Indian Defence Review*, February 02, 2019, www.indiandefencereview.com, accessed on May 18, 2019.
7. S D Goswami, "How Artillery Changed the Tide of Kargil War", *The Economic Times*, 13 July 2018, www. economictimes.indiatimes.com, accessed on May 19, 2019.
8. Brig Gurmeet Kanwal, "Pakistan's Strategic Blunder at Kargil", *CLAWS Journal*, CLAWS, New Delhi, Summer 2009, www.claws.in.
9. Method suggested by Lt Gen VK Ahluwalia, Army Commander, "Weather Round", during Artillery Seminar conducted in 2010.

Paratroopers in Batalik

Colonel BM Cariappa

When it all started, I was in Bangalore, attached to the Parachute Regiment Training Centre (PRTC). My mother was suffering from cancer and was in the last stages of her life. My unit then was in Siachen and my Commanding Officer was magnanimous to get me attached to PRTC, to be by the side of my ailing mother since I had already finished the mandatory two stints on the forward locations on the glacier. While I was busy tending to my ailing mother, it was in the news that there was unusual activity in the Ladakh region bordering Pakistan. Patrols had gone missing; a MI-8 (helicopter) and a MiG-21 aircraft had been shot down. As the days went by, there was further news that the Pakistanis had crossed the LoC and had occupied the heights on our side that were vacated during the winters. Our patrols that had gone in when the snow levels had reduced were abducted and tortured. Things really seemed bad.

Soon after, my mother passed away. After I finished off with her last rites, I went up to the Deputy Commandant, PRTC, and requested him to terminate my attachment and send me back to my unit.

On 17 June 1999, on reaching back my unit, I was informed that two companies that had de-inducted from the Glacier were heli-lifted to Batalik and inducted into the operations to evict the Pakistanis who had occupied the heights on our side. That evening while we were sitting in the officer's mess, my Commanding Officer received a call from the higher Headquarters with orders that an officer from the unit is required urgently for operations with one of the companies from my unit that had inducted into Batalik earlier. I was tasked for the purpose and was given orders to move to Batalik early next morning.

Next day, 18 June 1999, while driving to Batalik, I came across several trucks with black flags moving towards Leh. I stopped one of them and enquired as to why were they flying black flags as it was the first time, I was seeing a convoy of vehicles with black flags. I was informed that they were carrying the remains of the martyrs who had lost their life in the ongoing battle in Batalik.

On reaching Batalik sector, I was asked to move further up closer to the LoC, to a location where an Infantry Brigade had established their tactical HQs. It was a trek of approximately 5-6 hours to the tactical HQs. Enroute I came across soldiers from my unit. I was informed that I am slated to take over one of the companies from my unit for operations. I was also informed that the Pakistanis occupying the heights were all regular soldiers wearing Pathan suits and track suits and were from the Frontier Force and Northern Light Infantry regiments, and not mujahideen as being propagated by the media. One of the soldiers also showed me some documents retrieved from the area, which included I-Cards of Pakistani soldiers and ration issue registers.

The First Major Success in Batalik Sector Pt 5203

On reaching the tactical HQs of the Infantry Brigade, I was briefed by the brigade commander and was tasked to capture Point 5203. Point 5203 is an imposing feature driving like a wedge in one of the sub-sector. To progress operations further towards the LoC, it was necessary to be cleared.

The plan was to bombard the feature for a day with artillery; thereafter, the assault was to commence at night from different directions simultaneously with one company of PARA and two companies of the Ladakh Scouts.

The operations began with artillery bombarding of the feature that commenced the previous day and went on till the next day. We were camping at the base of the feature with Khalubar to the West and Point 5203 to the East. Both these features were held by the enemy in insufficient strength and any movement in the open would draw fire from the enemy, causing casualties. We decided to go up from a steep route which was a very difficult and unexpected one. If successful, we would take the enemy by complete surprise. I was banking on the experience of my men who had spent close to two years in the area and in Siachen. My team comprised of self and another officer Lt Surinder, two JCOs and many men. We split up in two teams each with an officer to lead and a JCO and other men.

My only worry at that time was that I was not acclimatised for the operations since I had spent two months of leave and 20 days of attachment in Bangalore and it was only my third day in the area. However, the circumstances were such that I thought it would be shameful to even mention it to anyone, to be misunderstood to be giving an excuse to avoid the operation.

We commenced our operation at approximately at 8 pm that night. As we kept nearing the Arty shelling area, I would order for the Arty fire to be lifted up by another 50 or 100 metres. Lt Surinder's column was to be moving on to my right. The demarcation between both our teams was a clearly defined fold in the rock face. While climbing up, every time there was a landing, I would stop and take a report from Surinder's team. Around 1.30 am, Surinder reported that he has encountered an overhang and they could not negotiate it. I directed him to cross over the fold in the rock face demarcating our columns and fetch up with the tail of my column. Soon after that, the communication broke down between both the teams. Surinder could hear what I was passing on the radio, but I wasn't getting any of his messages. Every time he would try to speak on the radio, there would be a blank between the static. I then passed it to him that if he could hear me, he should press the presser switch three times repeatedly. He gave me the confirmation as asked. Standing on a ledge, I switched on the *Indiglo* light of my watch pointing it downwards and checked if Surinder could see it. *(Self and Surinder had picked up this watch from Leh market during one of our visits together in the past.)* He gave me a confirmation on the radio pressing the presser switch thrice confirming so that he could see the glow. I directed him to continue with the climb, link up with the tail of my column and try after a while to communicate again. The route was very steep and by about 4.00 am when dawn was just breaking out, we managed to reach the crest line. Our team tried calling Surinder, but there was no response, we looked down to check for the rest of my troops and there was a wide gap to the last man coming up. If we waited too long, we would be daylighted and lose the element of surprise. We were shielded by a huge rock on the crest line. Up ahead about 50 m away on a little raising, we noticed an enemy bunker beautifully made with the natural lay of the rocks. We had to eliminate this enemy position. The plan was to crawl close to the bunker and lob in hand grenades into the enemy bunker. To draw the enemy attention away from us, the Light Machine Gun (LMG) was to engage the enemy once we reached a particular open spot so that the enemy was distracted from observing us. Self and Yudhbir managed to reach the bunker unnoticed and Lance Naik Sher Singh who was manning the LMG carried out the orders and opened up the LMG as directed. Yudhbir clambered up on top of the flat rock above the bunker and I chucked in two grenades one after the other. One of the Paki soldiers ran out from the rear the moment the grenades were lobbed; he was shot by Yudhbir. However, the two grenades I lobbed into the bunker did not explode. Those moments waiting outside the enemy bunker for the grenades to explode were the longest moments.... All I could hear was my own heartbeat. We had to take a decision fast. So I turned into the loophole of the bunker and fired my rifle like a man possessed, till the rifle magazine was empty. I then went around the bunker and cautiously entered in. There were two more Pakis we found crouched up in a corner of the bunker, dead. We then heard the war cry of the Ladakhis reverberating from the other side of the feature. Once we linked up, I passed the code word for success of the operation. I could hear the cries of jubilation on the radio set. **Point 5203** was finally captured. This was the first major success in the Batalik sector. The morale of the soldiers was sky high, who were keen to go ahead with the next operation against the enemy.

Induction of PARA Battalion into Batalik

There was an urgent need for acclimatised troops for operations. So, towards the end of June, my unit was de-inducted from the Siachen Glacier and inducted into Batalik. My unit was given the first task to clear the remnants of the enemy on a feature called "Khalubar", which was recently assaulted by an Infantry Battalion, and thereafter clear the valley area further to the West upto "Area Spring" and then further up to "Area Muntho Dhalo". "Muntho Dhalo" is an imposing location which has a mountain feature surrounded by a large flat area from three sides, the approach to which rises steeply from the narrow valley West of Khalubar. This area was used by the Pakistanis as a stocking base for progressing operations deeper into our territory. Just beyond this location is the LoC.

The clearance of the area up to Muntho Dhalo was meticulously carried out by my unit. Ahead of Muntho Dhalo was the LoC where the Pakistanis had taken up defences on two imposing peaks: "Conical Complex" and "Ring Contour Complex". The deep "U"-shaped saddle formed between these two peaks was the gateway for the Pakistanis to infiltrate into the Batalik area. From both these peaks were spurs coming towards our side and criss-crossed each other as they merged with the ground. A bowl-like shape was formed between the two spurs, the peaks and the saddle. We camped at Muntho Dhalo base and the next few days recouped all our war fighting stores. Logistics was a challenging part; the local base was a 18-hr trek from where we used to get our food and other necessary equipment; another interesting part of this operation was we found huge piles of arms and ammunitions left by the Pakis, which was probably one of the largest discoveries of enemy arms and ammunitions, in the entire war. Soon after, my unit was given the task of capturing Conical and Ring Conical Complex and Ring Contour Complex. I was tasked to assault and capture "Area Conical" and Maj HS Jaggi was tasked to assault and capture "Area Ring Contour"; both these features are located on the Line of Control and were well defended by our adversary. I was to lead a Company, and to assist me in my operation as my second-in-command (2iC) was Capt SS Bisht (who all of us in the unit, including the soldiers fondly call as "Chotu" owing to his short height), who had walked up to the Commanding Officer and requested him that "if Carie (as I am called in the Army) is leading the next operation", he would like to be part of his team for the operation. Maj Jaggi was assigned Lt Aditya Kumar as his 2iC. Both the companies also had an artillery Forward Observation Officer (FOO) team of an officer, a surveyor and a radio operator, to direct artillery fire when needed.

I along with Chotu, the FOO and my platoon commanders decided to carry out a recce of the target peak that afternoon and decided on the routes to be taken for the assault. The plan was simple. The assault was planned more like a raid. We planned to bombard the entire area along the LoC during the day with artillery. The operations were planned to commence at 7.30 pm. Chotu along with a larger group of soldiers, carrying heavy equipment was tasked to climb up along the spur; I along with a smaller team of selected few volunteers planned to move into the bowl and zigzag our way through a treacherous but unexpected route. Secrecy and silence were to be maintained till the first bullets were fired. The idea was to take the enemy by complete surprise.

On return to the base, I assembled all my men, made a model of the target peaks, the spurs and the bowl formed, using stones and soil and gave out the plan. Earlier, I had asked for volunteers when all the senior JCOs had assembled. To my surprise, I had a whole lot of volunteers from various companies. Bulk of them were from other detachments of my unit who had served with me in Siachen and in previous operations. Nk Yudhbir Singh and Lance Naik Radhe Singh were selected as the scouts for the operation. During the day, I had tasked every soldier to zero their weapon. I had remembered an aspect from my Young Officer's Course wherein I had learnt that with every 2000 ft of altitude gained, the trajectory of the bullet changes. The last thing one would want in such operations is to have a weapon that does not shoot where aimed.

We commenced our operations as planned and moved up to a location where the firm base was planned to be set up. As we moved out of the firm base, I received a message on the radio set from my Commanding Officer, **"Cease fire has been declared, all columns are to fall back"**. We were disappointed to have missed the opportunity of some action. On returning to Muntho Dhalo, we were informed that a cease fire has been declared and the Pakistan had promised to pull back all their troops from the area up to 1 km behind the LoC. From Muntho Dhalo, the next few days we observed the enemy locations every day. We realized that instead of pulling back from the LoC, the enemy was in fact strengthening their positions. We also realized that they were laying land mines and fortifying their sangars and bunkers and also observed them bringing up a 12.7-mm anti-aircraft gun, which was positioned in the centre of the saddle. As we were given strict orders that there would be no firing carried out, we could but only watch the activities of the enemy in great despair.

After we returned back to Muntho Dhalo base, the very next day, a criticality had come up which demanded the requirement of an officer for another important task. Chotu was therefore pulled out of my team and sent for the task. A young officer, Lt Vaibhav Dixit, was given to me as my company 2iC.

Nine days passed by and it was really frustrating to just watch the enemy who was not keeping up its commitment of withdrawing back 1 km from the LoC but building up its defences further. On 20 July 1999, we were again given the orders to assault and capture the two features, "Area Conical" and "Area Ring Contour". The composition of the assaulting teams remained the same as planned before. Troops were assembled again and were briefed on the latest developments. This time they were strictly instructed not to walk on any open patch of ground as land mines were extensively laid by the enemy and that they should walk only over boulders, no matter how difficult it would get. The rest of the plan remained as planned before, i.e., to launch the attack with stealth.

Commencement of Operations Again

Bombarding of the enemy positions all along the LoC in the area, with artillery commenced during the day. We commenced our move at around 7.30 pm with Maj Jaggi's company leading, followed by my company. We established the firm base and proceeded ahead. All this while, artillery bombardment of the enemy positions continued. Maj Jaggi reached the location where both the spurs criss-crossed, dispatched his teams in the direction they were assigned to and waited for me to fetch up. When I reached his location, we hugged each other like brothers and wished each other luck. I then moved further ahead and waited for Dixit's team to fetch up. Once he did, I set his team off on their planned route and then slipped into the bowl with my own team.

We were facing challenges of logistics and weather in the high altitude. None of us had bathed for at least a month, all of us were wearing the same clothes that we wore when we got into the operations more than a month back and we were surviving on food being sent up through porters, cooked in village Dah, and which was 3 days old.

Despite being the month of July, it was overcast and there was light snowfall that night which helped us in maintaining our surprise as it was a totally dark night. We could see the flash of the artillery shells exploding ahead of us followed by the deafening nose of the explosions that followed.

At approx 2.30 am, I was having severe cramps in my stomach and had to relieve myself. Suddenly there was a deafening explosion from the neighbouring feature of "Area Ring Contour" followed by loud screams of someone in pain. The screams were echoing so loud in the bowl as if were happening somewhere close. Following the screams, we could see that the enemy had opened up with their small arms, RPG and mortars towards the location where the screams were coming from. The Air Defence Gun we had observed earlier was also firing in a direct role and we could see the tracer bullets bouncing off the rocky surface of the mountain. The intensity of the firing had become so strong that we could feel the whole area reverberating. Just as I finished what I was doing, a huge boulder from somewhere above got loose and went tumbling just next to me, missing me by a whisker. The next, I could hear someone from my column screaming out loud. I quickly zipped up and went down to where the screams were emanating from and saw that the surveyor, part of the FOO team with my company, was stuck below the boulder that had slipped down from the slope. We managed to gag the soldier in pain and all of us got together and pushed the huge boulder further down. This soldier was lucky as he fell into a cavity formed between two boulders when the boulder fell on him and the only injury he sustained was the skin from his nose had peeled off, exposing the bone and was hanging from the tip of his nose. Luckily for us, his screams got drowned in the immense noise caused due to the firing happening at that time. We were lucky that the enemy had still not detected our movements and there was still no enemy fire coming on to us.

We needed to focus on our task, so we resumed with our climb. At approx 3.45 am, I received a radio call from Dixit and he gave me the code for successfully reaching the peak. I checked with him again. He confirmed that there was no enemy on the peak and that they had secured it. We were in a way happy, thinking that the enemy would have probably abandoned their location and all we have to do is to go occupy the peak. Daylight would breakout soon and we were still about 30-40 minutes below the peak. As we got closer, I could sense that something was not right. I couldn't see any of my troops from Dixit's column around, which was a larger column. But what was even more surprising was we did not notice any enemy movement too. It was around 0430 hours and we had reached the crest line now. I halted my troops and started observing the area around. I directed my troops to build sangars all around since that was the only protection from enemy fire and shelling. Subedar Darwan Singh, with his moustaches twirled up, did a fantastic job of getting the weary troops to get into action immediately.

At a location approx 40 yards away, in between the snow fall and early morning haze, we noticed two stone walls (sangar) with a soldier comfortably sleeping in his sleeping bag. Between our position and where this soldier in the sleeping bag was, it was a narrow, razor edge-like crest line and one would have to rope up to negotiate it. For a moment I thought it was one of the soldiers from Dixit's column. So, I yelled at him as to why on earth was he relaxing while he should be taking up defences. The soldier lazily woke up supporting his head with his arm and looked towards us. This was definitely not the kind of reaction I would expect from one of my men. Just then we saw a soldier running from behind the sangar to the left, which was also a bit further away, to the sangar to the right and closer to us. This soldier was wearing khaki trousers, khaki jersey and a khaki balaclava. This is when we realized that they were Pakistani soldiers. Lance Naik Vikram who was by my side whispered in my ear, *"Sahabyeh toh Pakistani hai"* *(Sir, he is a Pakistani)*. This soldier who ran across was observing us from behind the sangar to the right. I directed Vikram to shoot the soldier in the sleeping bag and I shot at the soldier who ran across and was observing us. I fired a single shot and dropped the enemy soldier observing us from behind the wall; his body slumped and fell between the two sangars. Vikram also shot the enemy soldier in the sleeping bag. I was glad that we had zeroed our weapons before our operations as our weapons were firing with good accuracy. I then observed the dead bodies with a binocular and confirmed that they both were dead. Thereafter, all hell broke loose. We were under intense fire of artillery, mortars, small arms and RPG. By then we had taken up position in a sangar prepared by the enemy, now occupied by us.

We were now on the peak of "Area Conical". The peak was a huge rock (approx 10 ft high); one side of it (West) faced the location where the two enemy soldiers were shot by us and the other side (East) dipped down towards the saddle and then went up to join "Area Ring Contour". The LoC passed through the line joining the peaks of Area Ring Contour and Area Conical. Beyond the line joining these two peaks, towards the North was PoK and was a valley which we could observe into for a few kilometres. The spur from where my columns climbed up joining the crest line (LoC) or the peak formed a "T" with the crest line forming the horizontal of the "T" and the spur forming the vertical. Towards the West of the spur that led us to the peak of Area Conical is a steep cliff-like rock face that had a drop of approx 700 ft and to the East of this spur was the bowl. There was a sangar built by the enemy to the East and West of the rock on the peak. To move from West to East of the rock, one had to either climb up the rock to get to the other side or go around it which was dangerous, because a slip or misjudgement could mean a fall of 700 ft. The enemy could approach us only from the East as the approach from the bowl was a gradual slope. From the West the approach was difficult owing to the rock face and the narrow crest line.

As the daylight broke out in its full bloom, the snowfall stopped too. Now we could see the location beyond into the PoK area clearly. We realized that just behind the crest line was a huge camp of the enemy, tucked into the side of the mountain.

In between the firing I tried getting in touch with Dixit on the radio set and we realized that his column had hit a false peak on the craggy spur during the climb in the night and mistook it for the peak. With daylight breaking out, they realized that they were still way below on the spur but now could not move up as there was far too much of firing going on, on the peak and surrounding areas. Any attempt to move up to the peak would expose them and would invite unnecessary casualties.

On the neighbouring peak, the explosion heard in the night was when Maj Jaggi had stepped on a land mine. It was his screams in pain that we had heard while climbing up to our objective. Some soldiers from his company while trying to retrieve him from the area also blew up their feet in land mines.

The firing was intense, and it continued unabated for the next few hours. We had to scream to communicate even with the soldier next to us. We were being fired at from three different directions, from enemy locations to the West along the crest line, from "Area Ring Contour" to the East and from an enemy position further deeper into their area. There would be times when we would carry out intense firing and the other times when we would be pinned down. Mortar, RPG and artillery bombs were falling all around us, coupled with small arms fire.

At approximately 10.00 am, someone screamed that Naik Hemcharan has been hit. Hemcharan was a strong soldier and insisted on carrying the MMG all by himself. A mortar bomb had exploded in front of him and a large chunk of shrapnel had hit him on the face. His face had caved in and his eyeballs and brains had spilled out. Surprisingly his body kept quivering for a long time even after such a grievous injury. Lance Naik Sunil, who was in a neighbourings angar, rushed to give first aid to Naik Hemcharan but was shot several times and he tumbled and fell down the 700 ft cliff. Just then someone yelled that Naresh had been hit. Lance Naik Naresh was manning the LMG and sustained a gunshot through his chin. At approximately 10.30 am, someone from the other side of the rock shouted that there was a counter-attack being launched by the enemy. I was then on the other side of the rock on the peak; I screamed and asked as to how many of the enemy they could see. The reply I got was that there were too many to count. I took a quick stock of the ammunition left with us and realized that we were grossly low on ammunition and the required strength to fight the counter-attacking Pakistanis. I started screaming orders for everyone to conserve their ammunition and fire single shots. Naik Kaman Singh, who was in a sangar close by, crawled upto me and said, "Sir, don't you worry, I am carrying 500 rounds of ammunition extra in my pack". Naik Yudhbir who was next to me then noticed the worried look on my face and asked what the matter was. I told him that there is a counter-attack coming up by the enemy and someone has to man the LMG. Before I could say anything more, he jumped on the rock in front of us and climbed on the rock on the peak to move to the other side where the LMG was, all this while the enemy firing at us from just 40 odd yards away. While he was getting down towards the other side, he got hit in his left arm. He still somehow managed to reach the location of Naresh, pushed him aside and fired the LMG with one hand. The enemy was moving up fast and had reached close.

Meanwhile, I decided to call for artillery fire. The FOO was in the sangar next to me. He was terribly sick and shivering and kept repeating, "Sir, we all are going to die." I tried to snap him out of the thought, but he would not. I remembered then that all of us had decided that we should carry two bullets tied separately in our handkerchief, so that in our exuberance if we ran out of ammunition and a situation comes where we are outnumbered or about to be taken prisoners, we should not give ourselves up alive. All of us had heard how the Indian soldiers taken prisoners were tortured by the Pakis and some of us had also seen the tortured dead bodies. I then took the radio set of the FOO and spoke to Maj Gurpreet Madhok who was performing the duty of Battery Commander Observation Post located 2 km away at Muntho Dhalo; I gave him the instructions, "reference centre of the saddle as you see it, left 100 meters, get me whatever you can and get it soon". Gurpreet was surprised that we were asking for artillery fire from medium calibreguns firing at a near extreme range, at such an altitude, so close to our own location and advised me that it was not safe. But we had no choice. The Bofors guns fired really well that day. Every time I would get the count for the bombs to fall on target from Gurpreet, I would yell at my men to duck behind rocks. We followed this drill and the enemy was caught totally in the open. I also shouted orders for my men to change their location and fire so that our actual location was not pinpointed, and the strength would seem more than what it actually was. I kept yelling out our war cry "Har Har Mahadev, Shatrujeet Ki Jai", to get the sagging spirits up. We somehow managed to beat back the counter-attack and there were dead bodies of the enemy lying everywhere below us. Luckily, none of my men were grievously hurt in this episode.

The intense firing continued even after we beat back the counter-attack. From one enemy position to our West, we were drawing immense amount of RPG fire. We could not pinpoint where exactly was the RPG being fired from but had a general idea. So, I decided to fire a few rockets in the "Air Burst" mode in the general direction using the Carl Gustav Rocket Launcher we were carrying along. I prepared two rounds and asked Paratrooper Prakash Aswal to help me load the launcher. To fire the Rocket Launcher, I had to come out of the sangar, above the crest and expose myself for a few seconds. Just as I picked up the launcher on my shoulder, Naik Namdeo Dagdu Pawar caught me by the collar and pulled me into his sangar and with a lot of anger asked me as to why was I indulging in this stupidity? I asked him what he meant by behaving this way. And he replied that as long as I was alive, the troops will have their will to fight and that there was no need to expose myself to danger that way. Just then, a few more RPG rounds exploded behind me. Namdeo noticed the blood flowing from behind my head and informed me that I had been hit. In all that adrenalin rush and frenzy, I somehow did not realize when I was hit. It was only when the warm blood started flowing down to my neck, did I realize that I had actually been hit. I had sustained multiple splinter injuries in my head and neck. Namdeo along with a few other soldiers helped in stopping the blood flow by using "First Field Dressing". After a while, I informed my Commanding Officer of the situation and also informed him about my injury; he passed orders for me to de-induct immediately. I informed him that I could not do so since the enemy is likely to counter-attack again. All the effort and the life lost would be in vain if I did not hold on. Moreover, there was a requirement of an officer in the location to control the situation. He was terribly upset with me for not listening to him then, but later was glad that I remained stubborn in that situation.

By approximately 8.00 pm, Dixit's column fetched up to my location and I ordered all of them to build sangars at various places and take up defences. We re-distributed the ammunition amongst us, and I started de-inducting the wounded in buddy pairs passing instructions to each one of them to walk over boulders to avoid the land mines. There was further a counter-attack by the enemy which was successfully averted.

At approx 2030–2045 hrs, the enemy launched a counter-attack once again. But now we were present there in good strength and with adequate ammunition and support weapons. The artillery guns were also ranged to the exact location from where the enemy was assembling and climbing up. We managed to beat back the second counter-attack successfully too.

On 22 July 1999, Maj Sameer Anukul was tasked to move up to my location and relieve me. We waited for him to reach our location till about 3.30 am. He was still on his way. The Commanding Officer once again came on the radio set and informed me that Maj Sameer Anukul would be reaching my location in another 30 min or so and that I should de-induct immediately now.

Naik Yudhbir Singh, who was earlier hurt, had also refused to de-induct when the rest of the injured were de-inducting and insisted that he would de-induct with me. When I insisted that he should de-induct, he replied that I am also hurt and also in pain, and if I could hold on, then so could he. Now that I was de-inducting, we both supported each other and slowly managed to reach the valley below. We both were so thirsty that we drank water from a murky puddle in the valley. We were extremely tired and exhausted but somehow managed to reach our base at Muntho Dhalo. At the base I saw Maj Jaggi with his feet blown. I hugged him for a while and then passed out from all the exhaustion and loss of blood. When I came back to my senses, I was informed by the doctor that I have to be urgently evacuated for immediate treatment of my splinter injuries. So, I walked up to the makeshift helipad made at Muntho Dhalo.

We were waiting at the helipad for the Commander to arrive in a helicopter. At the helipad I saw a Pakistani soldier taken prisoner, waiting too. Soon after, the commander arrived. He met me and congratulated me for the capture of "Area Conical" and then informed my Commanding Officer that as per plan, the Pakistani was to move down with him on his way back, but now the Pakistani can wait and Carie will be evacuated on priority.

As soon as the helicopter returned, I got into it. I was not wearing any rank at that time and the dangree (overall) I was wearing was in tatters and torn at several places as I was wearing it for the last month or so. I was shabby and had a beard growing too. The pilots presumed I was the Pakistani prisoner since they were not aware of the switch of passengers as per the directions of the Commander. The moment I got into the helicopter, the pilots turned around, and over the rotor noise, started yelling the choicest of expletives at me. I was still weary and weak with bandages tied around my head. I waved at them to keep quiet, trying to tell them they had misunderstood, but they would not understand. Meanwhile, the Commander arrived, everyone saluted, and we took off. On landing at the helipad in the base, the Commander showed me the thumbs-up sign and went off on his way. A team from my unit was waiting there at the helipad; they were informed on the wireless set to be there to receive me and escort me to the medical centre. They were all emotionally charged up and the moment I got off the helicopter, I was being pulled from side to side as everyone wanted to know all the details of our operations and the casualties we had suffered. The pilots probably thought that the Pakistani prisoner was being mauled up by the Indian troops. One of the pilots opened the door of the helicopter and yelled over the rotor noise, "*saale ki acchi tarah se band bajana.*" *(thrash the hell out of him).*

In the battle for these two peaks, we witnessed the determination, bravery and grit of some of the finest men in the most hostile terrain. By the morning of 22 July 1999, Area Conical and Area Ring Contour were back as part of the Indian Territory and we had the tricolour flying on these two peaks once again.

Random Musings and Reminiscences of My Tryst With Kargil: Operation Vijay and Beyond

Colonel Vivek Murthy

It was the summer of 1999. The spring term was nearing its end at the National Defence Academy. I was in the fifth term and "End of Term" season was round the corner. The Academy was busy with exams. There was infact an uneasy calm before the proverbial storm when events exploded in one's face without any warning. Only in this case, it did not pertain to the academy alone. The destiny of the Indian Nation was intertwined with what had been happening inside the hallowed portals of my alma mater.

Cadets Perception

By mid-May, the news of an ill-fated missing platoon led by Lt Saurabh Kalia and detection of large-scale intrusions in the Kargil sector came about. Our instructors spoke in hushed tones. Few of the tough ones who were certified as "even their mothers cannot love them", due to their hostility to everything in life in general and cadets in particular, started behaving erratic. Instead of the usual banter and expletives with which they would relate to us as a matter of fact, they spoke philosophy in riddles and parables. We would later come to know that many of them – fighter pilots, Infantry and Artillery officers – had volunteered to "rejoin their units which were mobilizing and were on standby". There were whispers in the corridors about "war clouds looming". Except for the Navy guys, the excitement was palpable.

The month was nearing its end. In the frontiers, tempo was building up. The news and reports which emerged were not encouraging. The

Indian Air Force had by now lost two MiG-21 and MiG-27 fighters and a Mi-17 in just two days of commencement of air war. Flt Lt Nachiketa was now a Prisoner of War (PoW). Large-scale shelling by Pakistanis on NH1 and mounting casualties were in the national news.

Notwithstanding the above, the Passing out Parade (PoP) was on schedule and it was raining profusely. It definitely was not a good omen at Khadakwasla either. As per the academy myth, only three times it had rained before or during the PoP, 1962, 1965 and 1971 wars. It is a well known fact that a few newly commissioned officers from theses batches were martyred in these wars.

The term break commenced by the first week of June. I was in the comforts of my home keenly following the news bulletins. In that sense, Kargil became the first truly televised war in India. My family was no exception. The entire family gathered around the television sets to hear the updates of the ongoing war from famed war correspondents like Burkha Dutt, Vikram Chandra, Deepak Chaurasia and the ilk.

A Ring Side View of the War

One of the most vivid images of the war that left an indelible imprint on the national psychology during this period was that of the young Captain Jayashree saluting the mortal remains of her martyred husband Major Vivek Gupta, the hero of the first major victory achieved by the Indian forces at Kargil. Nothing could have personified better, the mood of the nation, at this hour than the pride and the pain of this young woman in uniform. At my home, and many more in the country, there was not one eye which did not shed a tear. The country was awakened. The mood was belligerent. For the first time in India, the general public directly confronted the biting realities of what constituted a modern war. Feeling for real, what was happening in Kargil changed the perceptions regarding the conflict zone, the indefatigable spirit of the Indian soldier and the resilience of the Indian Nation.

Capt Jayashree saluting the mortal remains of her husband, Major Vivek Gupta, who was martyred in the Army operations in the Kargil sector.

Only a few days ago, Major Vivek Gupta was having the time of his life in Dras. He said as much in a letter of June 8 to his father, Lt-Colonel (retd) B.R.S. Gupta. "You should feel proud of me ... I am contributing something for the nation in this uniform I have worn ... being a company commander at this time is the greatest experience one can have." Ironically, the elder Gupta was to receive the letter in his Dehradun house only at noon on June 17. By then the Army band had played out Dead Body Slow March. And his son's last rites had been completed, just half an hour before.

From the village schools where the children were carefully copying *"Kargil hamara hai"* and *"Jai Jawan"* on their slates, to the faceless widows of Vrindavan fasting for their unknown foster sons on the frontiers, the young girls in a college at Tiruchirapalli lining up to volunteer as suicide bombers, and the aging women and men pledging to donate one of their eyes and kidneys to the injured Jawans, the conflict had forced a rediscovery of India. The jawans fighting against insurmountable odds in the most inhospitable terrain and altitudes brought about a heavy emotional bonding. The national feeling and spirit, which had been partly lost in the sea of messy politics of Mandal–Mandir era of cynicism, disillusion and disgust, suddenly resurfaced. We were back in the Academy in the beginning of July. The pictures and letters from our seniors who had passed out only a few years back, some of whom we had so closely known in "flesh and blood", lined the notice boards of the central lobbies. Some of them turned out to be their last letters home.

One such letter was that of Capt Manoj Kumar Pandey, PVC (P), which read,

I have myself brushed boulders with death four times... I really don't know what would happen at the next moment but till now I can assure you and all countryman that certainly we would push back intruders at whatever we have to pay may be our life. . . . This Operation has certainly given some exposure which cannot be quantified. Like leading me on face of death, their fears, their loyalty and the stress and strain both physical and mental which human being can take but yaar Indian Army specially an Infantry Jawan is ultimate. He would do anything provided led properly. As I have always told you that what Infantry gives you cannot be told, but today I am so proud of my decision of "Infantry" that I can't explain.

Another young martyr Captain Vijayant Thapar's last letter home read,

By the time you get this letter I'll be observing you all from the sky enjoying the hospitality of the Apsaras. I have no regrets, in fact if I become a human again, I'll join the Army and fight for my Nation. If you can, please come and see where the Indian Army fought for you tomorrow.

At Point 5140, Captain Vikram Batra, a young officer who was to make the supreme sacrifice in a subsequent action, had proverbially radioed *"Yeh dil maange more"* (the heart wants more) and his interview with the journalist Burkha Dutt became the toast of the nation.

Capt Vikram Batra with his team

Meanwhile, at the academy there were rumours doing rounds of our training getting truncated and we heading to the units at the frontiers without the mandatory arm-specific training at Indian Military Academy, Dehradun, in case the war was going to be prolonged. It was not to be. On 08 July 1999, when the victorious soldiers of 18 Grenadiers hoisted the National Flag on Tiger Hill, the highest feature and the most formidable objective of the war, it became evident that the conflict was nearing its end. It came to an end on 26 July 1999 with the Indian Army announcing the complete eviction of all Pakistani intruders.

A Step Towards my Destiny

I eventually passed out from National Defence Academy in December 1999. But Kargil continued to shape my destiny. Our basic training at Indian Military Academy was cut short by 6 months. Inspired by the sound of Bofors guns thundering through the skies of Kargil, I opted for the "Regiment of Artillery", as my first choice of arm, and providence got me commissioned in a Bofors regiment. Most of us had to head straight to the Valley.

The immediate aftermath of Kargil was gruesome and chaotic. By the time I joined my *paltan* at Uri, at least a few of my immediate seniors who passed out barely months prior were no more. The young lives were extinguished by the bloodletting actions of the enemy Border Action Team (BAT) along with some of their own raids on both sides of the Line of Control (LoC). Raids, counter-raids, ambushes and artillery duels had become the order of the day. Hardly a week passed without our firing across the LoC.

As a young artillery subaltern without having done the basic mandatory young officers course, I was confined to the four walls of the unit in an intensely fuming counter-insurgency environment. As and when the guns opened up, I was asked by the adjutant to be at battery command post to learn the nuances of command post staff work and fire control. In this restricted space, without any technical knowledge to be of any assistance, I was more of a liability than of some help. Bored as hell, I ended up as part of a gun crew wherein I would carry ammunition from ammunition pits or shift them from one gun to the other and/or prepare the ammunition. During a particularly prolonged firing through day and night, I spent the better part of the time with the crew and in turn, became an inextricable part of their retinue and routine. After the firing ceased, the senior JCO, who was to hang up his uniform for good in a few days' time, walked up to me and blessed me. He said, *"Beta, in my more than 30 summers in this army, I have seen many officers come and go. I have been watching over you last two days and you are unique. Mark my words – you are destined to command this unit and much more. Do not get carried away by the trappings of your rank any time. Be the same "you". No force in the world can or will stop you"*. Twenty years on, here I am, writing this article from a remote frontier in a far corner of the country, as the commanding officer of the same unit. Yes, when I count my blessings, I count Subedar Angrez Singh's twice.

Soon after the young officer's course, I was launched as an acclimatised Commando Observation Post (OP) and served with seven Infantry battalions as an Artillery OP officer for a continuous 18 months. The privation, pain, hunger and death, which I experienced all along, would proverbially baptise me under fire. It forced me to question the very meaning of life, death and existence. This combined with reading all those famous war novels and military history literature (only pass time in those pre-social media days) changed me forever. I emerged as a different human being, fully conscious of what the "gift of normal life" meant. The simple pleasures of having three meals a day, wearing fresh clothes, sleeping on a hard bed, having the opportunity to even wash and bathe every day and, last but not the least, not seeing a dead body of a "dear and near" comrade every second month assumed a totally new meaning. However, the wounds continued to fester on the borders and the trend continued till the end of Operation Parakram in June 2003. For me, Operation Vijay ended with the culmination of Operation Parakram.

It was during one of these OP tenures that I had come across a tall, smart Brigadier from artillery, commanding an Infantry brigade doing rounds. Though I felt a ready connect and urge to meet him, I did not muster the courage to do so, as I feared being labelled a "Keen Kumar" by my colleagues and seniors. Destiny had other designs and in dramatic circumstances two years later, I met him at my unit mess at Ambala, where my unit was then located. He had come to donate his yearly honorarium from a gallantry award, to his village school. After coming to know that I served in the same brigade Area of Responsibility (AoR) as him, we discussed in detail the past happenings from our own different perspectives. He asked me after the drinks, if I would become his ADC when he takes over the command of a division at Kargil shortly. My date with Kargil continued.

Living my Destiny

In December 2004, I continued to embark on this inspiring journey. Since winter was peaking and routes were closed, the General, an illustrious aviator himself, visited the posts in the choppers. While the operations branch briefed him on the operational details, my task was to study the history of the posts and battles fought over the icy heights in all the wars since 1947 and about the protagonist heroes involved, and brief him on the same. We also carried gifts, magazines, letters from home, and some cooked food for the post commander, from the divisional mess. Initially, I accompanied him on the rides. But I had this terrible problem of going off to sleep once the chopper took off. No amount of prodding from the General on the landscape did any good to me. Yet, the show went on till one day, when not only did I sleep, but fell on him twice. He politely told me that from the next time onwards I could accompany him only during ground visits.

With the advent of summer of 2005, the time to visit the "Batra" post came about. We were not acclimatised and time was limited. Moreover, we had to fall back on the same day. Therefore, the battalion in question had arranged for ponies to take us to the posts. Given the time constraints, the General, an extremely fit soldier, alongwith the brigade commander and the battalion commander, climbed the mount. The fourth pony was meant for me, and I refused. No amount of threat and convincing could make me do so. Finally, I mustered the courage and told them that "the day lieutenants and captains of Indian Army started moving about in ponies and horses on these heights; it would not augur well for the army and country as such". There was a dumb silence. I walked the entire stretch of nine hours "to and from" the post, mostly ahead of the ponies. Though the general would not speak to me till we reached back Kargil, he offered me a drink in the evening and said "Boy, you make me proud". Only conversation we had had the entire day.

In one of these visits, the general was annoyed by the elaborate food arrangements. He would tell me that from the next time, we would carry our own lunch. Fresh from my tenures two years prior, I would tell him that it was only during these visits that the battalions paid real heed to the maintenance of these posts including OP parties like mine from outside resources, and that the *Bara Khana* would have been the first decent "full and fresh" food the rank and file would have had in months wherein battalions make the extra effort of buying fresh from own funds instead of the normal tinned stuff. He as usual liked the innocent counter-narratives and prodded me for more.

The General had also undertaken a huge plantation drive for strategic greening of Kargil in those stretches under direct observation from the enemy posts. My flirting with a budding actress from Mumbai and friendship with her father who was a member of Bombay Natural History Society would eventually give a lead to the formation receiving "National Green Award" from the Prime Minister in November 2005.

Kargil Remains Special

By December 2005, leaving the General in the Kargil heights, I headed to Indian Military Academy, Dehradun, as a platoon commander. Fresh from the pilgrimage to Kargil, having felt for myself both through books and visit to these places of worship, where my "Gods" – Vivek Gupta, Vikram Batra, Saurabh Kalia, Manoj Kumar Pandey and the ilk – had written the story of their lives in blood and ultimately found their final resting place, I had several stories to tell. In those typical mid-night sessions meant to toughen up the cadets where they would be physically stretched to their limits by the young platoon commanders, I would call them to the ante room and read them the letters of my heroes and tell them the stories as I perceived them. At the end of term, I would give them the famous "Forever in Operation Division's –Vijay Diwas" presentation, with my own perspective. The gentlemen cadets are emotionless beings as a matter of fact and principle. But my foray started taking its toll, and by the end of the second year, barely a few days before passing out, one of them would cite human rights abuse and violation of Geneva Convention. He said, "Captain Moorthy, why don't you be like others ... take these physical strengthening sessions for an hour or two and move on. In which case, we get our hard scale rationed quota of whatever is left of the night for ourselves. On the other hand, even after you leave, your stories haunt my thoughts and do not give me the privilege of even those minimal hours of sleep". Deeply concerned by the emotional well-being and safety of my cadets, my experiments with Kargil at the intellectual level thus came to an abrupt end.

I moved on to even better pastures. My unit in turn completed two field tenures back to back at Dras during the period of 2008-2016. Four of our comrades from the unit made the supreme sacrifice during this period in the line of duty. I write this story from the room aptly titled "Dras" as a commanding officer of a Bofors regiment.

Even as I conclude my musings spanning a period starting from my days as a "cadet with sparkle in his eyes, fire in the belly and passion in the heart" to the present day as the commanding officer of a unit "wherein the world remains an oyster to be opened with my sheath", there are three things I would have thought should have changed in these 20 years for better. I will confine my thoughts to three arms that played the most decisive role during Operation Vijay.

- **Infantry.** Without doubt, Infantry is the "bread and butter" arm of the Indian Army and the Infantry men proved it once again that they will remain the final arbiter of the battle in both conventional and sub-conventional contexts. Given its pre-eminence in the battle field, the modernisation of its weaponry and provisioning of better personal kitting to its rank and file is a non-negotiable obligation. Though a good beginning has been made in the last two years by the current leadership, it need not have waited twenty years after the war, for real changes to unfold. The latest procurement of 73,000 assault rifles from the United States is a bold and welcome step in this direction.

- **Artillery.** Being a land-based continental army, all things being equal, artillery will continue to remain the arm of decision in our regional conflicts as demonstrated during Kargil War. The procurement of 100 pieces of K-9 Vajra SP guns and 145 BAE Systems M777 Ultra-Light Howitzers are positive developments. However, the large-scale modernisation and mediumisation of **Field Artillery** needs to be fast tracked to stay more relevant to the ensuing operational and tactical framework. Notwith-standing the above, one acknowledges the fact that significant progress related to rocket artillery (Smerch and Pinaka), missiles (Prithvi, Agni and BrahMos) and surveillance equipment (UAVs and Weapon Locating Radar) has been made.

- **Indian Air Force.** While the IAF has acquitted itself with enormous glory in Kargil operations in the wider canvas and perspective, one story which has not changed from May 1999 to May 2019, for me, is that of our pilots becoming captive in enemy territory in the first or second day of contact. In this regard, I would like to draw a parallel between Kargil and Balakot. While the content and context of both these events are very different, I cannot help but ask myself and the wider audience of my country the following questions:

  (a) The ethics of pitting MiG-21s and MiG-27 against F-16s armed with AMRAAM beyond visual range air-to-air missile and/or current state of the Army Air Defence structures – How many Prisoners of War, technical snags are required before we replace the 10 squadrons of MiG-21 and MiG-27s with more contemporary platforms?

  (b) How long the fighter pilot, for all his bravery, resilience and unmatched courage under fire, would continue to be sent into combat with, at best, mediocre and increasingly obsolescent equipment?

- **HR Management**. While the civil–military divide is often fiercely debated, it is time we equally introspect on the state of affairs within the organisation on the growing combat arm–support arm–services divide. Nothing can illustrate better the meritocracy and equality in the calibre of the officer cadre than Op Vijay, where they answered the call of duty no matter which lanyard they wore at the moment of final reckoning. If we analyse the gallantry awards and supreme sacrifice made by the officer cadre, I think we will get the answer. Every Manoj Kumar Pandey and Vikram Batra was matched in motivation and leadership by a Padmapani Acharya, Anuj Nayyar or Vijayant Thapar. It was an integrated battle, fought as a homogeneous team – be it the infantry, artillery, Special Forces (SF), engineers, signals, army aviation, air defence and logistic elements, supported by the Air Force. In my personal view, often cited arguments on civil–military divide, "for and against", are equally applicable to the Indian Army. It is time we restore the equilibrium in the inter-arm and inter-service equations into more mature constructs where "justice and fair play" instead of "lanyards and tribal loyalties to own arm and service" forms the "bed rock and heartbeat" of organisational culture.

Conclusion

I would like to end this discourse on a positive note. They say, a nation without heroes, is a nation without a future. There were enough heroes, during this war, to inspire an entire generation. It reinforced our faith in all that is "bright and beautiful", "wise and wonderful" and more meaningfully, the "strength and sacrifice" innate to the illustrious young sons of India in redeeming her honour in their life and death. In these 20 years, I personally, and this country as such, have come a long way. For a soldier, there is no worse travesty than the "tyranny of complacency", be it war or peace. That we never will. I, therefore, conclude in my capacity as a commanding officer of a frontline combat unit and representative of a wider collective emotion, by pledging "Kargil will never fall again". You have our "our last bullet and last breath" as the guarantee.

VICTORY MOMENTS

PART IV
MOTIVATION

स्वधर्मे निधनं श्रेय

IT IS GLORY TO DIE DOING ONE'S DUTY

– Bhagawad Gita

Lest We Forget

Major Saurav Pandey

The Revelation

It was a lazy winter afternoon of December 2016, when the Head Clerk announced to the Adjutant that the battalion was next moving to Moscow. Flabbergasted and awestruck, the Adjutant re-checked the signal the SD branch only to find out that the actual location read: 'Mashkoh, Dras'. The unit was going to be a part 8 Mountain Division, famously known as "Victors of Operation VIJAY", as also 'Forever in Operations'. The tenure seemed to be rewarding especially because the GOC 8 Mountain Division during Operation VIJAY was Major General Mohinder Puri, who was an ex-Commanding Officer of our battalion. By evening, almost everyone came to know about the unit's next move. Boys sometimes, even though mockingly, still fantasized that the unit was being exposed to a foreign assignment in Moscow, Russia.

Within a few days, we all realized that it would be a challenging tenure in terms of our physical capacity, mental aptitude and emotional ability. While on one hand we all were excited that this would be a professionally satiating and enriching tenure, on the other hand, the memories of Operation VIJAY were so strongly etched in the Hippocampus *(part of brain responsible for storage of long-term memories)* of our well-wishers that they still believed that Dras was a disturbed sector. Apart from this, the fact that Dras was the second coldest inhabited place on earth, only accentuated their worries. Their anxiety was evident in almost every interaction including *Bara Khanas*, as well as informal interactions with their families (even Mandir Parades). It was only after "*CO Saab*" declared in the farewell (*Bara Khana*, hosted for the advance party, that their anxiety was alleviated altogether. He announced, "*Main Vaada Karta Hun Ki Battalion Ke Sabhi Logon Ko Surakshit Wapas Launga*" (I promise to bring back each individual of the Battalion safely). Thus, the advance party left on June 2017 for their mission.

The Journey

I was still enjoying the salubrious climes of Wellington when the unit moved to the new location. Thereafter, I was constantly in touch with the officers and my company-mates, trying to gain maximum information about the inhospitable terrain, inclement weather and the tough operational commitment, which was reasonably expected of me as it was my first Super High Altitude tenure (as the boys called it). Towards the fag end of the Staff Course, I began preparing myself both physically and mentally, for the next assignment by initially indulging in strenuous physical activities, later developing a habit of drinking a lot of water (one of the best survival techniques at High Altitudes), and subsequently reducing oil, salt and sugar content in my food. After all, I had to prove myself to my boys, one more time.

When I finally reached the battalion in June 2018, it felt as if I was back home. From my guest room in Dras, one could get a close glimpse of the mighty and renowned "Tololing" peak. Every morning as the bright sunlight touched the peak, I used to get goose bumps even if I was relaxing in my room. There seemed to be something more than just its name – I guess a mystical charm about that place had already overwhelmed me. Later that day, I was informed by the Commanding Officer that I had been slated for a winter deployment at a forward post. It was going to be a real test of one's worth and character as the post remained practically cut-off from the rest of the world for at least seven months during winters. Days passed quickly and finally the day of my induction to the post had arrived. After an arduous eight-hour-long journey amidst light snowfall and fast-blowing chilly winds, and religiously following my battalion's tradition of personally carrying one's own baggage and other belongings, I finally reached my post, dead tired. My post was located strategically and perilously close to an enemy post, barely 150 m, having nearly an eyeball-to-eyeball contact. Identification of Friend or Foe (IFF) had never been easier than this.

The Realisation

I can never forget the morning of 26 February 2019 when I got a call from my Commanding Officer letting me know about the "Balakot Air Strike" by the Indian Air Force. It seemed to me like a classic example of how things build up, in the Opening Narrative of Sand Model exercises in Junior Command Wing. I comprehended in my mind, "Incident in Pulwama", "CCS Meeting", "Air Force crosses over". I asked myself as to what could be next – possibly a WAR?

The days following the incident were painfully tough. To avoid any casualty, we were instructed to strictly restrict ourselves to our bunkers and be on a watch 24×7. More so, the proximity of the enemy post posed an additional risk. The temperature in the night was dipping below –35°C. Food, rest and even morning ablutions were restricted to bunkers and concrete structures. Living shelters were "out of bound". Even though adequate heating arrangements were made for making us comfortable during those freezing nights, it seemed that even the flame inside the Kerosene Heater had subdued and turned into yellow sleet (or may be, that was what we felt).

I had just finished my rotation of sentry duty and as I sat down on a chair, my body and mind slipped into a deep slumber. Suddenly memoirs of books, journals and war diaries of Operation VIJAY started flashing through my mind. Of all the wars fought by India, the Kargil War had caught the attention of the nation, second to none, as it was under constant media coverage, beaming the "ground zero" report directly to our "drawing rooms" (of course it did have its impact on the security of the ongoing operations). Tiger Hill, Tololing and Khalubar had become household names for the citizens of India.

I started probing myself as to how could someone endure such a cold climate and yet assault near-vertical cliffs in such a rarefied atmosphere, where even intake of a complete breath is a luxury. It was also a known fact that during the initial stages of war, the Army fought with scarce winter clothing, without adequate information about the enemy, and with truncated periods of acclimatization. Even these voids could not prevent the Army from achieving an objective each time it was given one, even if it came with a price. It would have been a difficult war to win had it not been the raw courage and the indomitable will of the Indian soldier.

What else than *"Naam, Namak aur Nishan"* would have forced Grenadier Yogender Singh Yadav to have an overwhelming desire of being alive and assisting his battalion capture Tiger Hill (by providing valuable input about the layout of the enemy camp), even after being wounded. He chose not to die for his country but make the enemy die for his. What made *"Luv"*, famously known Captain Vikram Batra say to his Commanding Officer, *"Yeh Dil Mange More"*, even though he had captured Point 5140, the most formidable feature in the Dras sub-sector? He could have comfortably settled for the recently achieved success. In all probabilities, he would have been recommended for a gallantry award for that conspicuous act too. Why did he risk his precious life while trying to rescue a young soldier who had been badly hit by bullets during capture of yet another objective? After all, each one of us in combat knows that casualties in operations are no exceptions.

Captain Manoj Kumar Pandey was a pure vegetarian and a teetotaler. On the occasion of his first Dusshera celebrations in the unit, as part of Gorkha traditions, he was challenged to prove his worth by cutting off the head of the sacrificial goat in one blow. Later he had washed his hands a multiple times to rinse away the guilt of his first kill. What could have possibly motivated such a noble soul to rise from the safety of a bunker, walk through the deadly enemy fire and slit the enemies' neck off, cutting swiftly through their skin, ripping through veins and sinewy muscles in one powerful strike? How could Riflemen Sanjay Kumar who had not slept for more than 30 hours, had been ascending a feature for the last 18 hours sitting just few feet below the enemies' Machine Gun Post, be so innovative in his thought (even in these testing times) that he generates a novel idea of wrapping both his hands with a medical bandage and then pulling out the enemy's Machine Gun by its hot and nearly molten barrel? I am quite sure that none of them had faced a similar situation in their training and even their military career. What made them act like superhumans especially when the "chips were down", with almost all factors working against them?

I think trying to find any pertinent answer to any of these questions is futile. Undoubtedly, the ethos of the Army instil, the *Jazba, Josh and Junoon* for undertaking any task under the sun. When someone crosses that threshold of physical and mental agony usually associated with humans, all other influences seem to be feebly insignificant, and what emerges strong is the will to achieve the "AIM", anyhow and anywhere. As I was just about sinking this newly discovered fact deep into my cerebral tissues, I felt a warm hand on my shoulder and faintly heard a hoarse voice seeming to be familiar to that of my Company Havaldar Major. As I opened my eyes, I saw him holding a cup of hot tea for me with a message, "*Saab aapki sentry duty ka dobara time ho gaya hai*" (Sir, it's time for your sentry duty again). I was now standing at the same sentry post yet again, only this time the weather seemed to be a bit warm, the atmosphere a bit less hostile and "Me" a bit more confident.

Vikram Batra, PVC (P)

Major General Ian Cardozo

The *Param Vir Chakra* is India's highest award for showing gallantry in a battle. Only an act of the most conspicuous bravery, daring, valour or self-sacrifice in the face of the enemy merits this award. Since its institution on 26 January 1950, only 21 have been given this award, and Vikram Batra is one of them.

This is his Story

Vikram Batra was awarded the Param Vir Chakra for his outstanding contribution to the Kargil War of 1999. This war was fought at heights ranging from 15,000 to 19,000 feet in a rarified de-oxygenated atmosphere. Troops had to scale near-perpendicular walls encumbered with heavy loads of arms and ammunition. The glaciated terrain was devoid of cover from the devastating fire from an enemy located at dominating heights. At times, the slopes were so vertical that their access required the use of ropes. The defending Pakistani soldiers were confident that they could beat back any attack by our soldiers; so great was their tactical advantage.

They, however, did not reckon with one factor in the Indian armoury – "Courage"! Courage of the infantryman whose bravery in battle must never be forgotten.

The media responded magnificently by taking front-line battles into every Indian home, thereby boosting the morale of the troops and encouraging them to even greater feats of daring. Media stories highlighted the fact that in no other war had young officers shouldered responsibilities well beyond their years. However, from amongst them all, the one who also captured the imagination of the public was a young officer, Captain Vikram Batra. His bold courage, and the daredevil risks that he took in mission after mission, filled the public with wonder and awe. He seemed to be invincible, but every time he sallied forth to meet new challenges and dangers, people prayed for his safe return. His code name, "Sher Shah", soon became his nickname and even the enemy soldiers came to know of it.

Vikram was commissioned as an officer of the Indian Army on 06 December 1997. On that day, he repeated the Chetwode motto that he would place the safety, honour and welfare of his country above all else, that he would place the safety, honour and welfare of his soldiers next, and that his own safety would be his last priority. It is by this maxim that Vikram Batra lived and behaved in peace and fought and died in war.

As young boys, Vikram and his twin brother Vishal used to watch the Param Vir Chakra televised series. These stories of courage ignited a fire in him that never got quenched. However, not even in their wildest dreams had Vikram, or Vishal, ever dreamt that one day Vikram would win the coveted Param Vir Chakra.

Vikram and his twin Vishal were born in 1974 to Girdhari Lal Batra and Kamal Kanta in the town of Palampur that nestles in the shadow of the Dhauladhar mountains. The boys were nicknamed "Luv" and "Kush". The Sanskrit word 'Vikram' means an abundance of bravery – a name that had a prophetic meaning.

Every night, before going to sleep, Vikram would ask his father to narrate a story. His father, being a patriotic person, would narrate stories of India's great revolutionaries and freedom fighters to the twin brothers. These stories of valour, patriotism and self-sacrifice became strongly imprinted in the hearts and minds of the brothers.

Even while in school, Vikram's attitude and behaviour indicated his bold and fearless nature. One day, while going to school, the door of the school bus flew open and a young girl fell out of the bus. Realising that she could be run over by another bus, Vikram jumped out of the moving bus and pulled the little girl to safety.

In college, Vikram was adjudged as the best NCC air wing cadet in the North Zone and was selected to take part in the Republic Day Parade in Delhi in 1994. On his return, he told his parents that he wanted to join the Army. He prepared hard for the Combined Defence Services Examination and got through in his first attempt.

In July 1996, Vikram joined the Indian Military Academy and was commissioned as an officer of the Indian Army in the 13th Battalion of Jammu and Kashmir Rifles (13 JAKRIF) which at that time was located at Sopore in the Kashmir Valley. After completing its tenure in the Valley, the unit was posted to Shahjahanpur and the advance party left for the new location under the second-in-command.

At that time, the Indian and Pakistani Prime Ministers were negotiating a peace settlement. However, the Pakistani Army was at the same time, secretly pushing its forces across the Line of Control (LoC) and occupying dominating locations along the Kargil hills. By early March 1999, Pakistan had infiltrated troops from the Northern Light Infantry and commandos from their Special Forces Group, and occupied large areas varying from 4 to 12 km across the LoC. Having consolidated their positions, Pakistan effectively dominated the Srinagar–Leh highway. It was a part of their strategy to cut off Ladakh from the rest of Jammu and Kashmir.

The advance party of 13 JAK RIF was recalled from Shahjahanpur and the battalion was ordered to move to Dras on 06 June. On 14 June, the Brigade Commander decided to task 13 JAK RIF for the capture of Point 5140.

Point 5140 was the highest peak and an extension of the Tololing Ridge. It was from here that the Pakistanis had brought down an Indian helicopter, using their Stinger missile. It thus became evident that unless Point 5140 was captured, Indian helicopters could not fly in that area.

Lieutenant Colonel Yogesh Kumar Joshi briefed Captain Vikram Batra and Lieutenant Sanjeev Jamwal for the capture of Point 5140. One Company under Vikram Batra and another Company under Sanjeev Jamwal were to climb for the assault under the cover of darkness. Both these companies were to attack from different directions, and their officers were given a free hand for their plans for attack. The only limitation given was that the feature needed to be captured before the "first light" of the following day. Both officers were asked to give their success signals. Jamwal said that his success signal would be "Oh! Yeah, yeah, yeah"! the slogan of Hunter squadron, which was his squadron at the National Defence Academy. Vikram Batra said that his success signal on the radio would be "Dil Mange More"!

When daylight faded on the evening of 19 June, the companies began their climb towards their objectives. They received artillery support from Bofors guns that attempted to keep the enemy's head down when the companies were approaching their objectives. The objective had two bunkers on the top and five bunkers on the eastern slope. The enemy seemed to be aware of the movement of our troops. The darkness got punctuated with para flares followed by artillery and machine gun fire against both the companies.

Captain Batra decided that he would attack his objective on Point 5140 from the rear, which would be an unexpected direction with a greater chance of success. However, the approach involved a climb that was nearly vertical. By early morning of 20 June, both companies were close to their objectives and the fire of the artillery guns that were supporting them were lifted. As soon as that happened, enemy fire recommenced making further advance impossible. Both the company commanders asked for the covering fire to continue till they were 100 m from their objectives. This was dangerous, as the companies could suffer casualties from their own artillery but the young officers took that risk, and the guns obeyed.

While Batra's company was approaching the top, the enemy commander shouted, "Why have you come here Sher Shah? None of you will return alive"! Vikram replied, "Within one hour, we will see who will remain on top"!

There was no time to lose. They had just one more hour to complete their assault otherwise they would be "daylighted" in the open, and destroyed. Vikram Batra fired three rockets at the enemy bunkers. All three found their mark. Company assaulted the enemy bunkers and shouted "Jai Durga" while they fell upon the enemy. Few enemy soldiers were killed, few fell into a deep gorge while trying to escape, while the rest ran away. Captain Jamwal announced the capture of his objective with his success signal, "Oh! Yeah, yeah, yeah"!

On the other hand, just as the sun was lighting up the mountain tops, Vikram Batra radioed his success with "Dil mange more", and hoisted the Indian Tricolour on the top of Point 5140. A cheer went up from the personnel of the Brigade Headquarter who were following the progress of the battle on the radio. What was exceptionally good was that the companies suffered no casualties. The capture of Point 5140 turned the tide of the battle in the Dras sector. After its capture, helicopters could land at Tololing top, which had by then been captured by 18 Grenadiers.

After the capture of Point 5140, 13 JAK RIF was deinducted from Dras to Ghumri for rest and recuperation. From here, Vikram spoke to his parents on a satellite phone telling them of his success, and that he was well. He was also able to speak to his girlfriend Dimple, who was at Chandigarh.

From Ghumri, Vikram wrote to his parents. He wrote,

Dearest Mom and Dad,

I am fine by the grace of God Almighty. I had come down from the top for a few days of rest and recuperation, but am again moving up today for another offensive action. So, all set to go.

I had undertaken a very big operation also, in which I got 100% success and it was the biggest success in this sector. I had also received congratulatory calls from the Army Chief and other senior commanders from all over. Was also interviewed on line by the media.

Don't know when I will be moving down again. So, whenever I will get a chance, I will call you up. So, please pray for the success of my next operation. ...

On 30 June, the battalion was moved to the Mushkoh valley for the capture of Point 4875. It was a feature of strategic importance that dominated a stretch of the National Highway 1A for 30 to 40 km from Dras to Matayan. Effective fire could be brought on this road by an enemy observation post located on Point 4875 and helicopters could not land on the Dras helipad because it was a registered target.

On 4 March, the Company Commanders, Major Gurpreet Singh and Major Vijay Bhaskar briefed the Groups about their objectives and company commanders began their climb towards their objective the same night. The night was pitch-dark and the gradient was very steep. Covering fire from the Bofors guns commenced in the evening on 04 July; but, when the companies reached about 200 m short of their objective, they came under very heavy fire from the enemy.. The companies responded with their automatic weapons but the enemy fire from Point 4875 was very heavy and the companies were in imminent danger of being "daylighted".

The enemy continued to bring very effective fire on the companies as it was daylight now and there was very little cover except for rocks and boulders. The company commanders spoke to the Commanding Officer, Lieutenant Colonel Joshi, who decided to take control of the situation. He personally fired two Faggot missiles at the enemy bunker from which heavy machine gun fire was emanating. Both were direct hits and the enemy was seen fleeing from the bunker which was holding up the attack.

Major Gurpreet immediately assaulted the position and by afternoon of 05 July 1999 "both the companies linked up on the objective. However, they realised that only a part of Point 4875 had been captured. The enemy position had more bunkers in depth which continued to bring effective fire on the companies. The firefight continued the whole night and by early morning of 06 July, one company reported that it was running out of ammunition; Subsequently, another company, which was in reserve, quickly brought up the required ammunition and the fight continued.

On the night of 06-07 July, close recce of the enemy position revealed that they had occupied a long and narrow ledge with several sangars echeloned one behind the other. Vikram Batra, with his company, was tasked to clear the position. He was ill with fever and wrapped in a blanket, but putting his health aside, he volunteered to lead the attack. His Commanding Officer hesitated to allow him to do that, but seeing the criticality of the situation allowed him to go. A message was passed to the other two companies that "Sher Shah" was on his way up to tackle the enemy position. Suddenly Vikram was possessed with a new energy. His fever vanished and he became a man with a mission.

Vikram spotted the bunker from where the machine gun was holding up the attack. Running from one rock to another, he closed in on the bunker, lobbed a hand grenade into it, and destroyed it. Leading from the front, he ran towards the next bunker, and the next, killing the occupants with his AK-47. At this stage, one of his jawans got wounded and called for help. A JCO volunteered to bring him back but Vikram pushed him aside saying that he was a married man. Instead, he himself decided to do the job. In the process of rescuing the soldier, Vikram was shot in the chest and fell. Enraged at seeing their leader fall, his soldiers charged the position and overran it killing all the occupants, and Point 4875 was captured. All observation of the road and in the air by helicopters, by the enemy, was removed.

Captain Vikram Batra had however passed away. Many young officers and soldiers had contributed to this victory. When Vikram's body was flown to Palampur, a crowd of over 25,000 had gathered to mourn the death of their young hero. **They recalled his prophetic words: "I will either come back after raising the national flag in victory or return wrapped up in it; but I will come back for sure".**

Captain Vikram Batra was just 24 years old when he made the supreme sacrifice for his country. He had continuously led from the front displaying unparalleled courage, commitment and dedication to his task. **His success signal, "Dil mange more" became his signature and his code name "Sher Shah" became known to all, including the enemy**. His image on TV screens caught the attention of the people of India and the "man in the street" mourned his demise. His memory will always live in the minds and hearts of the people of India and the message of his life will continue to motivate present and future generations.

Capt Vikram Batra's Citation

During "Operation Vijay", on 20 June 1999, Captain Vikram Batra, Commander Delta Company, was tasked to attack Point 5140. Captain Batra with his company skirted around the feature from the East and maintaining surprise reached within assaulting distance of the enemy. Captain Batra reorganized his column and motivated his men to physically assault the enemy positions. Leading from the front, he, in a daredevil assault, pounced on the enemy and killed four of them in a hand-to-hand fight. On 07 July 1999, in another operation in the area Point 4875, his company was tasked to clear a narrow feature with sharp cuttings on either side and heavily fortified enemy defences that covered the only approach to it. For speedy operation, Captain Batra assaulted the enemy position along a narrow ridge and engaged the enemy in a fierce hand-to-hand fight, and killed five enemy soldiers at point-

blank range. Despite sustaining grave injuries, he crawled towards the enemy and hurled grenades clearing the position with utter disregard to his personal safety. Leading from the front, he rallied his men and pressed on the attack and achieved a near impossible military task in the face of heavy enemy fire. The officer, however, succumbed to his injuries. Inspired by his daredevil act, his troops fell upon the enemy with vengeance, annihilated them and captured Point 4875.

Captain Vikram Batra, thus, displayed the most conspicuous personal bravery and leadership of the highest order in the face of the enemy and made the supreme sacrifice in the highest traditions of the Indian Army.

Disclaimer: It has not been possible to cover the acts of gallantry of all the PVC and MVC awardees in this book. However, it is proposed to do so in other CLAWS Publications later. This part has been modified from the article covered in CLAWS publication (Scholar Warrior, Spring 2019).

Manoj Pandey, PVC (P)

Major General Raj Mehta

Lt Manoj Pandey, PVC (P), 1/11 GR, challenged death at alpine heights during the Kargil War – and won

When bravehearts are martyred in India, we invariably compensate for the loss by naming residential colonies, roads, airports, auditoriums, tournaments after them. We rarely reflect over the intent that drove them to martyrdom. We do not understand why, when living was an option, they chose to die, fiercely upholding the timeless ethic of *Naam, Namak, Nishan* that has been in the Indian soldiers' DNA since the ancient killing battlefields of *Kurukshetra*.

Lt Manoj Pandey, PVC (P), 1/11 GR, was martyred at Bunkers Area en route to Khalubar Top. This story is about his selfless sacrifice on the night of 02/03 July 1999, his bloodied *Khukri* flashing as he exhorted his charged Gorkhas with *"Na Chhornu!"* as he fell. They did, several of them dying with him but neutralizing the entrenched Pakistanis with bullets, khukris, grenades – and grit.

The story of Manoj's heroism is available on the internet in narrative and video formats. A mainstream Hindi film covers his martyrdom. Nothing could, however, be better than hearing about him first hand from his then Commanding Officer (CO), Col Lalit Rai, VrC.

In June 1999, when the Kargil War had commenced, he was offered a chance to command 1/11 GR by his Colonel of the Regiment.

A crisis was unfolding in the strategic but primitively developed Yaldor Sub-Sector. Ordered to retake Khalubar Top from the infiltrating Pakistani Pathan troops, with non-existent road communications, his immediate task was to lead a 14-hour forced march into war, with all equipment/ammunition carried backpack, with whatever troops he could muster even as his second-in-command marshalled the balance men. This was on 02 July 1999 and this is where young Manoj entered the narrative. A word about him is necessary before the daunting terrain where his bravery – and Lalit's – manifested, becomes our point of focus.

Lt Manoj Pandey was born on 25 June 1975 in Rudha, Sitapur District, UP, to Gopichand and Mohini Pandey. Gopichand was a man of very modest means, but Manoj, the family elder, never put a financial burden on his parents as he blazed through Sainik School and Laxmi Bai Secondary School, both in Lucknow with a brilliant all-round performance in academics, NCC and sports. Asked during his SSB interview on why he wanted to become an officer, his convincing *"To win the PVC"* response got him selected for the NDA. Commissioned into 1/11 GR, a famous Battalion raised in 1918 in Mesopotamia, Manoj served in the Kashmir valley and Siachen before Kargil happened.

In the remote, near inaccessible Batalik sector, the infiltrators had occupied a number of ridges whose recapture was a must as these dominated the Batalik–Leh route. It took some time before the ingress routes to the four roughly parallel ridges were blocked by India. Among all, the most important was the recapturing of the Khalubar Ridge, which also had a Pakistani ammunition dump sited on it. It was the Gorkhas led by Col Rai and, on his vulnerable flank, Manoj, who did it.

Lalit recalls that it was the night of 02 July that he chose to head for Khalubar Top with his team. Directly under observation of the entrenched Northern Light Infantry's (NLI) Pakistani troops (Pathans among them), very effective fire was being brought down on his column from Khalubar Top and flanks, causing severe casualties. To prevent getting daylighted before he reached his objective and getting decimated, he ordered Lt Manoj Pandey to take his 5 Platoon, in order to neutralize **Pehalwan Chowki**, later named as **Bunkers Area**. The CO had by now sustained a bullet wound in his leg and splinter wounds in his calf, but slogged on.

Lt Manoj Pandey, with experience of the successful and gut-wrenching attack on Jubar Top behind him, rushed to carry out his CO's directive. Ordering Havaldar Bhim Bahadur Diwan to encircle the Bunkers Area with his section from the right, Manoj took on the main bunkers from the left with the battle cry *"Jai Mahakali, Aayo Gorkhali"* on his lips. He cleared the first two enemy bunkers with dispatch. While clearing the third, he was hit on his shoulders and legs but continued to lead the assault on the fourth bunker, neutralizing it with a grenade. *"Naa Chhornu"* he commanded his men, but, at that instant, got hit in the forehead by a Machine Gun bullet. The furious Gorkhas captured all six bunkers, killing the enemy and also sustaining serious losses in the brutal close-quarter combat. The brave young officer had led his men from the front. A compulsive diarist, he had lived up to his own handwritten prophecy that he would **"kill death before death overtook him"**. He was just 24 and had fully lived up to the timeless ethic of *Naam, Namak, Nishan.*

As mentioned earlier, Manoj was a compulsive diarist and wrote eloquently about things dear to him. A poem on his Mother states, *"She is the star which shines brightly in the darkness, someone who will always give and bless"*. Poignantly, just under this poem, he had written his

Doodle of Lt Pandey's act created after interaction with Col Lalit Rai, VrC. Made by chief designer, Ravi Ranjan. The doodle can be seen in gallery 8 of the Punjab State War Heroes Memorial and Museum, Amritsar, curated by the author and his 10 researchers, then working under DSW, Govt of Punjab

own epitaph: *"If death strikes before I prove my blood, I promise (swear), I will kill death"*.

Elsewhere in the diary, he had again reflected, *"Some goals are so worthy, it's glorious even to fail"*. Such thoughtful statements from a young man deployed in a war zone with death always lurking around go a long way to show that Manoj was a young man of great substance and courage, both mental and physical – a young man who had adapted to whatever hand destiny would deal out to him. His writings stated that this officer would contest whatever God had in store for him and put infinite value on his life before fate took over. He was a proud Indian and someone who in death has become deathless.

His younger brother Manmohan, on visiting the Dras Kargil Memorial, said,

> I had come here to pray at the place where my brother sacrificed his life in the line of duty. This place is a temple for me. My father and mother have visited the memorial several times and it was my dream to visit the place. I am so glad I have been able to visit it and remember my hero, my brother....

In 2004, Col Lalit Rai had arranged a visit by the parents and siblings of Lt Manoj Kumar to the NDA. It was a dedication ceremony during which a portrait of the braveheart was presented to Mike Squadron, the squadron where he spent his three learning years. Lalit spoke with pride and deep respect for his officer. His father made a brief, poignant address, asking the seated cadets to follow the path of Manoj and, if needed, sacrifice their lives for the Idea of India. The program left the family in tears of pride – and the cadets with an irresistible urge to *"do a Manoj"* when and if destiny called.

The sacrifice of Manoj has impacted on *aam aadmi* in different but positive ways. One example worth narration concerns excerpts of a telephonic conversation between a re-employed fellow officer and the father of Manoj. Col AK Jayachandran, 12 ASSAM, who became a senior Bank Executive post his retirement,

> In life, there are some days when one feels terrible and some days, when one feels really good from within. One such thing happened on a Friday evening in September. I was set to go home from the Bank. One clerk and an officer were all who remained. The phone rang. An old man was on the

other side. He was irate and quite fed up. He had approached his bank's branch to settle his dues from his son's pension, which had not been correctly calculated. They'd kept fobbing him off. Finally, he got my number from someone and called. I took his details – told my guys to take a look at it and tell me if he was really due. They did that and yes – there were arrears due to him. Looking at the printout, I saw the name, *Lt Manoj Pandey ... no wife ... pension to parents ... date of death, Kargil war days.* Speaking to the old man at 7:30 pm, I asked him if he was the father of PVC Lt Manoj Pandey. He confirmed.

We quietly went and switched on our system. We worked out his dues and arrears, which was around Rs 8 lakh. This amount was credited into his father's account at about 9 pm. I called up the father and told him that his account had been credited ... he was very surprised, said it could've waited till Monday. I apologized for the bank's delay and told him that having come to know, waiting till Monday would have been the biggest disrespect/dishonour to the PVC. The old man thanked us and broke down ... he said that this one act had accorded more respect to the memory of his son, than any other civilian award.

Lt Manoj Pandey, PVC (P), 1/11 GR, deserved that kind of rare respect – in life and in death.

Lt Manoj Pandey's Citation

Lieutenant Manoj Kumar Pandey took part in a series of boldly led attacks during Operation Vijay, forcing back the intruders with heavy losses in Batalik including the Capture of Jubar Top. On the night of 02/03 July 1999 during the advance to Khalubar as his platoon approached its final objective, it came under heavy and intense enemy fire from the surrounding heights. Lieutenant Pandey was tasked to clear the interfering enemy positions to prevent his battalion from getting daylighted, being in a vulnerable position. He quickly moved his platoon to an advantageous position under intense enemy fire, sent one section to clear the enemy positions from the right, and himself proceeded to clear the enemy positions from the left. Fearlessly assaulting the first enemy position, he killed two enemy personnel and destroyed the second position by killing two more. He was injured on the shoulder and legs while clearing the third position. Undaunted and without caring for his grievous injuries, he continued to lead the assault on the fourth position urging his men and destroyed the same with a grenade, even as he got a fatal burst on his forehead. This singular daredevil act of Lieutenant Manoj Kumar Pandey provided the critical firm base for the companies, which finally led to Capture of Khalubar. The officer, however, succumbed to his injuries.

Lieutenant Manoj Kumar Pandey, thus, displayed most conspicuous bravery, indomitable courage, outstanding leadership and devotion to duty and made the supreme sacrifice in the highest traditions of the Indian Army.

Disclaimer: It has not been possible to cover the acts of gallantry of all the PVC and MVC awardees in this book. However, it is proposed to do so in other CLAWS Publications later. This part has been modified from the article covered in CLAWS publication (Scholar Warrior, Autumn 2018).

Anuj Nayyar, MVC (P)

Rachna Bisht Rawat

It was a cold morning of 05 July 1999, in the wind-lashed Mushkoh Valley. On the barren brown mountain, where temperatures have dipped to 2°C even in peak summer, Col Umesh Singh Bawa, Commanding Officer, 17 JAT, stands facing 23-year-old Captain Anuj Nayyar, the icy wind whipping their unwashed hair and sunburnt faces. Anuj has been tasked with leading a platoon of men to reinforce the Company that has captured Whale Back feature but is facing ferocious counter attacks by the enemy. Maj Deepak Rampal, Company Commander, has sent a desperate message that ammunition has almost run out and Anuj is being sent to help.

"An opportunity to go for war comes to the most fortunate soldiers, Anuj," Col Bawa tells his young officer, who stands before him, his arms ramrod straight by his side. "You are very lucky it has come to you so early in your life." Looking into Anuj's eyes, Col Bawa rests an arm on his shoulder, "You have a chance to be remembered forever, don't miss it. Either you can be brave and be remembered forever; or you do not do your job and are called a coward for life. This is your chance to create history. Go and make a name for the battalion." Courage is stamped on Anuj's handsome face. His young eyes sparkle. They show no fear. But he slips off his engagement ring and takes his wallet out of his pocket. For a second he opens it and looks at the picture of his fiancée – a pretty schoolmate he fell in love with at Army Public School, Dhaula Kuan, between bunking classes and playing basketball. She is smiling up at him. He looks at her tenderly and then hands both his ring and wallet to his Commanding Officer. "Will you please keep these for me, Sir?" he asks.

"Wear the ring Anuj. It will inspire you to fight with even more courage," Col Bawa tells him but Anuj is adamant. "I don't want these to fall into the dirty hands of the enemy. Please keep them," he says. Col Bawa, who is from Delhi just like Anuj and has met the young bride to be when Anuj brought her over one evening, gets sentimental. "Nothing will happen to you my boy," he tells Anuj. "You will come back to us. Go and do your duty. I shall keep your belongings safe." Talking to me nearly 20 years later, Brigadier Bawa, VrC, SM, who has retired and is now settled in Gurugram, says Anuj probably had some kind of premonition about what was to come but none of them realized it then.

On 05 July morning, Anuj led his team to Whale Back. He covered the distance from the base camp to the post in just 2 hours, ensuring that he wasted no time in reaching the soldiers, who were then without sufficient ammunition. After reaching his comrades he found that the Company has managed to beat back an enemy counter-attack in early morning, but more than that the enemy soldiers were seen to be regrouping for another attack. By early afternoon ammunition has been distributed, Light Machine Guns were loaded and 17 JAT was ready for the enemy. After two successful attacks by the Indian Army, Whale Back was captured. It was a big win for the Army but Anuj's moment of glory was yet to come.

The last Battle

On 06 July 1999, 17 JAT was tasked with attacking the feature Pimple 2. Company Commander Major Ritesh Kumar was leading a platoon; Anuj was right behind him. The soldiers have been surviving man pack for 2 days. They only had shakkarparas, mathis and stale puris in their backpacks. Anuj was hungry and asked for something to eat. The soldier with him handed over some cold puris to Arun . "*Ye mujhse nahi khayi jaayengi yaar,*" Anuj told him with a wry smile. Arun then gropes his own backpack and pulls out a packet of biscuits, sharing it with those around. "*Chalen?*" he then asked and, slinging his rifle behind his back, starts climbing. Just 800 metres short of the objective, the soldiers were spotted by the enemy who started shelling them. Maj Ritesh Kumar got splinter injuries on his legs besides four other soldiers who were also injured.

When this was communicated to Col Bawa on the radio set, he asked the injured men to return and get treatment at the Regimental

Aid Post. Thereafter, Col Bawa asked Arun to take charge. As the men moved up further, they came under enemy machine gun fire, thereby restricting their movement. They bravely neutralised three machine gun positions one by one but the fourth continued to stay out of their reach, despite multiple efforts. An exasperated Anuj crawled forward on his arms and knees and managed to throw a grenade inside the loophole but the deadly machine gun kept blazing.

On 07 June, Col Bawa, who had been following the battle on his radio set, suddenly lost contact with Anuj. Every time he tried to contact the young officer, he met with a deafening silence. A worried Col Bawa ordered Major Punia, to take 30 men and contact Anuj. Soon he called Col Bawa. His voice was heavy with grief. "Sir I have very bad news. Anuj is no more," he says, "I can see him and other soldiers fallen on the ground". A devastated Col Bawa asked him to retrieve the men. "Drag them behind cover. Maybe they are alive," he says desperately. "No Sir, I can see them clearly. They are dead. The enemy is firing continuously. He is not letting us reach the bodies," Punia tells him. With a heavy heart, Col Bawa asks Punia to pull back. "I don't want to lose more men. The enemy is sitting at a height and he has spotted you," he says.

Col Bawa decided against launching another attack that night because he realised that the enemy will be waiting for it. Instead, he kept bombarding the enemy position through the night, ensuring that the Pakistani soldiers do not get any chance to sleep. The next morning he ordered an attack in broad daylight, soon after breakfast time assuming that the enemy soldiers who have been awake all night would have their guard down since they would be expecting the Indians to attack only in the night. Exhibiting extreme daring and courage, two platoons of 17 JAT – led by Major Deepak Rampal and Major RK Singh – climbed up from two different directions and managed to reach Pimple 2 undetected around the same time. They launched simultaneous attacks in the afternoon, therefore, surprising the enemy completely. A fierce battle ensued and the enemy post was finally captured on the evening of 08 July.

The deaths of their men had been avenged but there was sadness all around at the big losses they had faced. The battalion's first task was to retrieve the bodies of its martyred soldiers, including Captain Anuj Nayyar, who was called a surprise hero in the battle.

Anuj had also honoured his Commanding Officer's wishes. Col Bawa later learnt that he had led his men with complete disregard for his own life. He had been standing near a boulder, taking respite in a moment of peace in the midst of the battle. He had probably been planning his next move, aware of the fact that the dark sky was slowly turning orange with dawn breaking over the tall barren peaks. That was when a Rocket Propelled Grenade had come and hit him on the neck. Shocked that death had come to him before he could complete his next task, Anuj had looked up for a second to try and see where the treacherous fire had come from but for the first time he could not get his body to obey his mind. He had fallen to the ground and his eyes had shut forever, leaving unfulfilled his dreams of capturing Pimple 2, of a new car he had asked his parents for on his birthday in August and marriage to his school sweetheart in September. Anuj Nayyar was martyred. He was only 23. For its outstanding performance in the war, 17 JAT was awarded the Chief of Army Staff Commendation on the spot, the Battle Honour Mushkoh and Theatre Honour Kargil. The battalion received 41 awards that included a Maha Vir Chakra for Captain Anuj Nayyar; four Vir Chakras for Col US Bawa, Major Deepak Rampal, Captain SB Ghildiyal and Havaldar Kumar Singh; six Sena Medals; 20 Mention-in-Despatches and 10 Commendation Cards. The battalion suffered the highest casualty for a unit in the Kargil War. Looking back at the war, 20 years later, this is what Col Bawa had to say, "It is the dream of every soldier to go to war. When we were sent to battle I was excited at the opportunity. I thought I would have stories to tell my grandchildren. But after the war, when I saw the coffins of my boys, when I saw my soldiers maimed and disabled in hospitals, when I met grief-stricken parents and young girls widowed so early in life, my heart was full of sadness. I never want to see another war in my life. Wars only bring misery. They cannot solve any problems."

Nearly 20 years after the Kargil war, I also met Mrs Meena Nayyar, Anuj's mother, over coffee in Delhi's South Extension. We spent more than an hour together and with great affection and moist eyes she told me about the young son she had lost. When I asked her if she had ever gone to see the War Memorial at Kargil, her son's last battlefield, she said no. "I never wanted to. There is nothing for me there. My son is gone," she told me, her voice grief stricken. She smiled talking about the day Anuj (then a student of Army Public School, Dhaula Kuan) missed his school bus and decided to walk home all the way to Janak Puri, where the Nayyars lived in a joint family. "He was in class 7. He didn't know the way but he followed the same route that the bus used to take and reached home," she says. "His father and I had gone out for lunch so we didn't even know he had missed the bus." *"Aisa hi tha Anuj. Bas apne man ki karta tha,"* she said talking about the son who will always stay 23 for her. She remembered how he once fractured his foot in school and was advised by the doctor not to strain the leg. *"Par wo kahan kisi ki sunta tha"*, she stated. "I noticed his dirty shirt and scolded him for not listening to the doctor, and to avoid that, he used to take off his shirt on the playfield so that I wouldn't find out he was still playing. When I noticed that his vest stayed dirty, he started to take off even that and started playing barechested, putting on his clothes before returning home so that I never knew what he had been up to," she laughed.

One memorable morning, Anuj told his parents that someone special was going to come to see them. Soon after, the doorbell rang and a pretty young girl walked in. It was his schoolmate from Army Public School, Dhaula Kuan. She was the daughter of an Army officer. *"Choti si ladki thi per wo toh apna rishta khud hi lekar aa gayi,"* Mrs Nayyar remembered with a gentle smile. "After she left, we asked Anuj if he was serious about her. He coolly said, *'tabhi toh aap se milwaya hai'*. His father and I were happy about that too. We had never said no to Anuj for anything," Mrs Nayyar said. "Though sometimes I wish I had said no to him more forcefully when he had decided to join the Army," she added.

Mrs Nayyar remembers how she and Anuj's fiancée ran around getting goodies to send to him with an officer who was flying down to his location at the time of war. "We bought packs of juices and chips and hastily bound them in a parcel. I added an envelope with some money as shagun for Anuj and another for the young officer who was going for war. Anuj never got to see that because he never came back from that operation," she says. "The parcel was returned to us with his coffin, his engagement ring, his watch and wallet."

Young Anuj Nayyar, the boy who was the first in his family to join the Army, which he clearly saw as a career after joining Army Public School, ended up becoming one of the most famous alumni of his school. He might not have returned from war but soldiers never die on battlefields. They continue to live in the memories of their comrades and their countrymen. And Anuj shall also live forever in our hearts.

Capt Anuj Nayyar's Citation

On 06 July 1999, Charlie Company was tasked to capture an objective, which was a part of the Pimple Complex on the Western Slopes of Point 4875, in the Mushkoh Valley. At the beginning of the attack, the Company Commander got injured and the command of the company devolved on Captain Anuj Nayyar. Captain Nayyar continued to command his leading platoon into the attack under heavy enemy artillery and mortar fire. As the platoon advanced, the leading section reported location of 3 to 4 enemy positions. Captain Nayyar moved forward towards the first enemy position and fired rocket launcher and lobbed grenades into it.

Thereafter, the section, along with Captain Nayyar, physically assaulted and cleared the position. The enemy, which was well entrenched, brought a heavy volume of automatic fire. Captain Anuj Nayyar, unmindful of his personal safety, motivated his men and cleared two more enemy positions. While clearing the fourth position, an enemy rocket propelled grenade hit the officer killing him on the spot. This action led by Captain Anuj Nayyar resulted in killing nine enemy soldiers and destruction of three medium machine gun positions of the enemy. The success of this operation after a brief setback was largely due to the outstanding personal bravery and exemplary junior leadership of this daring officer. Captain Anuj Nayyar displayed indomitable resolve, grit and determination and motivated his command by personal example acting beyond the call of duty and made the supreme sacrifice in true traditions of the Indian Army.

Disclaimer: It has not been possible to cover the acts of gallantry of all the PVC and MVC awardees in this book. However, it is proposed to do so in other CLAWS Publications later. This part has been modified from the article covered in CLAWS publication (Scholar Warrior, Spring 2019).

This account has been recreated from conversations with Mrs Meena Nayyar, mother of late Captain Anuj Nayyar, MVC, and Brigadier Umesh Singh Bawa (Retd) VrC, SM, who was Commanding Officer of 17 JAT during the Kargil War.

PART V
WAY AHEAD

Emerging Challenges and the Way Ahead

Lieutenant General (Dr) VK Ahluwalia and
Colonel Rajeev Kapoor

"We need forces that are agile, mobile and driven by technology, not just human valour. We need capabilities to win swift wars, for we will not have the luxury of long drawn battles. . . ."

– Narendra Modi, Prime Minister of India, Combined Commanders' Conference on board INS Vikramaditya, 6 December, 2015.

Exordium

To commemorate the 20 years of our "Vijay" in Kargil, we have dedicated the previous parts, to the heroic motivational stories of our brave hearts for their exceptional courage and saga of valour. We have also briefly discussed the important battles in Dras, Mushkoh, Batalik, Kaksar and Turtuk sub-sectors, the role of supporting elements, and have obtained the opinions and perception of a few commanders and officers who were on the ground during the conflict. Kargil conflict was the first conflict between the freshly proclaimed nuclear weapon states, India and Pakistan, and fought in 1999 in super high-altitude areas of the Himalayas.

Following Kargil, a number of high-level security committees analysed the glaring weaknesses in our security architecture. While the effectiveness of Army's surveillance along the affected areas of intrusion was certainly examined, the roles of RAW, IB, military intelligence, and their inputs were also scrutinised in detail. A few important recommendations are as follows:

- Improvement in Intelligence system at all levels, organisational structures, capacity building, integration and coordination, and an oversight to provide resources to the intelligence agencies and to monitor their performance and activities.

- Integration of MoD with the Armed Forces HQ.
- Jointness among the Armed Forces.
- Appointment of a permanent Chief of Defence Staff (CDS) by the Kargil Review Committee (KRC) and the Group of Ministers (GoM), and Permanent Chairman, Chiefs of Staff Committee by the Naresh Chandra Committee.
- Better management of borders, by ensuring the principle of "One Border One Force".
- Emphasis on technology, innovations, and indigenisation of production.
- To streamline and improve the system of procurement of weapon systems and defence equipment to modernize our forces.
- A few actions that have been taken on the recommendations of the committees have been covered in the later part.

This Part aims to discuss the emerging world order, the present geo-political and regional dispensation that will have bearing on the future conflict scenario in the region, and also to revisit lessons learnt and actions taken to mitigate the Pakistani startle of 1999, in future. As the Kargil-like scenario is quite unlikely in future, the part would endeavour to speculate the envisaged threats and challenges of the future, and our preparations to face them.

THE EMERGING WORLD ORDER

Two decades is a long time during which a lot has changed, both at the international and regional levels. Therefore, when we look at the way ahead, it would be prudent to broadly understand and analyse four important aspects: emerging world order, regional geo-political environment, historical perspective of the security environment, and the threats and challenges to security. Undoubtedly, it is difficult to crystal gaze into the future with certainty due to constant changes taking place.

To analyse the emanating world order, it becomes imperative to understand the changing dynamics in the regional and global environment – particularly the developments in West Asia and North Africa (WANA), North Korea, South Asia, China, Russia and Indo-Pacific region – as also the security threats and the flash points in different regions. West Asia has remained unstable due to the rivalry for regional dominance, intra-regional armed conflicts, civil wars, sectarian and ethnic conflicts, religious fundamentalism, criminal networks and drug trafficking. The relations between Iran, Qatar, Saudi Arabia and the United Arab Emirates (UAE) are a major cause for concern regarding stability and security in the Gulf region. According to SIPRI Fact Sheet 2019, Iran, Qatar, Saudi Arabia and the United Arab Emirates (UAE) had high levels of military expenditure as a share of their GDP in 1994-2018. Saudi Arabia was the third-largest military spender globally ($ 67.6 billion) and the largest military spender in the Gulf region in 2018. Expenditure on military is also a good indicator of the prevailing apprehensions, fears and tensions in the region. The region continues to remain a global hotspot, and certainly affects the energy security and stability in the neighbouring regions.[1] These identified flash points are likely to witness conflicts in the future; thus, causing turbulence and instability in the geo-political environment.

Over the past two years, some of the events that bear testimony to an uncertain and complex global environment are as follows: USA's pull-out from the three years old multi-layered Iranian nuclear deal called Joint Comprehensive Plan of Action (JCPOA) in May 2018, re-imposition of sanctions on Iran, and the rising tensions due to shooting down of a drone of the US by Iran on 20 June 2019; USA's pull-out from the Paris climate change and threats to move out of WTO; US sanctions on Russia; the US-China trade war and China's efforts to offset the trade imbalance; and the expected turmoil due to Brexit. Two important events relating to Saudi Arabia – assassination of journalist Jamal Khashoggi and the colossal humanitarian crisis in Yemen following the Saudi-led offensive – have affected the stability in the region. President Trump's announcement to pull out US troops from Afghanistan and Syria, followed by another statement that he agreed "100 percent" with maintaining a small-troop presence in Syria has added to the complexity of the situation. The US has made an all-out effort to bring the Afghan Taliban to the negotiating table, to stabilise the situation and to pull out its troops.

The global security environment has remained linked to economics and trade. A climate of economic uncertainty is all too visible due to the ongoing trade war between the USA and China. In the recent past, the world has also witnessed large fluctuations in oil prices, and financial crises in Venezuela, Turkey, Iran and Pakistan. Venezuela, with the largest proven oil reserves of around 300,878 million barrels, has been affected by economic and political crisis.

The rise of regional powers has changed the character of geo-politics at the global level. With the progressive shift in the economic centre of gravity from the West to Asia and the resultant rise of China and India, we find that the Asian region has new dynamics of cooperation and competition between these two countries. This shift has also brought in Asia as the key player in shaping the geo-strategic environment of the future. Amongst all these, China's Belt and Road Initiative (BRI) covering different sectors and regions, and its likely impact has caught the attention of all stakeholders – political leaders, economists, political scientists and the strategic communities at large. Given the vast regions and the population base being covered by China's BRI ambitious project, it is, in fact an attempt to establish a new world order. Besides having an influence on major energy-producing countries, it is expected to have an impact on 65 countries and over 62% of world's population. How far will China succeed in its endeavour would only be known in due course.

The Indo-Pacific region is beset with a large number of challenges to security: territorial disputes both on the land and sea (maritime); piracy and security to sea lanes of communication (SLOCs); terrorism, insurgencies, religious fundamentalism; proxy war and state-sponsored terrorism; sectarian and ethnic-based conflicts, drug and human trafficking, displacement of people; environmental degradation; cyber security etc. While India has been propagating "Rule-based order" on sea navigation issues, it does not find acceptability due to vested interests of the nations. Given China's growing stature and strength, and its sensitivity to maritime areas of influence, it may not permit presence of extra-regional powers in the South China Sea in the future. This would have implications for the region and the world at large.

Recently, in response to the US "terrorism designation" of the Iran's Revolutionary Guards, Iran's Parliament overwhelmingly approved a bill labelling the US forces in West Asia as terrorists.[2] Thereafter, the tension between the two countries continued to mount on two counts;

one, Iran announced that its stockpile of low-enriched uranium would exceed the laid down limit; two, on 20 June 2019, Iran brought down a US Navy MQ-4C Triton Drone (spy drone, as stated by Iran) in the Gulf Region, the exact circumstances and area of the incident remain vague, due to different interpretations. Such actions and reactions add to the prevailing uncertainty and complexity of the geopolitical-economic-strategic situation, both at global and regional levels. These notwithstanding, the positive streaks in 2017-19 were the success against ISIS in Iraq and Syria, and the two rounds of talks – though unsuccessful – on the Korean Peninsula Peace Process. The nature and intensity of developments, both at the global and regional levels, suggest that we are living in a geo-politically unstable world.

Going by the current trends, it appears that the new world order is likely to be multi-conceptual and multi-lateral, and may not be necessarily multi-polar, as perceived. The present geo-political realm has four prominent underpinnings: intensification of strong state-centred politics, i.e. Nationalism; abrading of global norms; expanding relevance of regionalism; and aggressive geo-economic agendas. Today, "Nationalism" is the flavour of geo-politics, and the aspiring powers are seeking to adjust the rules of the game and international context in ways favourable to their national interests.[3]

Historical Perspective

Post–World War II, there has been a progressive increase in the intrastate conflicts. In fact, these conflicts started increasing since the 1960s, when decolonisation was nearing completion. There was a sharp rise in the intrastate conflicts towards late 1980s, when the signals of the end of cold war started emerging, and these peaked around 1994-97. The data below,[4] from year 1946 to 2016, further substantiates this belief.

It is well known that since the end of cold war, rapid changes in the political, economic, social, cultural, technological and environmental domains have had a profound impact on the geo-strategic environment. The emergence of asymmetric threats, revolution in technologies, emerging lethal autonomous weapon systems, economic challenges, and new strategic partnerships and alliances between nations have added a new dimension to the geo-political and geo-strategic environment. Resultantly, the envisaged threats and challenges to national security – both traditional and non-traditional – have also undergone a change, the complexities of which need to be analysed to formulate the future course of action.

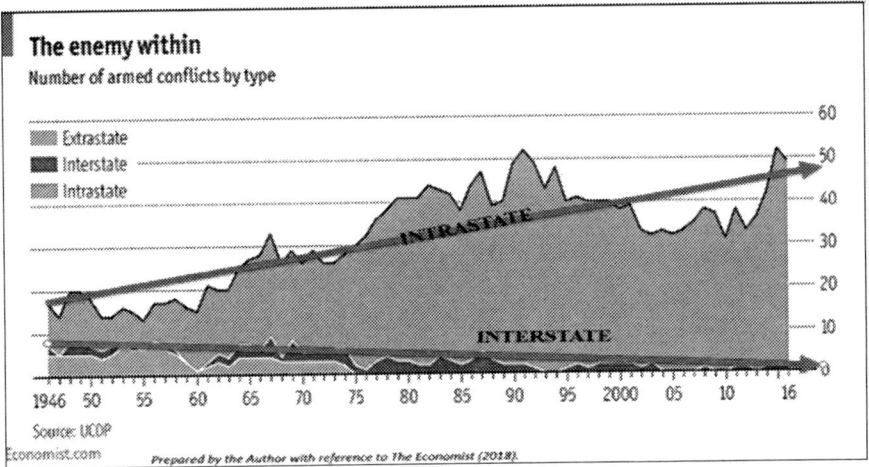

The enemy within
Number of armed conflicts by type

Figure 5.1: Number and Type of Armed Conflicts, 1946-2017

Source: United Nations Development Programme, 2017, and the Economist, Jan 2018, trends of conflict updated by the authors.

Let us primarily have a look at the landscape of global terrorist and extremist threats. It is likely to persist and is anticipated to be dominated by three major developments. First, Islamic State of Iraq and Syria (ISIS) is likely to enter a new phase in global expansion primarily due to depletion of its rank and file in Iraq and Syria from about 60,000 to 5,000-6,000 combat fighters, and the IS territorial control in its main theatre has shrunk to 1%, east of the Euphrates River.[5] Second, with the Islamic State Khorasan (ISK) threatening the present stakeholders in Afghanistan, i.e., Taliban, the Afghan government, and Pakistan, the sphere of influence of ISIS is getting more pronounced in the Afghanistan-Pakistan region. Third, with the worldwide rise of "nationalism," the communities are slowly and incrementally getting polarised on religion and ethnicity.

Besides external security threats, religious and ethnic extremism, population growth and unemployment, societal tensions, severe competition for natural resources, climate change and environmental degradation are likely to ensure that armed conflicts will persist, perhaps with greater intensity.[6] In a large number of cases, in Africa, West Asia and South Asia, trans-national neighbouring forces and non-state actors have been indulging in proxy wars, abetting insurgencies, terrorism, violence and organised crime, thus, perpetuating instability and conflicts.

SECURITY CHALLENGES

To analyse the future threats and challenges, it is important to briefly look at four vital aspects that have an impact on the security and economies of the countries: Fourth Industrial Revolution (4IR), additional security challenges at the global and regional levels, region wise armed conflicts, and the ranking of regions and countries given their peacefulness and the economic cost of violence.

The 4IR is the fourth major industrial era since the initial Industrial Revolution of the 18th century. It is characterized by a fusion of technologies that is blurring the lines between the physical, digital and biological spheres, collectively referred to as cyber-physical systems. As soldiers in uniform and civilians alike, we must take a note of the new technologies like internet of things (IoT), cyber security, simulation, lethal autonomous weapon systems (LAWS), artificial intelligence (AI) and Big Data, augmented reality, cloud computing, addictive manufacturing etc. These technologies would have a great effect on the emerging security environment in the coming decades.

Some of the security challenges at the global and regional level are instability in West Asia and North Africa (WANA); spread of terrorism and increase in intra-state conflicts; boundary disputes over land and sea; proliferation of weapons of mass destruction (WMDs); militarization of space; maritime security and piracy; cyber threat; environment degradation and climate change; intense competition over energy and fast-diminishing natural resources; water security; demographic inversion; drug trafficking; dilution in the effectiveness of the UN; and internal displacement of people.

Report by the Population Division of the United Nations Department of Economic and Social Affairs (UN DESA) states that nearly 80 million people are moving into urban areas every year globally. According to Census of India 2011, the urban population in India increased by 31.2% from 1991 to 2011. Therefore, hyper-urbanisation is the threat in being, as there has been a large-scale migration from rural to urban areas, particularly in Africa and Asia. The main drivers of hyper-urbanisation are poor rural infrastructure, unemployment, hunger, poverty, lack of basic facilities, poor quality of life in rural areas, rural crime and conflict and environmental degradation. History is replete with examples that if the basic aspirations of the migrant population are not addressed, it results in a conflict situation. Again, these could, either singularly or as a combination of two or more factors, add multi-dimensional threats to global security.

According to Global Peace Index (GPI) 2018,[7] published by Sydney-based Institute of Economics and Peace, examines 23 quantitative and qualitative parameters, "Peacefulness" has deteriorated by 2.38% over the past 10 years. South Asia is the second least peaceful region of the world, out of the nine regions that were evaluated, the least peaceful being WANA and South Asia, in that order. The armed conflict by region given by Uppsala Conflict Data Program (UCDP)[8] in year 2018 substantiates this fact and is depicted below in Figure 5.2.

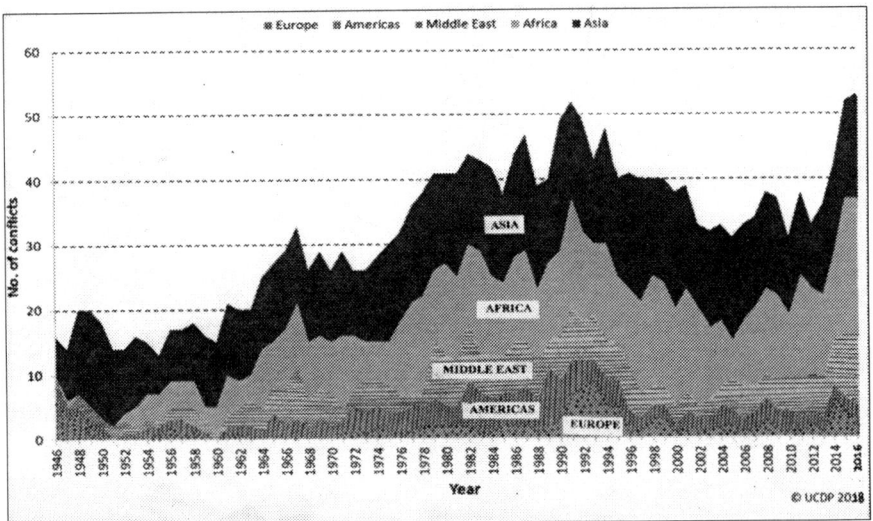

Figure 5.2: Armed Conflict by Region, 1946-2017

Source: UCDP, 2018 (annotated by the authors).

This graph shows that Asia has continued to remain at the forefront of armed conflicts since 1946, with varying intensities – low, medium and high. The conflicts in Africa have increased since 1960, wherein there was a spike in the armed conflicts during 1990-94, and then 2010 onwards. A scan of the recent conflicts in WANA, Afghanistan and Africa suggest that there is blurring of lines between war and peace, regular and irregular and conventional and non-conventional warfare. The non-traditional threats and challenges to security have also been gaining importance, due to which security environment is ambiguous, uncertain and complex.

Increase in Violence and Economic Cost

Based on their evaluations, GPI 2018 gives out the ranking of the least peaceful regions, and nations, and the economic cost of violence. Out of 163 countries, the ranking of the least peaceful nations in South Asia and our strategic neighbourhood is as follows: Afghanistan, 162; Pakistan, 151; India, 136; China, 112; Bangladesh, 93; Nepal, 84; Sri Lanka, 67; Bhutan, 19. The least peaceful nations at the global level are Syria (163rd, least peaceful), Afghanistan, South Sudan, Iraq, Somalia and Yemen.

The economic cost of violence refers to the direct and indirect costs incurred in preventing, containing, and dealing with the consequences of violence. The economic cost of violence to India has been 9% of its GDP. It merits a mention here that our defence budget of 2019 is about 1.51% of the GDP. It is time to address our internal armed conflicts, improve governance and bring about better social cohesion and harmony among the people so that the economic cost of violence can be minimised and the budget be allotted for improving the quality of life of our people. As a matter of interest, economic costs of violence for a few other countries as a percentage of their GDP are as follows: Syria, 68%; Afghanistan, 63%; Pakistan, 12%; Sri Lanka, 8%; Nepal, 6%; China and Bangladesh, at 4% each (GPI 2018). The following table gives out the GPI ranking for South Asia in 2017 and 2018.

Table 5.1: Global Peace Index for South Asian Countries, 2018

Country	Rank	Global Position (2017)	Global Position (2018)
Bhutan	1st	13th	19th
Sri Lanka	2nd	80th	67th
Nepal	3rd	93rd	84th
Bangladesh	4th	84th	93rd
India	5th	137th	136th
Pakistan	6th	152nd	151st
Afghanistan	7th	162nd	162nd

Source: Institute for Economics and Peace

Source: Institute for Economics and Peace, 2017 and 2018.

It is true that owing to the cost incurred by war, the intensity and frequency of conflicts need to be checked. However, as Plato, the Greek philosopher, had said 2,400 years ago, "Only the dead have seen end of war". He did not say "end of the war", but said "end of war". War is, therefore, part of the human nature, as he/she attempts to dominate the other human beings for want of power, territorial control, wealth, resources, control of society, etc. Therefore, while we will continue to witness conflicts, manifesting in different forms; resultantly, the international relations may also remain less than stable in the future.

REVISITING THE KARGIL CONFLICT

The Kargil conflict was the first conflict between freshly proclaimed nuclear weapon states, India and Pakistan, since the Ussuri River clashes between the Soviet Union and China in 1969. This high-altitude mountain conflict fought in the summer of 1999 lasted longer than the earlier three wars that India fought with Pakistan (1947, 1965 and 1971). The Kargil conflict can be conjectured as a conflict wherein the sanctity of the LoC was violated, and the Indian Territory was occupied by a mix of Mujahideen and predominantly Pakistan's Northern Light Infantry (NLI) soldiers, which necessitated the mobilisation of virtually a fair portion of the Indian Army. After more than two months of "bloody fighting" and loss of precious lives, the Indian Army wrested back the posts that were theirs. Thus, this victory at best can be termed as a tactical one as it primarily involved recapturing of our own lost territory. Till the time we do not understand the variance between tactics and strategy, we as a nation would keep celebrating our victories in battles but may not win a war.

We need to comprehend that mere tactics at best can win a battle, but for winning a war, strategy is a pre-requisite. Though Kargil can surely be claimed as a "victory" when gauged purely on the "War Parameters", yet, can we thump our chests in saying that in this war we were able to damage Pakistan's war-waging capabilities? Or can we claim that we removed our vulnerabilities by gaining territorial advantages? The short answer is "No", partly because the aim we set for ourselves was limited: it was to push back the intruders and restore the sanctity of LoC. Accordingly, this victory can candidly be termed as an incomplete operation, where we did not plan to defeat the enemy in detail. However, it may also not be forgotten that the Armed Forces conducted operations with a great sense of urgency, as there was an outcry from the nation to achieve results at the earliest. The Armed Forces need to be complimented for pushing back the intruders and restoring the sanctity of the LoC against all odds, including the strategic restraint of not crossing the LoC.

In military parlance, it was perhaps a "once in a lifetime" opportunity that India squandered. Although we were reacting to a situation, we had the initiative and the latitude to achieve and put in real-time practice, our aims set during the "war games" rather than just regaining our territory at a heavy price. More so, as Pakistan had disowned their NLI troops claiming them to be mujahideen, we had the "retaliatory window" available to target the terror camps in Pakistan-occupied Kashmir (PoK) and Gilgit-Baltistan that would have found acceptability in the world. Again, this has to be seen in light of the geo-political forces at play, and our preparedness and capability during Op Vijay.

With accelerated changes in technology and the character of conflicts, India, in the next two decades, is likely to face an ultra-high technology adversary in the North, with hybrid warfare as the key feature; or a medium technology adversary in the West with greater focus on the sub-conventional threats including proxy war, cross-border terrorism and information warfare. The conflicts could well be a combination of both, against a nuclear backdrop. Due to the territorial disputes and 'no loss of territory' resolves of the contesting nations, major compliment of the war or the conflict would be land oriented, which will progressively increase the fighting in urban terrains. We should, therefore, be prepared to effectively fight, against both the emerging external, internal and hybrid threats in the future.

As we stand two decades later, with many lessons in national security, higher defence organisation, diplomacy, warfare, strategy, modernisation of the armed forces, border management, collation, gathering and analysis of intelligence, and reviewing our nuclear doctrine, it is time to take a stock of actions taken by us to improve our national security apparatus. Based on the recommendations of various committees, a centralised communication and electronic intelligence agency, the National Technical Research Organisation (NTRO), Defence Intelligence Agency (DIA), Integrated Defence Staff (IDS), Defence Acquisition Council (DAC), Andaman and Nicobar Command, Nuclear Command Authority, and Strategic Forces Command (SFC), have been established. A full time National Security Advisor (NSA) has also been instituted, whose organisational structure and responsibilities have been reviewed recently. An improved aerial surveillance using Indian Radar Imaging Satellite (RISAT) satellites, UAVs and Electronic Intelligence Satellite (EMISAT) have been put in place and are functional. Unfortunately, a large number of recommendations have remained largely ignored and have still not been implemented due to a number of reasons. All those aspects, which are detrimental to national security, must be addressed with a sense of urgency.

India-Pakistan Dynamics Post-Kargil

Unfortunately, despite the well-publicised victory, justifiable by every count, it neither diminished the Pakistani Army's adventurism nor helped our cause to attain peace on our Western borders. It did little to change Pakistan. Beyond a few months of international isolation, the rogue state continued its misadventures by attacking our Parliament in 2001, Kaluchak massacre and attack on Akshardham in 2002, Mumbai in 2008, Pathankot and Uri in 2016, Sanjuwan in 2018 and Pulwama in 2019, to name the prominent ones.

Thus, it is quite debatable to conclude that Pakistan will not try a "Kargil-like" operation in the future. Nothing seems to have changed in the basic fabric of Pakistan since its Kargil misadventure. It still nourishes all the longstanding factors of animosity with India like its general revisionism and the perceived unfinished business of partition and 1971 operation. The military's dominant role in Pakistan's national security policy still remains firm and intact. The other factors challenging the Pakistani Army's institutional interests are the concurrent improvement of general situation and the life in Kashmir Valley, inconclusive status of confidence building measures between India and Pakistan on terrorism post-Kargil, and the regional and global trends favouring India post-Balakot strikes. All these factors, therefore, can serve as an impetus for Pakistani agencies to pursue fomenting trouble on the Indian side in future.

Future Conflict Scenario

So, what does the future conflict scenario hold for India and Pakistan? It seems an enigma but can be deciphered with certain constructs that are likely to dominate and influence both the nations in times to come. It needs to be realised that inter-state relations presently are no longer purely bilateral or standalone as they are heavily influenced by the changing geo-dynamics.

As Chanakya said, *"There is some self-interest behind every friendship. There is no friendship without self-interests. This is a bitter Truth"*. The narrative of future Indo-Pak relations therefore would remain "prisoner" to the following aspects:

- Impact of global geo-politics on Indo-Pak Relations.
- China-Pakistan collusion.
- Future Indo-Pak Relations: Growing China's Stakes.
- Regional dynamics in Indo-Pak relations.

Impact of Emerging Global Geo-politics on Indo-Pak Relations

In current security dispensation as highlighted earlier in this part, demography, energy and religious extremism are the main and potential triggers. Semantically, all nations especially the global powers would try to attain their national objectives and aims through means that are short of an outright war. The net effect of rising tensions within and between countries, and the growing threat from terrorism will be greater global disorder. The threat of terrorism, from Lashkar-e-Tayyiba (LeT), Jaish-e-Mohammad (JeM), Tehrik-e-Taliban Pakistan (TTP), and Al-Qaeda and its affiliates as well as the ISIS expansion and sympathy for associated ideologies has gained prominence in the area. The tolerance of the world including India in absorbing successive waves of state-sponsored terror attacks is declining precipitously, and Pakistan's emergence as the "ground zero" in the terror landscape is slowly being realised by the world.

But in this new world order influencing the Indo-Pak relations, supporting the concept of "good and bad" terrorists is also becoming a norm with countries flagrantly supporting and condemning terrorism in the same breath. Eventually, countries like India who historically are ethical and work according to the rule books would therefore suffer, albeit they embrace these changes and play by these new rules.

Hence, factors like globalisation, the prospects of economic gains, selective aversion to terrorism are more likely to determine alliances rather than the intention to gain power and friends merely for the sake of being militarily powerful. No alliances are likely to remain permanent and would be national interest based. Hence, flexibility in diplomacy and guarding one's interest will be the key requirement. The examples of this "new game of Chess" are galore and can be seen in opportunist relations like that of China and Russia, the erstwhile foes and now friends for benefits, confounding China-Pak bonhomie and ingrate Turkey's swaying away from the US, to name a few.

This new world order is having a direct impact on Indo-Pak relations. To start with, more than this new world order, actually it is the rise of China in the geo-political and geo-economic mosaic of the world, which has ushered a new dimension impacting the Indo-Pak relations. In the next decade or so, China will remain the epicenter around which the world geo-economics and the future conflicts would orbit. This meteoric rise of China is attributed to the growing uncertainty about America's role in the world; a hobbled Europe; a turbulent Middle East; aspiring South Asia; and weakening of international forums like United Nations Security Council (UNSC). These dynamics have facilitated China to fill up the vacuum left by Russia, in the international system.

This emergence of China coupled with China-Pakistan Economic Corridor (CPEC), which has increased China's presence in Gilgit and Baltistan, makes CPEC a greater cause of concern in the region as a whole and on India-Pakistan dynamics in particular.

The brewing US-China rivalry at the world geo-political level is the second aspect that is adding fuel to the already turbulent Indo-Pak relations and both are slowly becoming main players influencing the Indo-Pak rivalry. On one side the geo-strategic location of Pakistan is keeping it relevant and on the other side, India is emerging as an important US ally in the region because of its huge potential of markets, and also as it provides an opportunity to the US to contain China's growing influence in the Indian Ocean Region (IOR).

China, to check both India and the US, is nurturing its bonhomie with Pakistan despite its dubious credentials.[9] China is trying to keep India fully committed to its problems in South Asia so that it remains "boxed in", leaving no leeway for it to concentrate on issues beyond its immediate neighbourhood. Pakistan therefore has become an important cog in China's surreptitious and low-cost, high-returns game against India. Simultaneously, analysts also reckon that the US and China are probably using India and Pakistan as "pawns" to test each other's reactions and capabilities.

The future Indo-Pak relations are thus likely to remain fluid and dynamic owing to rapidly changing alliances driven by self-interest and erosion of ethics in the diplomatic arena. The relations in coming days would unfold under the risk of conflict that is likely to increase due to diverging interests among major powers; an expanding terror threat; continued instability in weak states; the spread of lethal, disruptive technologies; and under the shadow of growing US-China rivalry for world hegemony.

India: China-Pakistan Collusion

While examining the China-Pakistan collusion, it is prudent to briefly look at India's relations with China. The Sino-Indian relationship is a complex mix of competition and cooperation, which remains characterised by mutual distrust. While India is one of the fastest growing large economies, it has boycotted China's most publicised project of the 21st century, BRI, but at the same time is also part of the Quadrilateral Security Dialogue. China views India's actions with suspicion. On the other hand, it has remained a persistent obstacle to India's membership in the UNSC and the Nuclear Suppliers Group (NSG). Also, it had remained firm in not allowing the blacklisting of Masood Azhar as a global terrorist on three occasions. During the past decade, China has increased its footprints in India's strategic neighbourhood, carried out military modernisation and exploited hybrid tactics in the grey zone. These developments portend increasing competition between the two regional powers. Equally important is the fact that both countries have a lot to gain from each other by maintaining cordial relations. This could be by way of penetrating some of the emerging markets to improve our economies, and by taking measures to guard against rising trade protectionist actions in the emerging world order. Some of the areas of common concerns are as follows: keeping their respective peripheries secure and stable, and addressing the non-traditional securities threats like food, water, energy etc.

China-Pakistan relations have always been close. For China, Pakistan serves as a leveraging tool to assist in containing India and thus Pakistan has always been used as part of former's strategy in maintaining equibalance in the sub-continent. Both nations have been treating India as a collective target, with China acting contrary to India's interests as also in light of rising Indo-US strategic leverage. The fact is that these two nations are an "odd couple" with nothing in common except a shared enmity against India and have been claiming vast swaths of Indian Territory. Investment in CPEC serves China's two-pronged motives and benefits, one being economic and the other, strategic, by having a naval hub intended to project power in the Arabian Sea and the Indian Ocean.

Militarily, due to the growing presence of Chinese troops in Pakistan and its energy needs being dependent on CPEC, it can be irrefutably deduced that India's future endeavours on its Western front would not be devoid of India crossing China's path, thereby making two-front war a reality for India. Moreover, the increased Chinese boot-prints in Pakistan-occupied Jammu and Kashmir (J&K) also means that India faces the dilemma of Chinese troops on both flanks of its portion of J&K, given that China occupies one-fifth of the original princely state of J&K. This presence further substantiates as to why India must contemplate the unpleasant possibility of a "two-front" war.

Future Indo-Pak Relations: Growing China's Stakes

In the Indo-Pak rivalry, one area that is most talked about and where India could try a meaningful riposte to Pakistan-sponsored insurgency in Kashmir is Baluchistan. But, is it? The dynamics seems to have reversed and the so-called window of opportunity, as perceived by the Indian strategists, has been substantially diminished. Baluchistan now has become the "Geo-strategic fulcrum" for China because of CPEC and if meddled, it would definitely draw its reaction. In the future, it would be extraordinarily difficult for India to make any aggressive move without threatening Chinese interests. In fact, any Indian overture endangering thousands of Chinese citizens working on the CPEC project will certainly give China the *loco standi* to initiate hostilities against India. One can perceive that the operational or strategic options for India have been substantially reduced. Anything beyond shallow skirmishes would have the risk of drawing China into a two-front war.

Stakes of China have increased so much in Pakistan that in future it appears inevitable that China perhaps would decisively take sides with Pakistan, even if pushed against the wall by the world. China's repeated vetoing UN action against Masood Azhar, the Pakistan-based chief of the Jaish-e-Mohammed, is a sad glimpse of the same. India surely would find it extremely difficult to break the China-Pakistan nexus however hard it may try. So, can India fight both China and Pakistan simultaneously? The answer is quite clear and brute that given the present capacities and force levels, India cannot fight and win. There are no definite terms that imply that India can't achieve this in future, but it surely does require concerted efforts if it intends reaching that capability and military deterrence.

The most concerning facet of China-Pak alliance remains their interoperability, as both the armies now claim to have achieved this capability to execute joint missions against a common target. As mentioned earlier, through Chinese assistance, Pakistan is gaining access to advanced weaponry and new-age technologies such as cyber and drones, which could be a concern for India.

Strong economy is one of the most powerful weapons in the world. Therefore, currently both China and India have set their aims to achieve economic development without compromising their security and strategic autonomy. India has the window available to take actions: firstly, prevent and weaken collusion to minimise its adverse impact on our security, and secondly, deal with a warlike or war situation, if it occurs. Since China–Pakistan strategic embrace is not likely to change in the near future, there is a need for India to take measures that are bilateral as well as multilateral. A multifaceted, multi-layered national strategy, with synergised political, diplomatic, economic and military measures will have to be worked out. Pending that, as peace cannot be assured and ensured, India should be ready to support its military strategy of ensuring a "deterrence" against Pakistan, and "dissuasive deterrence" against China, by developing its capabilities and force structuring in the future. Given the financial constraints, to begin with, we need to look at the most likely threat scenarios rather than the most dangerous one, albeit the forces must have the resilience, flexibility and adaptability to face a difficult scenario, when required.

Regional Dynamics in Indo-Pak Relations

The future of South Asia is in the hands of three powers – China, India, and to a minimal extent Pakistan who hold the keys to this region's stability and prosperity. These three powers would further gain prominence and become complicated once the US withdraws from Afghanistan and its influence in the region declines. The various questions which gain importance at this juncture are as follows: How will the rise of China and India affect Indo-Pak relations in Southern Asia? Could a combination of crises trigger conflict between China and India, given their historical relationship and future ambitions? What might change the nuclear escalation scenario in South Asia, particularly between India and Pakistan? How could China and the United States encourage de-escalation? How would a U.S.-China collision affect regional stability (for example, in the South China Sea and trade war), and how will India respond to China's expanding maritime activities in the IOR?

"The conventional wisdom is that China will intensify support to Islamabad amid rising India-Pakistan tension," said Michael

Kugelman, senior associate for South and Southeast Asia at the Woodrow Wilson Centre, a Washington-based think tank.[10]

The US, however, is steadily losing its influence in South Asia. It has virtually lost its Afghan war and is looking for a respectable exit. This has in turn given an opportunity to China to gain hegemony in the region. Islamabad, on the other hand, has seen the best of both worlds – being China's closest ally, while remaining a non-NATO ally of the US. But, with India's emergence as a trusted ally in the making for the US, it has antagonised China, and has, thus, further strengthened the China-Pak ties.

Another axis of China-Pakistan-Russia is set to play a dominant role in the regional geo-political order as all three are anti-US. The anticipated loser of this axis could possibly be Indo-Russian ties. Leaving US therefore would hurt India's cause, as the Russia-China-Pakistan ties without the balancing effect of the US in the region could push India further to the wall. Though Russia is anticipated to remain neutral towards India due to its economic interests, but the erstwhile Indo-Russian bonhomie would remain relic of the past. The role of Iran – which also has hostile relations with the US, even as it maintains a crucial strategic partnership with New Delhi – would have to be closely watched.

Religious Fundamentalism

Religious fundamentalism is continuing and will continue to pose serious threats to regional and global peace. ISIS, as a terrorist geo-political entity, has been defeated in its strongholds in Syria and Iraq; but its virulent idea, identity and motivation to achieve its aims and objectives continue to remain vibrant and active. Even today, thousands of IS jihadists are spread over different parts of Syria. IS is progressively spreading itself into different parts of North Africa, South Asia and South East Asia. It will continue to carry out random terror strikes by its affiliated groups. IS Khorasan has already spread to Afghanistan since 2014 and has been carrying out deadly terrorist attacks. Attack in Sri Lanka on the Easter in 2019 is a case in point. According to a UN Report, Al-Qaeda is also reviving itself to spread its influence in other parts like Sahel region, South East Asia and South Asia. India has to take measures to prevent the spread of influence of ISIS or Al-Qaeda, which may happen with the support of terror groups in Pakistan.

Finally, amidst present global dispensation, China-Pak collusion, rising religious fundamentalism and extremism and the regional dynamics, there is a need to ponder, as to what would happen if there be an India-Pakistan crisis like the Kargil conflict of 1999. There is a very thin line distinguishing the proxy and the conventional operations and actually it is the response that can turn any proxy war into a wider conflict. The attack on the Indian Parliament in December 2001 nearly leading to a war is a case in point. India, therefore, needs to prepare well for all the eventualities to avoid getting surprised as the threshold level and sentiments of Indian public psyche have been enhanced post-surgical strikes.

LONG UNFINISHED WAR AND THE WAY AHEAD

"War is a very expensive way to learn lessons and hence wasting opportunities to learn from past operations is a criminal dereliction of duty."

– Raghu Raman

Kargil imbroglio can easily be tipped as a watershed in the Indo-Pak relations. This conflict not only became a *point de depart* for our defence policies but also for preparing as a nation, for a secure existence within inviolable frontiers. Besides, the issue of nuclear overhang on a conventional conflict had been well settled after Kargil, and subsequently after the surgical strikes. However, this conflict still remains a long unfinished war for both the warring nations, as, perhaps, both the nations were not able to achieve their aims. Pakistan, having become a nuclear weapon state in May 1998, just a year before the intrusion, was confident that with flare-up of situation and war hysteria between the two nuclear states, the US and other powers would intervene to resolve the J&K issue in its favour. It did not happen. Also, it could not consolidate its foothold and achieve its strategic aim of cutting off NH1A (now NH1D), and the attendant advantages that were to accrue. India, on the other hand, in spite of having an upper hand at the later stage of the conflict, showed restrained strategic response. India, even after two decades, is yet to fully mitigate the challenges of "Op Vijay", and Pakistan is still "licking its wounds" and continues nurturing its devious aims in Kashmir. These reasons therefore should underpin our "Way Ahead" and future course of actions.

How should we "celebrate" the Kargil Conflict?

Though the issue of unresolved border disputes with China and Pakistan would always remain under the clouds of conventional operations, but there are reasons enough to believe that an all-out war is unlikely. However, if it breaks out, it is likely to trigger in mountains (disputed boundary and territorial areas) and then spread over to other regions.

So how should we "celebrate" the Kargil conflict? Twenty years on, this question lingers every year, but it somehow gets subdued under its own weight. This war surely needs to be celebrated for our unflinching resolve as a nation; for the junior leadership exploits of one of the finest Armies of the world; by paying tribute to the gallant officers and jawans who dedicated themselves to the nation; and for our Armed Forces who worked steadfastly to protect the unity and integrity of our nation. But more importantly, Kargil also needs to be celebrated by safeguarding and making sure that complacency in national security and the mistakes of year 1999 do not happen again and the inescapable requirements of national security are not compromised in future. It would also be in order to conduct an audit of what has changed for the better since then, and what continues to constrain the armed forces.

Security Review Committees

Post the Kargil Conflict, a number of national level and service-specific committees have given their recommendations to improve our operational effectiveness: be it about one border one force; jointness, theaterisation and integration; integration of MoD with the three services; having a CDS, as recommended by GoM or a Permanent Joint Chiefs of Staff as recommended by the Naresh Chandra Committee in 2011-12; whether to have theaterised commands or functional commands; reducing army's commitment in internal security; and to lay emphasis on technology, innovations, and indigenisation of production. A fair number of KRC and GoM's recommendations still remain unfinished and continue to fester. [11] Lt Gen Satish Nambiar observes in his article published by the USI, "Restructuring and Integration of the Ministry of Defence With the Three Service Headquarters," that despite having seen five wars, multiple insurgencies, proxy war, state-sponsored terrorism, changes due to Revolution in Military Affairs and emergence of new nuclear-powered states, the original structure of India's national security system has, by and large, remained unchanged.

The bottom line is that we should be effective operationally, with the ability to ensure synergistic application of all available resources for that operation in the very limited window of opportunity. Unfortunately, a fair number of these recommendations have not been implemented. Yes, we have taken some actions to lay emphasis on indigenisation, make in India, and to create new organisations to improve our intelligence at the national level. Given the evolution in technology and new systems available to conventional forces and to the non-state actors, there is still a need to improve the intelligence system by way of the organisational structures, capacity building, integration and coordination, and an oversight both to provide resources to the intelligence agencies and to monitor their performance and activities. Equally important, if not more, is the need to develop ISR capability, which would ensure that our territorial integrity and the hinterland remain safe and secure.

India still needs to acquire state-of-the-art military satellites and aerial and ground surveillance systems to guard against repetition of the Kargil-type intrusion or a similar situation. We have still not ironed out issues pertaining to manoeuvre and fire power in mountains including the air power and its equipment profile to effectively fight in high-altitude areas. Concept of lighter formations is yet to be tested and the faster decision-making at the tactical level that can only be achieved by jointness between the forces is still eluding us. A total review of weapon and equipment according to the terrain and changing battlefield requirements is still a work in progress. We still have miles to cover in terms of developing the infrastructure, operational tracks, ammunition stocking and other logistic nightmares of Kargil. A tailor-made logistics that fits the requirements of each sector requires to be worked upon. We have many benchmark measures that yet need consideration 20 years down the line. Shying away from them would be tantamount to repeating the mistakes of Kargil 1999.

Path-breaking innovations in the field of information technology, artificial intelligence, big data computing, communications, data storage and data processing have enhanced the ISR capabilities. But with imported systems, we run the risk of embedded platforms, which can compromise our security system at crucial moments. It is time to indigenously develop ISR capabilities for ground, aerial, sea and space-based systems to improve our response mechanism.

Unresolved Boundary Disputes: No Loss of Territory

The territorial and boundary disputes on our sub-continent are a result of its unique geo-strategic location, its neighbourhood, its history and the legacy of the partition. These disputes finally translate to external threats to India. We, on our sub-continent, have an extraordinary responsibility towards territorial integrity, as loss of any territory is not acceptable under any circumstances. We have to take a number of lessons from the Kargil conflict of 1999, where from initial knowledge of the intrusions in early May 1999, it took us almost 70-80 days to complete the operations (26 July 1999), notwithstanding a few constraints like not crossing the Line of Control, induction of troops from counter-insurgency into intense mountain-warfare environment and their mindset, acclimatisation of troops, problems faced in supply of logistic support at high altitudes etc. Therefore, in a short and intense nature of conflict, we will not have the luxury of delayed decision-making, delayed mobilisation and delayed application of forces. Timely and synergistic application of forces can only take place if we have unity of command, which would further ensure unity of effort. How can we achieve an effective unity of command and effort (joint war-fighting capability) in such short and intense conflicts? It remains unanswered to our satisfaction so far. Surely, this needs to be examined urgently, with due seriousness.

Twenty years have gone by but Pakistan's stance of abetting proxy war and state-sponsored terrorism, intrusions across the LoC, radicalisation of Kashmiri youths, and psychological warfare have not changed, and they continue unabated. The only change has been the Indian response mechanism that has seen an upward trajectory along the escalatory ladder, from subdued responses to the aggressive and proactive ones.

Understanding Pakistan's Psyche and Indian Mindset

India should factor-in the existence of Pakistan along with its deep state, and hence be prepared to deal with its two power centres, namely, military and polity. This essentially means that we need to engage Pakistan Army for any worthwhile negotiations.

We need to have a better understanding of Pakistan's "psyche". It would be futile to hope that internal instability, international pressure or economic compulsions will dissuade the Pakistani army from embarking on such ventures in future. In less than two years after the Kargil conflict, Pakistani-trained terrorists attacked the Indian Parliament in December 2001, and then the 26/11 happened followed by Pathankot, Uri and Pulwama. This clearly depicts that such misadventures are unlikely to end. Though recent Indian reactions certainly have surprised them, but Pakistan Air Force (PAF) misadventures post-Balakot testifies the belief that they would retaliate, even if we hit known and justified targets like terror camps. Unless we adopt strong punitive military actions, immediately, and follow up with actions at multiple levels, Pakistan will continue with such misadventures.

Apparently, Indian mindset also requires to understand two important actions of Pakistan which have an impact on India: one, that Pakistan's Inter-Services Public Relations (ISPR) has been most effective in manipulating the social media, TV and internet extensively, and in issuing propaganda narratives, to influence the perceptions of the populace, both within its country and outside; two, that there is a need to understand Pakistan's "Nuclear bluff", which has permitted our conventional military capability to get neutralized and made us perpetually "Defensive" in our approach. This has led to our responses to be nothing more than "Limited Aims". Starting from 1947/48 operations, India chose to limit the duration of operations (many today believe that had we carried on, the history of the sub-continent would have been different); in 1962, we did not employ our air force; in 1971, we again limited the war to the capture of Dacca and did not consider the settlement of our disputes with 93,000 prisoners in India; and now in Kargil conflict again we tied our hands and did not plan to defeat the enemy in detail. Currently, when future conflicts are anticipated to be "short and intense", we need to be dynamic in our thinking and suitably tailor our forces to meet the impending challenges and not compromise on our conventional capability.

Military Deterrence: What does it Mean?

This brings us to an all-important aspect of Military Deterrence. Strangely, one has often been asked a question that if India is unlikely to fight a conventional war, then why should there be so much focus on building conventional capabilities? First, given our territorial disputes and seven decades of hostile attitude of Pakistan, in particular, the probability of war with our adversaries continues to remain high. This myth that India is unlikely to fight a conventional war should be removed from our thoughts. Given Pakistan's indulgence in proxy war-cum-state-sponsored terrorism, the probability of a sub-conventional conflict converting into a conventional one remains high. And our adversaries should understand that India will react with full force if provoked by Kargil- or Uri- or Pulwama-like incidents, and that India will not hesitate to escalate because of the nuclear weapons status of the adversary. Second, if India does not maintain its superior/credible conventional capabilities, it will be kept engaged by our adversaries in sub-conventional and hybrid war at multiple levels, with impunity. They would take full advantage of our weaknesses. Hence, rather than being reactive, India should seize the initiative and become proactive. This can happen only if we have the requisite capabilities.

"Peace through strength" is an expression that suggests that military power can help preserve peace. It is an old expression that has been used by many leaders from Roman Emperor Hadrian in the first century AD to former Presidents of the US, namely, the first American President, George Washington (1793) and Ronald Reagan in the 1980s. Therefore, conventional deterrence should be developed to a credible level, and the soft and hard power should be demonstrated to exhibit our capabilities. This form of deterrence would also help to prevent conflicts.

What does "military deterrence" mean? It means that a country has the capability that is qualitatively and quantitatively, in that order, far superior to that of its adversary, and that it would take a timely decision and action(s) to deal with a situation. Therefore, effective military deterrence can only be achieved by improving our military capabilities in both conventional and non-conventional war-fighting mechanisms, soft power and demonstrated power. Military deterrence would be credible if it is backed by comprehensive national power (CNP): political will, strong economy, social cohesion, vibrant industrial base, integrated logistics system, supportive public information system, and a strong technology and innovation culture. Thus, India needs to progressively build capabilities of hard military power, soft power and demonstrated power that can deter threats to its stability and territorial integrity from potential adversaries. Besides taking actions to build a strong economy, we need to understand that political clarity and political will are required to achieve Military Deterrence.[12]

Politico-military synergy is essential to ensure a seamless defence planning in consonance with our national objectives. It is time to have adequate civilian staff who, along with the armed forces officers, form a good team of specialists to holistically examine all issues pertaining to changing nature and character of warfare, latest technology in defence industry, weapons and equipment, ammunition, trials at different levels, ISR platforms, and the defence procurement procedures. Considering the envisaged threats and challenges in the next 10-15 years, integrated procurement and modernisation plans in terms of Long-Term Integrated Perspective Plans (LTIPP) should be approved by the Cabinet Committee on Security (CCS). This would also ensure firm commitment of financial resources for the approved projects. This also means that there should be meaningful discussions on national security issues, including our defence preparedness, our deficiencies and the defence budget in our Parliament.

Peoples' Support in J&K

India needs to understand, accept and factor in the present Kashmiri dispensation. Todays Kashmir is starkly different from the one during "Op Gulmarg in 1947" and "Op Gibraltar in 1965". The deficiency of intelligence needs to be fixed in which locals play an invaluable role, else we would be surprised again like we have been before. To "win" back the trust of the local Kashmiri, we seem to be running against time. Given the current conditions prevailing in the Valley, in particular, India would face heavy odds to win against Pakistan's charade in a future, conventional or hybrid operations, without the local's support. Thus, this strategic asset of local population, in all regions – Jammu, Kashmir and Ladakh – needs to be nurtured to play a positive role in India's integrity and growth.

Develop Strategic Partnership

It is important to pronounce that the dynamics of any future Indo-Pak conflict will be considerably different from that which was witnessed during "Op Vijay". While nuclear deterrence did not stop the crisis from occurring, it certainly played an indirect role in escalation management by way of ensuring a US role. This third-party overhang surely would stay in future crisis too, requiring persistent readiness of proactive and total dominant diplomacy to ensure conflict termination, which is based on our terms. But with China-Pakistan getting closer and US-India alignment in making, a new scepticism is expected to crop up as to who would actually be the third party? Nobody who is influential enough in the region appears as an arbitrator or even a remotely trusted party. Thus, more alliances have to be forged and old ones nurtured.

India should not shy away from openly accepting that China-Pak strategic alliance is unequivocally the most daunting national security challenge for India. Accordingly, to attenuate the "two-front dilemmas", India should not restrain from investing in alliances like "Quad" and India-Iran-Afghanistan strategic partnership.

In keeping with India's enhanced political, economic and military status, it would be prudent to develop defence cooperation and build cooperative partnership at strategic levels with leading global powers and strategically located countries. While we have developed strategic level cooperation with the US, we need to further enhance our economic-cum-strategic partnership with Russia, the UK, France, Germany, Japan, Australia, Vietnam etc.

Sphere of Influence

The aim should be to analyse the envisaged threats and find measures to counter them. This would help us maintain peace and stability in the affected regions and thus ensure that our national interests are taken care of. Therefore, India should progressively develop a separate sphere of influence of its own in South Asia, South East Asia, West Asia, Africa and the Indian Ocean in order to move ahead to become a global power in the future.

The above aspect should in no terms encourage soft-pedalling as an alternative for India with China. India should gear up to take some hard decisions and until India does this, it is quite pointless to expect China to deliver on India's concerns. Strategically, Uri and Pulwama have changed India, but this is yet to display in its China policy.

As a part of military diplomacy, the Indian Armed Forces have been conducting training exercises with a number of friendly countries, both in India and abroad. This needs to be given further impetus by the government to enlarge our sphere of influence.

Grey Zone Conflicts and Hybrid Warfare[13]

As the "Grey Zone" operations take precedence over conventional operations, India should enhance its punitive deterrence capabilities. If we analyse closely, our recent responses to Pakistan's terror attacks have actually squeezed options for Pakistan. What can we expect next from them? Possibilities of a conventional or Kargil-like option have been partially foreclosed. Pakistan will have to think twice before doing a Mumbai-like attack again. So, the options for them have really been narrowed down to a very low level of non-state actor attacks on military targets within Kashmir and the hinterland. Consequently, India needs to up the ante to raise the cost of proxy war for Pakistan at multiple levels. Exploitation of non-contact and non-kinetic warfare domain needs to be assiduously addressed.

A new era of Indian assertion has been heralded with surgical strikes against terror organisations across the LoC and in Pakistan. This trend surely is a strong deterrent and needs to continue. However, it should be based on tactical feasibility, operational readiness and strategic necessity, combined with political acumen. Such strikes require judicious employment as they lie at the extreme end of "Grey Zone response Matrix".

Pragmatically, there exists a wide disparity between India and China in terms of economy, military strength, defence industry, and science, technology and innovations.[14] China is the biggest factor or impediment in India's relations with Pakistan as well as in India's economic prosperity. Therefore, it would be prudent for India to evolve a *modus vivendi* with China to minimise the mistrust and dilute the growing China-Pak nexus. There are clearly several ways in which a growing India will have the power to impose some limits on Beijing's expanding influence in the broader region.

Defence Industrial Base: Transformation is the Need

It is ironic that even after 72 years of Independence, India still imports about 60-70% of its defence requirements from various countries. The primary reasons for India's huge military import are its under-developed organisational structures and defence industry, inadequate capabilities, and lack of accountability. In addition, excessive bureaucratic controls that dissuade initiative and support inefficiency, lack of fair competition and poor work culture also add to the problem. Although India has done reasonably well in IT, nuclear energy, missile and space technology, it is not a global leader in any of them. Just as Israel has revolutionised its industry due to the confluence of "Big Data, Connectivity and Artificial Intelligence", it is time for India to holistically and pragmatically review the existing system of defence procurement as well as defence production in India, with greater focus on accountability and innovation. It requires an urgent "Transformation – Review of the complete structures, organizations, processes and procedures", with better accountability. Cosmetic changes will certainly not help.

As per the vision of Mr Modi, the Indian PM, *"A transformation in mind-set cannot happen without transformative ideas"*. Thus, in order to produce state-of-the-art weapon systems in India, innovation has to be accorded very high priority, with substantial investment in R&D to revolutionise our industry. Given the huge potential of our private industry, a much greater role must be given to the private sector in defence production, with adequate incentives and a level playing platform. Thus, we may encourage a culture of innovation and indigenisation in the country.

There have been many long-pending, over delayed cases pertaining to infantry weapons, tanks, guns, aircraft, etc., due to which we have not made much headway either in procurements ex import or in their indigenous production. However, the "Make in India" initiative of the Government has given a much needed push to the development of sustainable ecosystem of defence production, R&D and technology absorption in the private and public sectors. The recent successful induction of 155 mm/52 calibre K-9 Vajra (SP) gun system, which has been manufactured through transfer of technology (ToT), and Advanced Light Helicopter (Utility Helicopter) and Weapon System Integrated (WSI) versions designed, developed and manufactured in India are a few good examples of success in defence production. The induction of 155 mm/45 calibre Dhanush Gun system and 155mm/52 calibre ATAGS are around the corner, with trials being conducted of the systems. The push to indigenous production and R&D is a step in the right direction and will certainly bear fruit in time to come. However, we have a long way to go in the area of niche technologies of surveillance, AI and autonomous systems

Focus on Information, Technology and Speedy Decision-Making

In operational domain, putting an effective Command, Control, Communications, Computers, Intelligence, Information, Surveillance, and Reconnaissance (C4I2SR) system has never been as critical, given its impact on speeding up the Observation, Orientation, Decision, and Action (OODA) loop and potential to enhance shared situational awareness and speedy decision-making. There is also an immediate need for military satellites with a sub-one-meter resolution and multi-spectral (optical, infrared and radar photography) capability, so that they are effective both by day and night.

AI technology has tremendous applications in social, economic, medicine, transportation, mining and military fields. USA and China are far ahead in their research on AI and its application, especially in the military domain. The Chinese have been refining the autonomous systems to undertake swarm attacks by UAVs. Looking at the future, Cyber, space and AI and their military applications should form an essential part of our national security strategy.

Periodically Review Nuclear Doctrine

India needs to realise that Nuclear weapons have fundamentally changed the nature of war. Nuclear weapons are not for war fighting; they are to prevent conflicts. The destructive power of nuclear weapons is so great that states understand the awful consequences, thereby resisting from its use. Therefore, India should not hold back due to the threat of nuclear overhang, and continue the bold reactions to Pakistan's terror actions in future. Recent Indian engagements, post Uri and Pulwama, have amply proved this point beyond doubt.

India promulgated its nuclear doctrine in January 2003, which is defensive in nature, but with a sound deterrent capability. With two nuclear armed states as our neighbours, with whom we have unresolved border disputes, reservations have been expressed at different forums on whether our nuclear doctrine, being 16 years old, needs a review. Credible minimum deterrence (CMD) capability should be based on Triad (precision delivery means) survivability and second-strike capability, and a sound command and control system. With changes in the geo-political environment and regional security matrix, it would be prudent to review our doctrine periodically.

Also, there is a need for "threat perception and scenario-building exercises" to be held periodically with the concerned stakeholders, to make them aware of the envisaged threats and our capabilities. Such an exercise would certainly facilitate taking timely decisions during various contingencies that may arise in the future.

Management of Borders

As future conflicts with either Pakistan or China are likely to commence in disputed territories, there is an ardent need to focus more on two vital aspects: one, ensuring better management of our borders; and two, enhancing our war-waging capabilities in such regions.

India has land borders with seven countries, and extends over 15,106 km. While the Sino–Indian border is 3,488 km, the border with Pakistan is 3,323 km, including 742 km of LoC and 126 km along the Actual Ground Position Line (AGPL) in the Siachen Glacier sector. Deployment of multiple forces on the same border has often led to problems of command and control, responsiveness, sharing of intelligence and accountability. In addition, while a large segment of the land borders is not demarcated on the ground, the maritime boundaries are also not clearly defined.

In India, a plethora of armed police forces has continued to guard our borders (BSF, ITBP, SSB and Assam Rifles). As each border has unique threats and challenges, "One Border One Force" was recommended by the KRC, which has actually not happened, particularly along the LAC.

The aim of border management strategy should be to effectively maintain the territorial integrity of the borders, and to take care of the multi-faceted threats and challenges along each border. Besides utilising technology to manage borders (smart management), it is vital to have clarity in responsibility, command and control, authority and accountability for each border, more importantly the borders under dispute.

In our case, ideally, the management of disputed and unresolved borders must be the responsibility of the Indian Army, functioning under the Ministry of Defence (MoD). In fact, in principle, BSF and ITBP, the border guarding forces on the Pakistan and China borders, respectively, should be placed directly under the MoD till the time our disputed borders are resolved. Alternatively, at least all forces and agencies deployed along the disputed portions of the border should be placed under the MoD. The management of the remainder borders should be re-adjusted with the other police forces, under the MHA. It requires a call at the national level. To further improve operational effectiveness, the equipment profile of all forces deployed on the disputed borders must be "sector specific" to ensure better logistics, uniformity and synergy among the forces.

Infrastructure and Environment

The pace of infrastructural work, especially close to the border areas, has been rather slow due to a number of constraints. It certainly has an adverse impact on operational preparedness, of which logistics are a vital part. While integrating the national and military logistics grid into a well-planned architecture, we need to improve our work output towards development of infrastructure along the borders in terms of roads, helipads, airfields, rails, telecommunications, power facilities, infrastructure for logistic nodes in critical areas. Strategic roads and infrastructure should be prioritised to complete them. A holistic review of Comprehensive National Logistics Power merits serious consideration.

Connected with the infrastructure development is an equally important subject of environmental degradation and its impact on our plans towards our territorial integrity. Environmental degradation occurs due to a host of factors: land degradation (deforestation, desertification, and soil salinization), atmospheric degradation (climate change, greenhouse effect, and ozone depletion), water degradation, biodiversity degradation, and pollution. Given the tasks of the armed forces, the army in particular, we have to understand that environmental degradation has huge implications on our security at strategic, operational and tactical levels. To analyse the long-term impact, it would be prudent to analyse environmental degradation on the Indian sub-continent and its effects on security at various levels.

Robust Logistics System

"Logistics is the unseen hand that shapes the army's punch."

Mountain warfare is a logistician's nightmare. Without detailed planning, forethought, and flexibility, successful attrition by the ground troops can come to a grinding halt. The rapid induction of troops into Kargil sector necessitated the same speed of assuring artillery ammunition, rations, kerosene oil, medical supplies, and heavy dozers, to be moved there for sustaining the warfront. The problems of establishing logistic bases well forward were further compounded by being targeted by accurate Pakistani Artillery firing. Water management is a case in point. It was a major task as snow on south-facing slopes had melted and even at heights, the remaining snow was unfit for consumption due to explosives contamination.

On the other hand, till the actual commencement of war, the Pakistanis appeared to have catered for a strong logistic backup. But once the onslaught of the Indian Army commenced, their administration simply collapsed and broke their resolve and fighting abilities. On the Indian side, the fact that so many guns, helicopters and equipment remained in a constant state of usage is a tribute to the professionalism of the logisticians.

The battles of the future will be shorter, intense, complex, and multi-dimensional, compressed in time and space, with high tempo of operations, and will be conducted in the backdrop of the nuclear overhang. Therefore, at the national level, there is a need to integrate military infrastructure development and essential logistic requirements with the national logistic development plan, with higher priority to development of strategic infrastructure. In addition, logistics should focus on absorbing technology, inventory management, capacity building based on appreciated requirements, and is also integrated with the other two services and based on tri-service operational philosophy, where feasible. However, in mountainous and difficult terrain and operational environments, it would be prudent to plan tailor-made logistic grids to serve the troops deployed in the forward areas.

Strong Punitive Actions with Strategic Balance

When faced with situation such as in Kargil in May 1999, a strong nation must first punish the intruders militarily, and then seek world opinion and their support. We did not do that. Of course, concurrently, actions should be taken to maintain strategic balance at the national level. We must raise the cost of such misadventures at multiple levels; this also includes shaping of world opinion from a position of military strength. This can happen only if we achieve effective military deterrence by improving our military capabilities in both conventional and non-conventional war fighting mechanism. Secondly, if our neighbour violates the sanctity of the LoC or the International Boundary (IB) by indulging in intrusions at several places, like it did during Kargil conflict 1999, then we should not bind ourselves to not cross the LoC to conduct military operations. In such situations, it should be our endeavour to defeat them in detail, with minimum casualties to our troops. This part requires political will to enable the armed forces – transformation of defence structures, modernisation and jointness – to give a befitting reply.

NATIONAL OUTLOOK FOR NATIONAL SECURITY

India is one of the fastest growing economies of the world, as also the sixth largest. As the third largest military, and one of the leaders in information, missile and space technology, India is an undisputed emerging power. Therefore, India's strategic aim should be:

- One, to maintain a conducive and secure environment for human security and country's growth;
- Two, to build CNP, which requires sustained high economic growth, among other parameters;
- Three, aspire to become an undisputed regional power by 2030, and a global power in the next two to three decades.

The writing is clear that India should focus on building its CNP, with highest priority to achieve sustained high economic growth, as that alone will give the desired impetus to address a host of threats and challenges to our national security. Simultaneously, India needs to transform its national security architecture: higher defence organisations, integration of MoD with the service HQ, integration and jointness, strengthening the defence industrial base and operational preparedness.

India and China have held 21 rounds of talks to resolve differences over the 3488-km long Line of Actual Control (LAC). President Xi and PM Modi met on the side-lines of the Shanghai Cooperation Organisation (SCO) summit in Bishkek, on 13 June 2019. On the vexed boundary issue, Xi Jinping said, "We need to make good use of the meeting of the Special Representatives on the boundary issue and other mechanisms, strengthen Confidence Building Measures (CBMs) and maintain stability at the border areas". It is a positive development. As a country, we must make an all-out effort to resolve our territorial disputes with China, as that would help us to maintain security and stability in the region; and focus on addressing the non-traditional threats to improve the quality of life of population at large, amongst other advantages.

Most of our schools of instruction impart professional skills, which concentrate on preparing officers in service specific subjects, and command and staff duties at different levels. It is important for the strategic leaders to comprehend the emerging politico-economic-social scenario, along with changes in the technology, and analyse their impact on the strategic scenario under different contingencies. This is important because the leader would be required to operate in such environment in the future, and would be required to analyse the strategic risk profile of various options available, and then make strategic choices. Subsequently, while the operations are in progress, managing the emerging uncertainties would be the core function of the leader. Therefore, to deal with complex situations, a leader needs clear vision, clear direction, agility of mind and high tolerance for ambiguity. Development of strategic culture and strategic thinking has not got the requisite impetus it deserves. Despite recommendations by national level security committees to achieve jointness, integration of the three services, appointment of CDS etc, these have remained unaddressed to the desired levels. Undoubtedly, these have an impact on our operational preparedness. It is expected of our strategic leaders to formulate strategies and make recommendations for the betterment of national security, with a **national outlook**. National security should not be held hostage to preservation of turfs or attempting to reach consensus. Matters like national security, which are well deliberated, require tough calls to be made, and implementation ensured in a time-bound manner.

The basic question, therefore, is whether we are prepared to face the challenges of the future threats – external, internal and hybrid – on the Indian sub-continent. Considering the scale and pace of changes in the warfare of the future, we need to analyse our response both conceptually and from the capabilities point of view. It is evident that we have to look at transformation of our current systems with due seriousness, and urgently. While military modernisation is an essential subset of transformation, it requires a change in thought process, review of our doctrines, strategy, war-fighting concepts, organisational and force structures, training concepts and logistics periodically, and, more importantly, preparedness of the strategic leadership to drive the change for improving our national security.

Having stated the operational necessity and the transformational requirements, we need to broadly examine the likely challenges to transformation, both from within and outside the Armed Forces. Transformation is a long-term continuous process. It should be sustainable. Therefore, the armed forces would require the support of the political leaders, bureaucratic setup, industrial support especially from the defence industrial base, DRDO and the armed forces themselves. We have to address the fundamental issue of achieving "interoperability and integration" within and among the three services. Second, even if we are able to bridge the technological gap by introducing state-of-the-art technologies, absorption of technology is an equally important part which must be planned for in a deliberate manner. To put all this together, military leaders have to not only keep themselves abreast with the latest changes in technologies, but also the geo-politico-economic-strategic environment to drive the change.

For a country like India, with multifaceted security threats and challenges, and the emerging strategic scenario, national security strategy would be far more complex. Therefore, formulation of Comprehensive National Security Strategy (CNSS) would be of utmost importance to give a clear direction to its national security. It is a well-established fact that no single authority or agency can address the complex nature of threats to our national security. As all elements of national power have certain responsibilities, either directly or indirectly, towards national security, CNSS should spell out major responsibilities of each element, both in the short- and long-term perspectives. This should be both for external and internal threats being faced or likely to be faced. This would also ensure timely decisions to take actions against an erring adversary. If the responsibilities are not defined, every element is not really clear about its short- and long-term responsibilities, and hence is not accountable.

Twenty years down the line post Kargil, and with a number of security committees having given their recommendations, it is time to transform all organs of the defence structures (not the Army alone) like the Armed Forces, HDO, MoD, defence production agencies, DRDO and defence procurement procedures, in a calibrated manner, to make them more responsive and operation oriented. Transformation alone would help us to achieve Military Deterrence. Rather than imitating another country's model, the aim should be to formulate an India-centric model for the integration of the Armed Forces, MoD, and other agencies of national power.

Internal security is one of the most crucial facets of national security. A thorough review of the internal security apparatus is required to create a secure environment, to facilitate India's growth story to flourish. In the larger interest of the country, it is important to address the causes of internal armed conflicts and resolve them on a mission-oriented basis.

> *"The character of war in the 21st century has changed, and if we fail to keep pace with the speed of war, we will lose the ability to compete."*
>
> – *Gen Joe Dunford,* 19th Chairman of the US Joint Chiefs of Staff, 2017[15]

Conclusion

In the present narrative, lasting peace with Pakistan seems unlikely. At best, we can expect an armed truce, that too dictated by Pakistan's internal fault lines and economic constraints. It would be utopian to think of friendship till the time Pakistan stops promoting Islamic fundamentalism and de-radicalises the affected population; the latter part would take at least a generation of re-education and intellectual purgation. Thus, this should underpin any *modus vivendi* we work out in future with Pakistan. Kargil should not be forgotten for the anguish it caused to the nation and its lessons should continue to be a beacon to the new avenues and opportunities that lie before this country. The sacrifices of those who died for the nation and the mourning of those left behind cannot be allowed to go in vain.

Though India lost the fleeting opportunity available to it in 1999, but it should be ready in the next round to secure optimum results. Therefore, it goes without saying that whatever is worked out with Pakistan in the foreseeable future, we must on no account, let down our guard as there is no question of trusting Pakistan's words again. Besides, our military power has to be decisively superior that the riposte to an adversary's misadventure can be swift and devastating.

Considering the threats and challenges of the future, India needs to focus on building its CNP, whose edifice should be based on sustained economic growth. Simultaneously, it should progressively build capabilities of hard military power, soft power and demonstrated power which can deter threats to its internal security, stability and territorial integrity from potential adversaries. Cosmetic changes will not help. We can take hard decisions only if look at "national security with a national outlook".

"In all fighting, the direct method may be used for joining battle, but indirect method will be needed in order to secure victory."

– Sun Tzu

NOTES

1. Cordesman, Anthony H. (2018), Stability in the Middle East: The Range of Short and Long-Term Causes, Center for Strategic and International Studies (CSIS), Washington DC, 22 March, Available at: https://csis-prod.s3.amazonaws.com/s3fs-public/publication/180403_Stability_in_MENA_Region.
2. Iran's Parliament labels US troops in Mid east terrorists, *Times Global*, April 17, 2019, Pp 22.
3. Kapoor, Rajeev, "Indo-Nepal Ties: Transmute From Dominance to Equality," Available at: www.CLAWS.in.
4. USDP, *"Number of Armed Conflicts by Type"*, The Economist.
5. "After the Caliphate: Has IS Been Defeated?" BBC News, December 20, 2018, Available at: https://www.bbc.com/news/world-middle-east-45547595.
6. VK Ahluwalia, Claws Journal, Imperatives of Transformation, Changing Character of Conflict in the Emerging World Order, June 2019.
7. Institute for Economics & Peace (2018), *Global Peace Index 2018: Measuring Peace in a Complex World*, Sydney, June 2018, Available at: http://visionofhumanity.org/app/uploads/2018/06/Global-Peace-Index-2018-2.pdf.
8. Uppsala Conflict Data Program (UCDP) (2018), "Number of Conflicts, 1946 to 2017", Uppsala Universitet: Department of Peace and Conflict Research, Available at: https://ucdp.uu.se/.
9. Kapoor, Rajeev, "Banning of JeM Chief: China's Quandary," Available at: www.CLAWS.in.
10. Tom Hussain, "How India-Pakistan Tensions (and US-China Rivalry) Are Raising Nuclear Stakes", Available at: https://www.scmp.com/week-asia/geopolitics/article/2026150/how-india-pakistan-tensions-and-us-china-rivalry-are-raising.
11. Indian Defence Research Wing (IDRW) (2019), "20 years after Kargil, where do we stand?", 18 May, Available at: http://idrw.org/20-years-after-kargil-where-do-we-stand/. See also, Air Marshall Anil Chopra (2019), "20 Years After Kargil, Where Do We Stand?", *The Tribune*, 18 May, Available at: https://www.tribuneindia.com/news/comment/20-years-after-kargil-where-do-we-stand/774508.html.
12. VK Ahluwalia, India's National Security Challenges and Priorities, Short- and Long-Term Perspectives, Manekshaw Papers No. 80, 2019.
13. VK Ahluwalia, Claws Journal, Imperatives of Transformation, Changing Character of Conflict in the Emerging World Order, June 2019, and Abhijit Singh, Between War and Peace: Grey-Zone Operations in Asia, 13 Feb 2018, Australian Institute of International Affairs.

Two terms – hybrid warfare and grey zone conflicts – have been added to the glossary of terms of International Relations (IR). Hybrid warfare, also known as ambiguous warfare is a blend of regular and irregular warfare. In other words, hybrid warfare is a blend of economy, military, information, psychology and cyber, with a view to achieve political objectives, and to achieve economic advantage. Warfare has graduated to the fifth generation in the form of hybrid warfare. It has been used in the recent conflicts in West Asia and Afghanistan. Although the Indian sub-continent continues to face sub-conventional war in the form of proxy war and cross-border terrorism, it has not experienced the full dimension of hybrid war so far. Grey zone conflicts are conflicts which oscillate between war and peace and are generally waged by the great powers who do not want to cross the threshold of an outright war due to the nuclear threat, and yet aim to achieve their political and territorial objectives.

14. Lintner, Bertil, "Great Game East", Harper Collins, India.

15. Robert Kozloski, **Commentary "War on the Rocks,** The Path To Prototype Warfare",** 17 July 2017, Available at: https://warontherocks.com/2017/07/the-path-to-prototype-warfare/.

Honours and Awards

Award	Awardee	Battalion/Armed Force
PARAM VIR CHAKRA (PVC)	• CAPTAIN VIKRAM BATRA (P) • RIFLEMAN SANJAY KUMAR	13 JAMMU AND KASHMIR RIFLES (13 JAK RIF)
	• LT MANOJ KUMAR PANDEY (P)	1/11 GORKHA RIFLES (1/11 GR)
	• GRENADIER YOGENDRA SINGH YADAV	18 GRENADIERS
MAHAVIR CHAKRA (MVC)	• CAPTAIN ANUJ NAYYAR (P)	17 JAT
	• MAJOR VIVEK GUPTA (P) • MAJOR PADROAPANI ACHARYA (P) • CAPTAIN NEIKEZHAKUO KENGURUZE ASC (P) • NAIK DIGENDRA KUMAR	2 RAJPUTANA RIFLES (2 RAJ RIF)
	• LT KC NONGRUM (P)	12 JAMMU AND KASHMIR LIGHT INFANTRY (12 JAK LI)
	• SEPOY IMLI AKUM AO	2 NAGA
	• MAJOR RAJESH SINGH ADHIKARI (P) • LT BALWAN SINGH	18 GRENADIERS
	• CAPT GURJINDER SINGH SURI	AOC, 12 BIHAR

During the operations, several soldiers made their supreme sacrifice and were awarded 04 ParamVir Chakras, 10 MahaVir Chakras and 70 Vir Chakras among others for gallantry.

(National War Memorial, New Delhi. Inaugurated on 25 February, 2019.)

BATTLE HONOURS

CORPS OF ENGINEERS

* 108 ENGR REGT   (DRAS)

INFANTRY

* 18 GRENADIERS   (TOLOLING AND TIGER HILL)
* 2 RAJ RIF   (TOLOLING AND DRAS)
* 17 JAT   (MUSHKOH)
* 8 SIKH   (TIGER HILL)
* 17 GARH RIF   (BATALIK)
* 18 GARH RIF   (DRAS)
* 1 BIHAR   (BATALIK)
* 13 JAK RIF   (MUSHKOH AND DRAS)
* LADAKH SCOUTS   (BATALIK)
* 1 NAGA   (DRAS)
* 2 NAGA   (MUSHKOH)
* 12 JAK LI   (BATALIK)
* 1/11 GR   (BATALIK)

THEATRE HONOURS

CORPS OF ENGINEERS

* 2 ENGR REGT   (KARGIL)
* 106 ENGR REGT   (KARGIL)
* 108 ENGR REGT   (KARGIL)

INFANTRY

5 PARA   (KARGIL)
9 PARA (SF)   (KARGIL)
10 PARA (SF)   (KARGIL)
18 GRENADIERS   (KARGIL)
2 RAJ RIF   (KARGIL)
17 JAT   (KARGIL)
8 SIKH   (KARGIL)
17 GARH RIF   (KARGIL)
18 GARH RIF   (KARGIL)
1 BIHAR   (KARGIL)
13 JAK RIF   (KARGIL)
LADAKH SCOUTS   (KARGIL)
1 NAGA   (KARGIL)
2 NAGA   (KARGIL)

12 JAK LI	(KARGIL)
3/3 GR	(KARGIL)
1/11 GR	(KARGIL)

HONOUR TITLES

REGT IN ARTILLERY

- 41 FD REGT (KARGIL)
- 141 FD REGT (KARGIL)
- 197 FD REGT (KARGIL)
- 315 FD REGT (KARGIL)
- 2122 RKT BTY (KARGIL)
- 108 MED REGT (KARGIL)
- 158 MED REGT (KARGIL)
- 286 MED REGT (KARGIL)
- 1889 LT REGT (KARGIL)

ARMY AVIATION

- 666 R&O SQN (KARGIL)

UNIT CITATIONS

1. 141 FIELD REGIMENT
2. 197 FIELD REGIMENT
3. 108 MEDIUM REGIMENT
4. 663 R&O SQUADRON
5. 666 R&O SQUADRON
6. 106 ENGINEER REGIMENT
7. 5 PARA
8. 6 PARA
9. 2 RAJ RIF
10. 11 RAJ RIF
11. 17 JAT
12. 8 SIKH
13. DOGRA
14. 18 GARH RIF
15. 14 ASSAM
16. 1 BIHAR
17. 12 JAK LI
18. 13 JAK RIF
19. 1 LADAKH
20. 2 NAGA
21. 5/1 GR
22. 1/11 GR
23. 22 RR (PUNJAB)
24. 874 AT BN
25. 18 GRENADIERS

Source: AG's Branch, Army Headquarters

Conclusion

Colonel Narjit Singh

"God is on the side of the battalions with bigger cannons."

— *Napoleon Bonaparte*

Though our operations picked up momentum rather late even after detecting the Pakistani intruders, but once the troops were committed to the ground, they, with their sheer grit and determination, fought fiercely against all odds and started throwing them back with heavy losses to the enemy. And so, by 11 July 1999, the guns started falling silent along the LoC. Seeing the Indian government's unrelenting resolve to evict every single Pakistani army soldier from Indian soil, the Pakistani establishment asked for a meeting between the Director General Military Operation (DGMO) of India and Director Military Operations (DMO) of Pakistan. Both functionaries met at Wagah border on 11 July 1999 where the Pakistanis agreed to withdraw from their side of the LoC by 16 July 1999. Pockets of resistance still remained in Dras, Mushkoh Valley and Batalik, and were forcefully evicted by 25 July 1999.

Our troops were still cut off from mainstream civilisation as newspapers were taking a week to reach the men. However, at base camps of the units, televisions provided them with the latest ongoings. Some officers felt that closure of such hostilities would minimise further troop losses. Anyway, 11 July 1999 also marked the beginning of a much bigger and daily task of now occupying, massing and guarding the LoC, perhaps for forever. A few diaries captured from dead Pakistani officers reflected that they had possibly intruded in early May 1999. On the contrary, Nasim Zehra, in her book *'From Kargil to the Coup: Events that Shook Pakistan'*, states that NLI troops had started moving onto unoccupied heights opposite Dras by end of October 1998. In a shocking revelation by Capt Hussain Ahmad and a diary recovered from a bunker in Mushkoh, their Chief, General Musharraf, had paid a visit to their post, Pt 4815 on 7 February 1999.

Operation Vijay was a high-intensity operation in high-altitude mountainous area which involved the usage of a large quantum of Artillery in an unconventional manner. Without doubt the lion's share of the credit for the military victory in Kargil must go to the brave Infantarians, who displayed unparalleled grit, determination and raw courage in inflicting defeat after defeat to their Pakistani counterparts. Heroes were born every day, who symbolised the undeterred will of an entire nation. What to say of their households and families? They also, with so much trepidation and weight in their hearts, showered encouragement to raise their kin's indomitable spirits.

The Kargil Conflict escalated from a reading of 0 on the scale of 10 without any intermediate figures. First, it was just throwing out a few "intruding rats", and then with the turn of a page, this "snowballed" into a full-fledged war. Such a situation needed an enhanced logistic mobilisation that was established and built up rapidly to cater to the daily growing number of troops inducting into the war. In support of the ground forces, the Airforce threw in their full weight. Despite the presence of active air defence missiles and difficult terrain, it always supported the troops on the ground.

Despite these shortcomings, the Indian soldier focused on mission accomplishment that carried him to the final chapter of victory. By mid-June 1999 and with no tangible battle results in sight – like status quo since commencements of operations in mid-May 1999 – the thought process shifted to enhancing the conflict. The then security advisor Brijesh Mishra informed the US national security advisor that India would not be able to show restraint much longer, and it was only a matter of time before it crossed over the border. A short while thereafter, victory came with Tololing and Pt 5140, and the victorious chain started to build up with more enemy defeats and reversals. Indeed, an all-out war had been averted and the US too acknowledged the Indian stance with seriousness, resulting in diplomatic pressure being brought to bear on Pakistan. Besides individual acts of sheer courage, collective gallantry at the company and battalion level was on display with regularity. The Indian soldiers were in a win-win situation being able to safeguard the honour and integrity of the country to re-enforce the *izzat* of their units, and thereby stamp personal examples of raw courage like their predecessors for future generations to emulate.

Looking at Kargil after 20 years suggests that we should analyse the changing geo-political environment and regional security matrix, and the operational preparedness of our Armed Forces. From the lessons of the Conflict and the deliberations in the book, it is evident that we have to address vital aspects of doctrine, strategy, war-fighting concepts, tactics, and a whole range of issues pertaining to higher defence organisation, jointness and integration, defence industrial base, indigenisation and innovation, border management, intelligence gathering and interpretation, and periodic review of our nuclear doctrine. On balance, all these would require political clarity and political will to formulate a road map to achieve them in a progressive manner.

It has been very aptly said that *"a nation without heroes, is a nation without a future."*

List of Contributors

General VP Malik, PVSM, AVSM,Former COAS (Retd), General VP Malik was the Chief of the Army Staff (India) from 1 October 1997 to 30 September 2000. Concurrently, he was Chairman, Chiefs of Staff Committee, from 1 January 1999 to 30 September 2000. In both these posts, he played a vital role in planning, coordinating and overseeing the military operations that enabled India to evict the Pakistani intruders in Kargil; and thus turn the tables on Pakistan. A graduate from the Defence Services Staff College and Madras University, General Malik is an alumnus of the National Defence College, New Delhi. He has been a member of India's National Security Advisory Board and has delivered lectures in many prestigious civil and military institutions in India and abroad.

General NC Vij, PVSM, UYSM, AVSM, Former COAS (Retd), Gen Vij was the 21st Chief of the Army Staff from 31 Dec 2002 to 31 Jan 2005. He was the Director General of Military Operations (DGMO) during the Kargil War in 1999. Another feather in his cap as DGMO was a visit to Sierra Leone to formulate and thereafter execute an operation (OP KHUKRI), wherein over 455 Indian Soldiers serving as part of UN Peace Keeping contingent, who had been taken hostage, were rescued in a dare devil operation. His tenure as the Army Chief is remembered for many notable improvements in operational & administrative postures of the Army. After his superannuation from the Army, he was appointed Founder Vice Chairman of National Disaster Management Authority, in the rank of Cabinet Minister, for five years from Sep 2005 – Sep 2010. He was also the former Director of the Vivekananda International Foundation (VIF).

Lieutenant General Mohinder Puri, PVSM, UYSM (Retd), was commissioned into the 5th Battalion of the 3rd Gorkha Rifles in June

1966. He Commanded his battalion in Mizoram and later an Infantry Brigade in the Akhnoor Sector of J&K. In his command of the 8 Mountain Division, his formation spearheaded the Army's offensive in the Kargil Sector and restored the sanctity of the LoC by capturing Tololing, Tiger Hill and Point 4875. Later he commanded a Corps in the Punjab-Rajasthan Sector. Before superannuation, he was the Military Secretary and later side stepped as Deputy Chief of the Army Staff.

Air Marshal Anil Chopra, PVSM, AVSM, VM, VSM (Retd), was a pioneer of Mirage-2000 fleet. He commanded a Mirage 2000 Squadron and IAF's Flight Test Centre, Aircraft and Systems Testing Establishment (ASTE). He was also the Team Leader of MiG 21 Bison Upgrade project in Russia. He has been a member of the Armed Forces Tribunal (AFT) and the Executive Council of JNU.

Lieutenant General BS Pawar (Retd), is a Gunner and an Aviator. He was head of the Army Aviation Corps and commanded the School of Artillery during a carrier spanning four decades. A defence analyst, he writes for a number of defence journals and publications. He is currently the President of the Northern Region of Helicopter Society of India.

Lieutenant General Rajeev Sabherwal, AVSM, VSM, Signal Officer-In-Chief, was commissioned in December 1981. The General Officer has been instrumental in the ongoing capability development towards Net Centric Capabilities and Information Warfare. The officer has also been the Commandant of Military College of Telecommunication Engineering and have also served in the Military Operations Directorate.

Major General Ian Cardozo, AVSM, SM (Retd), was commissioned into the 5th Battalion Gorkha Rifles (FF) in 1958 and has taken part in the wars of 1962,1965 and 1971. Severely wounded in 1971 in East Pakistan, he overcame the disability of losing a leg and is the first war-disabled officer to have commanded an infantry battalion and brigade.

Major General Raj Mehta, AVSM,VSM (Retd), is Chief Mentor Sarathi Museum Consultants; a consultancy which he set up in January 2018 along with his Research Team and which is also involved in creating a War Museum for a famous old Infantry Regiment. He also has a number of publications to his credit.

Major General (Dr) PK Chakravorty, VSM (Retd), an alumnus of National Defence Academy was commissioned into the Regiment of Artillery. He has served as the Defence Attaché to Vietnam. Post retirement, the officer was appointed as an Advisor to BrahMos Aerospace Private Limited .Currently he is a Senior Fellow (Veteran) at CLAWS.

Major General Alok Deb, SM, VSM (Retd), is the Deputy Director General of the Institute for Defence Studies and Analyses, New Delhi. He commanded 197 Field Regiment (KARGIL) during Operation Vijay. Maj Gen Deb is a highly decorated officer and also has a number of publications to his credit.

Brigadier Akhelesh Bhargava (Retd), was commissioned into Army Air Defence in June 1983 in 501 Air Defence Group (Self Propelled). He later commanded an Air Defence Unit in the Rajasthan Sector and the Eastern Command Air Defence Brigade. The author has also held various staff and instructional appointments.

Colonel Sushil Chander, an ordnance officer, has served as a director in the Integrated Headquarters (IHQ) of the MoD (Army). He is presently Senior Fellow at the Centre for Land Warfare Studies (CLAWS). The officer has commanded a Field Ordnance Depot and has been the alumnus of the College of Defence Management. He has written extensively on 'Make in India' and various other topics.

Colonel Rajeev Kapoor, has the distinction of actively participating in'Op Vijay' and Counter Insurgency Operations in both J&K and Manipur, including astintwith the Rashtriya Rifles.He has been on a UN mission andcommanded an Infantry Battalion in Counter Insurgency and High-Altitude Area along the LoC.The officer is arecipient of COAS-Commendation Card (**CC**), GOC-in-C Northern Command CC and UN Force Commanders commendation.

Colonel B M Cariappa, VrC, SM, was commissioned into the Parachute Regiment. The officer part of operations like OP ORCHID (Nagaland & Manipur), OP MEGHDOOT (Siachen), OP VIJAY (Kargil War-1999) and OP RAKSHAK (J&K). The officer was wounded in action during the Kargil War.

Colonel Madhusudan Dave, was commissioned in the Indian Army in Dec 1983. During the Kargil Operations, the author was commanding an Independent unit of the Parachute Field Company. He has also authored a book titled "India's Faultlines and Assymetric Threats".

Colonel Vivek Murthy NS, was ADC to the GOC of the Kargil Division in the year 2005. Some of the commentaries in the article are based on this tenure. A voracious reader and a military historian, the officer is presently commanding a Medium Regiment as part of a Mountain Division in the North East.

Major Saurav Pandey, was commissioned into 5th Battalion of the 3rd Gorkha Rifles (5/3 GR) in Dec 2007. The officer has held important appointments in the battalion and in the schools of instructions. After graduating from Staff College, he is currently posted as the company commander in High Altitude Area (HAA).

Mrs Rachna Bisht Rawat, has authored many books on the Indian Army's heroic and famous battles besides a book on PVC awardees. She is a 2005 Harry Brittain fellow and winner of the 2006 Commonwealth Press Quarterly's Rolls Royce Award.

Raghunandan M C, presently works as Web Manager and Researcher in The Centre for Land Warfare Studies (CLAWS). The author holds a Graduate degree in Business Management from Bangalore University and a Master's degree in Diplomacy, Law and Business from OP Jindal Global University. The author has research interest in National Security focusing mainly on the Internal security issues.

Shreya Das Barman, holds a Graduate degree in Sociology and a Masters degree in East Asian Studies. The author have research interest in China and also have a basic knowledge of Chinese (Mandarin) language. Presently, she works as Publications Manager in CLAWS.

Tejusvi Shukla, presently works as Research Assistant in The Centre For Land Warfare Studies (CLAWS). The author holds a BA Programme Degree in Economics and History from Miranda House, Delhi University. The author have research interest in Internal Security with a focus on Left Wing Extremism. She aspires to build career on peace, conflict and strategic studies.

EDITORS

Lieutenant General (Dr) VK Ahluwalia, PVSM, AVSM**, YSM,VSM (Retd), The General commanded an infantry brigade, mountain division and corps in Uri- Baramulla, Kargil and Leh-Ladakh sectors respectively. After his retirement as the Army Commander, Central Command in 2012, he served as Member Armed Forces Tribunal till 2017. He has authored a Book, titled, 'Red Revolution 2020 and Beyond'. Currently, he is the Director, CLAWS.

Colonel Narjit Singh (Retd), commissioned into 2 Lancers (1978), served in 2005 in the 8 Mountain Division Headquarters. The officer was entrusted with the project of making a documentary on Kargil War. The documentary named "The Kargil War" was widely released within the army formations and other institutions and was well appreciated.

OTHER CONTRIBUTORS

A large number of headquarters, units and formations have contributed towards the successful compilation of the book.

Glossary

Military Terms

1. **Section:** The smallest fighting sub unit of the infantry consisting of 10 soldiers and is led by a Non Commissioned Officer (NCO).

2. **Platoon:** An infantry platoon comprises three sections. It has approximately 32-35 soldiers, and is led by a Junior Commissioned Officer (JCO).

3. **Company:** An infantry company comprises three infantry platoons and specialist support weapons (medium machine guns, grenade launchers and mortars) platoon. It consists of 110-135 soldiers and is led by an officer (Major).

4. **Battalion:** A cohesive infantry unit capable of undertaking operations by itself. It comprises four companies, a support weapon and administrative support company. It is led by a Colonel.

5. **Brigade:** It comprises three-four infantry battalions and elements of supporting arms and services. It is led by a Brigadier.

6. **Division:** It comprises of three-four infantry brigades, an artillery brigade, and units of supporting arms and services. It is led by a Major General.

7. **Corps:** It comprises two-three divisions and is led by a Lieutenant General.

8. **Acclimatisation:** Owing to lower oxygen content in the air for breathing at high altitudes, it takes some time for the human body to adjust to the change. A gradual exposure helps in overcoming this problem considerably.

9. **Artillery Regiments:** Battalion-size units, each commanded by a Colonel. Each of these has 3 batteries.

Other Terms

10. **Jehad/Jihad**: A struggle or holy war against the infidels, on behalf of Islam

11. **Jawan:** Colloquial term for an Indian soldiers

12. **Mujahideen:** A term used for those who fight in an Islamic holy war

13. **Nullah:** Ravine or water course

14. **Sangar:** Defensive walls with loopholes to fire weapons, made of stones and boulders with or without the use of mud-plaster, or cement-like material

15. **D-Day:** The day upon which an operation is launched

16. **H-Hour:** The time at which the operation begins

Index